Praise for *Surgeon in Blue*

"As a medical director of the Army of the Potomac during the American Civil War, Jonathan Letterman made important innovations in the battlefield evacuation and treatment of wounded men that changed the history of military medicine. With sensitivity and insight, Scott McGaugh presents the story of this fascinating figure and his legacy, which has saved uncounted thousands of lives of soldiers wounded in many wars."

— James M. McPherson, author of *Battle Cry of Freedom*

"Jonathan Letterman's revolutionary medical innovations touch lives every time 911 is called for a trauma incident, a patient arrives at an emergency room, a medic treats a wounded warrior, or medical supplies are delivered to a disaster zone. Thanks to Scott McGaugh, Letterman can be introduced to a world that already benefits from his legacy."

— George Wunderlich e director,
Nati Medicine

"This is an important book, nd ably researched the underside of wa ounded soldier from being abandoned ...g the object of compassionate care."

— John S. Haller Jr., emeritus professor of history
and medical humanities, Southern Illinois University

"In this eloquent and engaging portrait of the legendary medical strategist, Scott McGaugh reminds us that Jonathan Letterman's spirit lives on today in every corpsman and medic, at every forward medical facility, and at every hospital in theater."

— André B. Sobocinski, historian, Office of Medical History,
Bureau of Medicine & Surgery, United States Navy

"Stirring . . . In addition to being an incisive portrait of the great doctor and leader, McGaugh's history is a testament to the brave men to whom Letterman dedicated his life."

— *Publishers Weekly*

"Solid, well-researched . . . A nicely crafted biography that also offers Civil War buffs an unusual ambulance-wagon view of the great conflict."
—*Kirkus Reviews*

"Verdict: McGaugh provides military history buffs, particularly those interested in military medicine, with a well-rounded picture of a man who greatly influenced our delivery of medical care for wounded warriors."
—*Library Journal*

"Adds a sobering tone to the 150th anniversary of a conflict that advanced medical care at a terrible cost. . . . McGaugh provides telling details within a concise narrative to give Letterman's personal story the context necessary for appreciating his influence."
—Associated Press

"*Surgeon in Blue* is a meticulously researched, totally fascinating narrative of Dr. Jonathan Letterman's pioneering of modern battlefield medicine in the midst of the nightmare carnage of the Civil War. Scott McGaugh's extraordinary work of military history documents a life-saving legacy that still echoes through Iraq and Afghanistan."
—Richard Setlowe, author of *The Experiment* and *The Haunting of Suzanna Blackwell*

"Mr. McGaugh nicely blends a narrative of the contributions made by Dr. Letterman with the various battles fought . . . This book fills a neglected spot in our understanding of great advances in medical treatment during the Civil War."
—*New York Journal of Books*

"McGaugh provides a finely written account of what [Letterman] accomplished . . . Shines a light on the inspired and truly innovative efforts of this remarkable man who greatly improved the quality of care given to soldiers. For readers interested in something more in-depth, beyond the stories of major Civil War battles, this well-written book provides insight into the efforts of one man working behind the scenes."
—*Washington Independent Review of Books*

SURGEON
IN BLUE

Also by Scott McGaugh:

Midway *Magic*
Midway *Memories*
USS Midway: *America's Shield*
*Battlefield Angels: Saving Lives Under Enemy Fire
from Valley Forge to Afghanistan*

SURGEON IN BLUE

Jonathan Letterman, the Civil War Doctor Who Pioneered Battlefield Care

Scott McGaugh

ARCADE PUBLISHING · NEW YORK

Arcade Publishing books may be purchased in bulk at special discounts for sales promotion, corporate gifts, fund-raising, or educational purposes. Special editions can also be created to specifications. For details, contact the Special Sales Department, Arcade Publishing, 307 West 36th Street, 11th Floor, New York, NY 10018 or arcade@skyhorsepublishing.com.

Arcade Publishing® is a registered trademark of Skyhorse Publishing, Inc.®, a Delaware corporation.

Visit our website at www.arcadepub.com.
Visit the author's website at www.scottmcgaugh.com

10 9 8 7 6 5 4 3 2 1

Library of Congress Cataloging-in-Publication Data

McGaugh, Scott.
Surgeon in blue : Jonathan Letterman, the Civil War doctor who pioneered battlefield care / Scott McGaugh.
    pages cm
Includes bibliographical references and index.
ISBN 978-1-61145-839-8 (hardcover : alk. paper); ISBN 978-62872-529-2 (paperback : alk. paper); ISBN 978-1-61145-830-2 (ebook)
1. Letterman, Jonathan, 1824-1872. 2. Surgeons–United States–Biography. 3. United States. Army–Surgeons–Biography. 4. United States–History–Civil War, 1861-1865–Medical care. 5. Medicine, Military–United States–History–19th century. 6. United States. Army of the Potomac–Biography. I. Title.
E621.M36 2013
973.7'75092—dc23
2013010329

Jacket design by Danielle Ceccolini
Cover photo courtesy of the Library of Congress

Printed in the United States of America

*To all in the military medical corps
who bring our sons and daughters home*

"It requires a man with a steel nerve and
a case-hardened heart to be an army surgeon."

—James Houghton, 4th Maine Infantry

CONTENTS

An insert of sixteen pages of photographs can be found between pages 166 and 167.

ACKNOWLEDGMENTS

E ach time I embark on a book project, I find myself enormously grateful for the many people and organizations dedicated to preserving our nation's history. I am reminded just how much of history binds our cultural identity. Our history is woven into the fabric of our culture, and without its preservation, the tapestry of our values, beliefs, and shared experience would unravel.

When I first approach a book's topic, the vista it offers can be as broad as it is overwhelming. An endless number of paths stretch out before me. Some lead to unexpected forks and side paths that yield enormous treasure. Others become box canyons. *Surgeon in Blue* is no different from my other books in this respect, for its research led me to rural towns, dusty archives, and generous strangers who quickly became kindred spirits, colleagues, and sometimes good friends.

Many people helped me set a research course at the outset. Brett Kelley and Janice Mullin of the National Civil War Museum suggested several routes of inquiry. Renowned Civil War devotee Michael Echols was a marvelous online resource, while Dr. Dale C. Smith, professor of medical history at the

Uniformed Services University of the Health Sciences, articulated the challenges and opportunities inherent in my book concept.

The gracious people of Canonsburg, Pennsylvania, were remarkably helpful. Michael McCoy, Phi Kappa Psi's historian; Jim Herron of the Jefferson College Historical Society; local historians Maryann Magra and Gina Nestor; and Jefferson Medical College's archivist, Michael Angelo, all were as responsive to a stranger's request for information as they were supportive.

When I reached the National Civil War Medicine Museum in Frederick, Maryland, I discovered a dedicated group of people devoted to this largely overlooked aspect of Civil War history. Gordon Dammann, a retired dentist in Illinois, founded the museum. He and his wife, Karen, welcomed me into their home, a den of irreplaceable historical documents and artifacts that included Jonathan Letterman's desk. George Wunderlich, Terry Reimer, and Adele Air at the museum were enormously helpful.

When my odyssey reached Fredericksburg, staff historian Donald Pfanz provided letters, diaries, and reports. Beth Malmquist and Jake Struhelka at the Chatham House extended personal courtesies, as did Randy Washburn, Rebecca Welker, and David Elrod at the Fredericksburg Visitor Center. Chief historian John Hennessy's review of the manuscript was greatly appreciated.

At Gettysburg, Phil Lechak provided a personal and inspirational tour of the battlefield. To sit in a forest clearing where Letterman's surgeons treated bleeding men took my breath away. Imagining the cries of battle brought tears. Dru Anne Neil connected me with historian John Heiser, who provided archival Gettysburg materials and later offered manuscript feedback. Gettysburg guide Tim Fulmer clearly spent a great deal of time reviewing and improving the Gettysburg chapter.

Meanwhile, other strangers became greatly appreciated colleagues. Marjorie R. Bardeen provided key historical perspective from the Lancaster Historical Society, while David Haugaard, Sara Heim, and Don Rolph at the Pennsylvania Historical Society in Philadelphia delivered a treasure trove of historical records otherwise out of my reach.

When the odyssey reached California, Joe Sanchez of the National Archives in San Francisco and Dr. Terence Allen, who wrote a history of the San Francisco's coroner's office, provided insights I never would have developed. Medical history author John Haller was especially helpful in reviewing the manuscript from the larger military medicine perspective.

Of course, all this was to document Jonathan Letterman's life's path and legacy. Regrettably, almost none of his personal papers remain. Only a handful of official reports and some handwritten notes have been found. Graphologist Sheila Kurtz was enormously helpful in "reading between the lines" and in helping me develop a more personal understanding of one of the Civil War's great unsung heroes.

None of their contributions would have seen the light of day without the sage counsel of my agent, Scott Mendel, and the unerring editing and manuscript polishing by Arcade Publishing's Cal Barksdale. Finally, as I write this on Valentine's Day, 2013, I know in my heart that each of my books has been made possible only by the unwavering support of Marjorie, my best friend, wife, and mother of my son.

I am indebted to all who helped me chart this course of discovery. Each has contributed to the preservation of an important part of our nation's military history. Thus, each has added to our understanding of who we are as Americans.

INTRODUCTION

"We are almost worked to death."

One out of nine of America's sons, brothers, and fathers fought each other in the Civil War. The human carnage was unimagined. For many, decades passed before the scars began to fade. Our civil war has been well chronicled, from its orders of battle to its sociological implications. Its history, one hundred fifty years later, is well preserved through the wealth of contemporary first-person accounts, a remarkable compilation of military medicine's medical records, and unending study and analysis in the ensuing fifteen decades.

I have always been fascinated by the building blocks of history, the individual human experience. *Surgeon in Blue* is the result of a personal journey that began when I became involved in saving the retired *USS Midway* aircraft carrier as a museum. I discovered its unprecedented forty-seven years' service to America represented the collective legacy of an estimated two hundred thousand men who served aboard *Midway*, at an average age of only nineteen. Their legacy became *Midway Magic*, my first book.

Midway Magic led to other books, including *Battlefield Angels: Saving Lives Under Enemy Fire from Valley Forge to Afghanistan. Battlefield Angels* chronicles the remarkable heroism and compassion of fourteen individual corpsmen and medics, emblematic of many others charged with saving lives in battle. It spotlights the American spirit in the dust and debris of the war. The book also weaves the story of the remarkable legacy of military medicine and how it has influenced civilian health care today. Anesthesia, blood banks, transfusions, antibiotics, hospital design, life flights, microsurgery, certain medical specialties, X-rays, and much more have been either validated through widespread use or pioneered on the battlefield.

Buried in the middle of that book is Jonathan Letterman, a young military doctor from Canonsburg, Pennsylvania. After spending thirteen years at army outposts in the Far West, where he tended sick soldiers, mended broken bones, and treated the periodic arrow wound, he was thrust into the heart of the Civil War. He became responsible for the survival and health of the Army of the Potomac's 100,000 men. He was given medical charge of an emaciated, exhausted, dispirited army in which nearly four of ten soldiers were sick or wounded.

In only eighteen months, he recast military medicine into a strategic element of an army's order of battle. He served as the medical director of an army that fought three of the Civil War's bloodiest battles, including America's single day of greatest loss of life. Against that backdrop, Letterman pioneered military preventive health standards of diet, sanitation, and hygiene. He became known as the "Father of Battlefield Medicine" after he established the first professional ambulance corps, restructured military hospital care to bring it closer to the battlefield, recast the medical supply chain to more closely match the realities of battle, and developed a system of officer accountability to make all that possible. His approach to medical command and control is echoed by the military medical command structure of today.

The impact of Letterman's remarkable accomplishments can be seen today, which makes it all the more remarkable that no full-length biography has been dedicated to him before now. It has been my honor to work with the National Museum of Civil War Medicine and a wide range of Civil War experts to remember the man and call attention to his legacy in this book.

Surgeon in Blue is not intended as a compendium of Civil War medicine. That subject has been studied thoroughly. Excellent books, including *Gangrene and Glory*; *Civil War Medicine: Challenges & Triumphs*; *Doctors in Blue*; and the multivolume *Medical and Surgical History of the War of the Rebellion*, offer extraordinary analysis and first-person data for study. Nor is my focus on Letterman's role intended to disregard the role of women in Civil War medicine, Navy medicine, military medicine in the South, prisoner-of-war health care, or a myriad of related aspects of mid-nineteenth century military medicine. *Surgeon in Blue* focuses on a single man who rose above the hell of battle to craft a vision of more humanitarian and effective care for the sick and wounded in uniform.

Approximately 10,000 engagements were fought in the Civil War. Surgeons treated thousands of wounded from a single battle, taking little time to meticulously record each treatment or procedure, much less document all the walking wounded who reached a field hospital. Diarrhea and dysentery were considered nearly synonymous in the Civil War, and other conditions and illnesses were similarly confounded, so statistical compilations of disease are difficult to analyze. The War Department might list an army's strength at 108,000, while that army's commanding officer might consider the 80,000 troops who were available for duty to be a more realistic description. Did a few skirmishes on one day mark the start of a battle or was an armed collision of tens of thousands of men the following day the true start of a battle? Dates of some Civil War events periodically vary.

As a result of such factors, many statistics and dates can be fodder for discussion and disagreement. When variances came to light, I relied on either the most commonly reported figure or version or the one from what I considered a reliable source. I've footnoted many figures and quotes for the reader's additional edification. Regrettably, a disastrous fire in Richmond in 1865 destroyed the bulk of Confederate medical records. Any errors or omissions are mine, and I always welcome suggested corrections.

Much of Letterman's organizational work focused on the corps, division, and brigade level, so a brief description of military organization is in order. The Army of the Potomac where Letterman served as medical director is a good example. It generally was comprised of three corps, each with about 30,000 men. A corps was divided into three divisions of about 10,000 soldiers each. Each division was comprised of three brigades of about 3,500 men each. Each brigade was comprised of three 1,000-man regiments. To be sure, the size of each component varied greatly throughout the war depending upon circumstance, the arrival and departure of volunteer regiments, and the health of soldiers.

Line officers, the men who led the troops in battle, answered to an army's commanding officer. However, medical officers were not only members of the fighting army but also part of the army's medical department, led by the surgeon general. Their participation in two chains of command could create tensions. In addition, equivalencies in rank between military officers and surgeons in the medical department could be confusing or problematic. A surgeon held the rank of major, and an assistant surgeon was either a captain or first lieutenant. In practice, military officers often disregarded suggestions by surgeons as unimportant or threatening to their authority.

The Union army was comprised of career military men, a force far too small to fight the Confederates. Regiments of volunteers were therefore organized by individual states to supplement the so-called regular army. Volunteer regiments would consist of approximately 1,000 men—untrained farmers, craftsmen, merchants, lawyers, doctors, and others—who often furnished their own uniforms. They selected their officers, sometimes on the basis of popularity or political connections. While necessary to the war, volunteer regiments were a source of great frustration among career military officers such as Letterman, who chafed at the volunteer soldiers' lack of training and discipline.

Terminology can sometimes be confusing, given the changes of usage over the years. In *Surgeon in Blue* I've relied on contemporary terms for diseases, drugs, and treatments. To simplify and clarify, I considered *physician* and *surgeon* synonymous, given the realities of battlefield medicine and its organization in the Civil War. Our nation's capital at that time was Washington, one of several cities in the District of Columbia. It became Washington, DC when those cities were consolidated in 1871. Finally, the term *hospital* wasn't what we view as a hospital today. During the Civil War, a field hospital could have been a commandeered barn or a collection of tents in a ravaged cornfield.

On a more personal note about Letterman, a quirk of his life is how the spelling of his last name changed. The original family name, of German origin, was Lederman, "leather man," reflecting the family's tradesman past. Jonathan Letterman's father, a physician, went by Leatherman. Records of Jonathan's early life include Leatherman and Letherman references. In 1856, Letterman submitted a report to the Smithsonian Institution under the name Letherman. Shortly thereafter, in military records, the form of the name became exclusively Letterman. Regrettably, the written historical records discovered to date do not reveal the reason for the change. In the interest of clarity, I use Leatherman for Jonathan's father and Letterman for Jonathan.

It is especially important to note that *Surgeon in Blue* is not a detailed account of the Army of the Potomac's major battles. Antietam, Fredericksburg, Chancellorsville, and Gettysburg were the canvases on which Letterman developed a new concept of battlefield medicine. I've offered descriptions of those battles in order to provide context for Letterman's achievement but have not tried to be comprehensive. Certainly, there is a wealth of other material for readers interested in battle plans, corps commander strategies, troop movement, fighting, and heat-of-battle decisions.

This is a book about Jonathan Letterman and the hundreds of doctors he commanded, about his leadership and their collective legacy. His innovations were possible only through the dedication of the sort of men he considered to be good medical officers, who, in his view, ". . . should possess a thorough knowledge of the powers, wants, and capabilities of the human system of food, raiment, and climate, with all its multiplied vicissitudes, the influences for evil which surround the health of any army, and the means necessary to combat them successfully. They should also possess quickness of perception, a sound judgment, promptness of action, and skill in the treatment of medical and surgical disease."[1]

The wounded in Letterman's charge survived because of the compassion and bravery of individual surgeons—surgeons who must first endure battle. "While the excitement of the battle lasts, and we hear the roar of the artillery, and the shock of contending armies, the terrible reality of the occasion hardly presents itself to our minds, and it is only when we survey the bloody field, strewed with the mangled, lifeless remains of friend and foe, or walk through the hospitals, where the unfortunate victims of battle writhe in the agony of their wounds, that we realize the terrible nature of battle."[2]

It was then, long after the guns fell silent, that Letterman's leadership inspired countless surgeons to wage private battles for survival: "We are almost worked to death; my feet are terribly swollen; yet we cannot rest for there are so many poor fellows who are suffering. All day yesterday I worked at the operating table. That was the fourth day that I had worked at those terrible operations since the battle commenced, and I have worked at the tables two whole nights and part of another. Oh! It is awful. It does not seem as though I could take a knife in my hand to-day, yet there are a hundred cases of amputations waiting for me. Poor fellows come and beg almost on their knees for the first chance to have an arm taken off. It is a scene of horror such as I never saw. God forbid that I should ever see another."[3]

Of course, war continues to plague our society. Following the Civil War, approximately 38 million Americans have served on or near the battlefield. More than 1.2 million have been wounded and likely owe their lives to corpsmen, medics, physicians, and specialists.[4] That is why Jonathan Letterman deserves recognition and his legacy is worthy of preservation. It is part of military medicine's legacy, one that represents the finest ideals of the American spirit: courage, compassion, and devotion to duty.

SURGEON
in BLUE

1

NOT A LEARNED
PROFESSION

"Open-hearted frankness"

In a sense, surgeon Jonathan Letterman's Civil War began when the enemy's guns fell silent. His planning and preparations for his first battle as chief medical officer of the Army of the Potomac had come down to this moment. Hundreds of surgeons under his command stood ready in primitive field hospitals as the moans from thousands of broken and dying men strewn across the battlefield replaced the whine of bullets splitting the air. "Over here!" punctured the eerie calm when searchers came upon a man in agony or found a pulse in a body curled behind a rock or straddling rows of shredded cornstalks.

The gory, writhing battlefield at Antietam in western Maryland on September 18, 1862, appalled the survivors, including Benjamin Cook. "Rifles are shot to pieces in the hands of soldiers, canteens and haversacks are riddled by bullets, and the dead and wounded go down in scores. The smoke and fog lift; and almost at our feet, concealed in a hollow behind a demolished fence, lies a rebel brigade pouring into our ranks the most deadly fire of the war. What there are left of us open on them with a cheer; and the next day, the burial parties put up a board in front of the position held by the Twelfth (Massachusetts) with the following inscription: 'In this trench lie buried the colonel, the major, six line officers, and one hundred and forty men of the (13th) Georgia Regiment.'"[1]

Thousands of wounded men littered farm fields, stands of timber, and creek beds. Though few could possibly know it, an untested newcomer to their army had become responsible for their survival. Jonathan Letterman had held medical command of the sick and beaten Army of the Potomac for two months before facing his first major battle at Antietam. He had taken command shortly before the army went on the march in search of the Confederate general Robert E. Lee. The thirty-seven-year-old had learned of the battlefield's location only a few days in advance of the fighting. After a single day's battle, Letterman became responsible for half again as many wounded men as the total number of those wounded in the Revolutionary War.

Letterman had been born toward the end of the so-called Era of Good Feelings in our nation's early years. The son of a small-town physician, he had grown up in southwestern Pennsylvania. He joined the army upon graduation from a first-rate medical school. Thirteen years of outpost medicine subsequently bore almost no resemblance to the carnage at Antietam. Letterman would have to rely on his instincts, untapped talents, and basic medical training if the wounded now in his charge were to stand a chance of survival.

On November 3, 1824, more than 365,000 white Americans voted for their sixth president. None of the five candidates received a majority of votes, casting the country into uncertainty. Three months later, on February 9, 1825, the House of Representatives selected John Quincy Adams over Andrew Jackson. Although Jackson received more popular votes, the House elected Adams on the first ballot.

When Adams named Speaker of the House Henry Clay (who had been one of the five candidates for president) as his secretary of state, political opponents charged that a backroom deal had been made by Adams and Clay at the expense of Jackson. The controversy over the appointment marked a new chapter for a nation that had been created only forty-eight years earlier. It closed what Boston newspaper reporter Benjamin Russell had first termed the Era of Good Feelings, eight years of muted political bickering in a young nation finding its way. The raucous bipartisanship that returned was both divisive and sectionalist, influencing national debate and election results.

In the midst of this political turmoil, on December 11, 1824, Jonathan Letterman was born in Canonsburg, Pennsylvania, a young town that had been incorporated by the Pennsylvania legislature on February 22, 1802. Set at the bottom of a hill alongside Chartiers Creek, it lay about twenty miles south of Pittsburgh.

Its roots stretched back to the 1740s, when Peter Chartiers established an Indian trading post on a creek that fed the Ohio River thirty miles to the north. The son of a French father and Shawnee mother, Chartiers trapped, traded with Indians, and supported the French. He was a harbinger of the immigrants who later arrived in western Pennsylvania, many of them coming from northern Maryland, Virginia, and Europe.

The pioneers settled in the heavily wooded and hilly region. Creeks meandered through isolated valleys. Dense forests held white-tailed deer, wolves, and bears. Forested slopes gave relief from hot summers punctuated by thunderstorms that occasionally drove creeks and rivers over their banks. Long and sometimes brutal winters brought snow as early as November.

Irish, Scot, British, and German pioneers carved farms from the forests and settled alongside rivers in communities that grew to become Pittsburgh, Wheeling, Wellsburg, and Brownsville. Celtic settlers tended to be farmers, while many of the English pioneers opened general stores. Some had fled political turbulence in Europe. Some northern Irish carried a price on their heads from opposing the Church of England before coming to America and establishing homesteads in its western wilderness. A settler could build a cabin, raise a crop of corn, grain, or vegetables, and apply for a four hundred–acre parcel of land as well as a preemption right to another one thousand acres.[2] Many squatters simply settled a piece of land without bothering to check on or file for ownership. Self-reliance and sweat equity were critical to surviving isolation, disease, and unforgiving weather.

Sustenance farming, fishing, and hunting followed the seasons. Once a year, some settlers loaded their horses and traveled more than 200 miles east by pack train to Baltimore to trade their grain alcohol, wool, fabric, and pelts for gunpowder, lead, salt, iron, and other farm and living essentials.[3]

Isolated pockets of farms spawned communities. Hardworking and frugal Scot and Irish placed a high priority on school and church. While most education took place in the home, sometimes itinerant teachers were hired to teach the children of several neighboring families that had settled along a creek or in a remote valley.

John Canon arrived in the late 1700s. Within a few years Canon owned twelve hundred acres on Chartiers Creek. An entrepreneur and officer in the local militia, in the early 1780s Canon built a flour mill and sawmill on the creek. He obtained a contract to provide rations to the local militia and turned his sights to creating what became Letterman's hometown. With Chartiers Creek as the southern boundary, Canon laid out a town on a portion of his property with the main street starting near his mill and proceeding north up a hill. Canon's first known plat of Canonsburg bears a 1787 date. It lists the names of lot owners but the date of the lots' sale is unclear.[4]

For several years, Virginia and Pennsylvania had claimed the portion of America's western Pennsylvania wilderness that included Chartiers Creek. Both states issued property ownership rights for the same land. The Mason–Dixon Line established in 1781 to resolve the border dispute placed the Canonsburg area in Pennsylvania. Canon and other Pennsylvania residents found they held land patents issued by Virginia. Although it took Canon several years to obtain Pennsylvania patents for his town lots in Canonsburg, he continued selling lots. His conditions of lot purchase required the buyer to build within two years a frame or log house that was at least twenty feet wide across the front and had a stone or brick fireplace.[5] Buyers also received free access to a coal outcrop not far away.

By that time, a rudimentary, one-room log cabin had been converted into a school by Presbyterian minister John McMillan, a graduate of what is now Princeton University. He expected many of its graduates to establish schools to educate and prepare young men as candidates for the ministry. McMillan hired teachers to teach the classics while he taught theology. By the early 1790s, most of McMillan's graduates enrolled at an academy in Canonsburg. Canon gave the academy's trustees a 2.1-acre lot almost across the street from his house and built a new, two-story stone schoolhouse for them (Canon's son was a stone mason).[6] Although Canon donated the lot, he gave the trustees the deed only after they had paid for the stone building in 1796. They soon began offering college-level courses after the state legislature chartered the school as the Academy and Library Company of Canonsburg.[7]

By the late 1790s, Canonsburg was firmly taking root. It had become a market town on the weekly stage route between Pittsburgh to the north and Washington to the south.[8] Property owners along the town's main street, Market Street, included weavers, tavern keepers, merchants, and lawyers as well as a doctor,

tanner, cooper, hatter, brewer, miller, and shoemaker.[9] Canonsburg was well on its way to becoming the college town where
Jonathan Letterman, the son of a local physician, could prepare
to become a doctor.

The paternal side of Letterman's family traced its American
roots to September 27, 1727, when Letterman's great-great-
grandfather, Hans Lederman (a linenweaver), two brothers, and
Lederman's nine-year-old son, Daniel, arrived from northern
Alsace, Germany, aboard the ship *James Goodwill*. Daniel, Letterman's great grandfather, grew up to become a minister and
lived in southern Pennsylvania and Frederick, Maryland. His
son, also named Daniel, went by the name Leatherman and
lived in Washington County, Pennsylvania. He settled four hundred acres along Pigeon Creek southeast of Canonsburg. Daniel
and his wife, Elizabeth, married in 1772 and a year later their
first son, Theobald, was born. The family grew quickly with the
births of Jonathan (1775, Letterman's father), Elizabeth (1777),
Hannah (1779), Mary (1781), and Joseph (1783). All were
German Baptists, commonly called Dunkards at the time.

Letterman's father, Jonathan Leatherman, arrived in Canonsburg around 1815.[10] By that time, the market town had become
an established municipality. Incorporated as a self-governing borough in 1802, the town had grown to encompass four school-
masters, four tavern keepers, four shoemakers, four carpenters,
three distillers, three tailors, two millers, two harness makers, and
two wheelwrights as well as a clockmaker, mason, and tanner.[11]
The same year, it issued a charter to the Canonsburg Academy
to become Jefferson College, authorizing it to grant college
degrees. Five young men received degrees the same year from a
college whose leadership was dominated by Presbyterian min-
isters and elders.[12]

Leatherman married Anna Ritchie on July 21, 1818. Anna's
father, Craig Ritchie, had been one of the first purchasers of the

town lots offered by Canon. Ritchie started a successful mer-
cantile business, had fourteen children, and served as a legisla-
tor from 1793 to 1795, then as justice of the peace. On January
29, 1819, Ritchie sold the lot next door on Market Street to
Leatherman and his wife for $300. Soon Leatherman lived next
to his father-in-law and was building a medical practice.

Leatherman made an immediate impression on Canonsburg
residents. Five years after his arrival, he served a two-year term
as a borough burgess. He functioned much like a modern-day
mayor but also had limited judicial authority and could levy
fines and issue short sentences for relatively minor legal offenses.
Both Leatherman and his father-in-law served on the borough
council as well.

Two years later, Leatherman formed a partnership with
Dr. George Herriott. On March 10, 1823, Leatherman announced
the new practice in the local newspaper, offering services "in all
the various branches of medical . . . (and) likewise informs the
publick, that he keeps himself supplied with fresh medicine, of
the best quality, from Philadelphia."[13]

Herriott had married Mary, another daughter of Craig
Ritchie. That made Herriott and Leatherman brothers-in-law as
well as business partners. As the practice grew, Anna Leatherman
gave birth to the family's first child, Jonathan. By that time, his
father had completed a medical apprenticeship and had received
his formal medical degree from Jefferson Medical College in
Philadelphia. The degree was largely honorary. Leatherman was
not required to attend medical school and had been practicing
as a physician as early as 1819.

Jonathan Letterman was born in a brick house on the southwest corner of Pike and Green Streets in the heart of Canonsburg.[14] When he reached school age, a private tutor educated him,
a common practice among financially secure and wealthy families at the time. Many families considered education a paramount

priority, either in the home or in a one-room schoolhouse with a teacher hired by the community. Typically the teacher was a man and modestly educated. He focused on reading, writing, and arithmetic.

The nation in 1824 was less than five decades old and in transition, as it sought to assert its identity and position in the world. The previous year, in a speech before Congress, President James Monroe outlined what became the Monroe Doctrine, a warning to European powers to stay out of national affairs in the Western Hemisphere. He promised to stay out of Europe, although his promise must have rung hollow as America did not have a viable army or navy.

The Missouri Compromise of 1820 proved to be a temporary armistice between pro- and anti-slavery factions. It authorized statehood for Maine as a free state and allowed the voters of Missouri to opt for slavery. That kept the number of free and slave states the same in a nation whose 1820 census counted a total population of 9.5 million, including 1.5 million slaves.[15]

Education emerged as a responsibility of government. In the early 1820s, local communities established school districts in Ohio, Indiana, Illinois, and New York. At the same time, America's leading colleges began debating whether higher education should be based on classic literature or focus on more contemporary subjects in the belief that learning should reflect the needs of modern life.

The fledgling nation was in a period of widespread expansion. In 1824, the Erie Canal neared completion. The canal was a commercial waterway that cost $7 million to build and would expand the nation's commercial base by reducing shipping times between the Midwest and northeastern states by one-third and cutting freight transportation costs by more than one-half. On the Mississippi and Ohio Rivers to the west, the gateway cities of Cincinnati, St. Louis, and New Orleans became portals to a vast, largely unexplored wilderness, with Chicago to follow within a decade or so. Stephen F. Austin recruited pioneers to settle Texas. Territories in the process of being settled included Missouri, Michigan, Arkansas, and Florida, in many of which Indian wars loomed on the horizon.

In 1825, the first steam locomotive appeared, and two years later the nation's first railroad, the Baltimore & Ohio Rail Road Company, utilized horse-drawn rail lines. As railroads began to connect cities and as small towns developed along post roads, turnpikes, and navigable waterways that provided transportation in remote regions, life in America evolved as well. Native authors such as James Fenimore Cooper (*The Last of the Mohicans*) and Washington Irving (Rip Van Winkle) became established. Families tended to entertain at home with games, music, and conversation. The minuet was gaining in popularity and the newest brass instruments, the coronet and French horn, were popular among musicians. Traveling circuses became popular.

Canonsburg evolved from a simple market town to a renowned college town. Jefferson College became one of the ten largest colleges in the nation, with a commensurably enhanced reputation. Leatherman joined its board of trustees in 1820 and remained a member for twenty-four years. Located on the corner of Main and College Streets, the college sat two blocks away from the Leatherman household after Leatherman bought a lot at the corner of Pike and Green Streets and built a home. There he likely saw patients and dispensed medicine between house calls.

His practice continued to grow. By 1830, Leatherman had the highest tax valuation in Canonsburg. At $2,636, his holdings included a $2,000 house, $500 in property, and $136 worth of horses and cows.[16] Jonathan lived and was educated in that home until 1838, when the family sold the property for $3,100 and moved a few miles outside of town.[17] Four years later he enrolled at Jefferson College in Canonsburg.

The college's admission requirements had stiffened in the late 1830s and early 1840s. By 1842, admission required Letterman to be familiar with arithmetic and geography, as well as possess a solid education in the classics. Letterman had to demonstrate knowledge of Caesar's Commentaries, Sallust, Virgil, the Greek Testament, and *Greaca Minora*, among others.[18]

Since his family had moved out of town four years earlier, Letterman may have lived in one of several dormitories available in Canonsburg, including one on campus, or in one of several private boarding houses within a few blocks of campus. The most desirable, only a block from campus, was named for Mrs. Armstrong, who ran it, and nicknamed "Fort Hunt." Like many students, Jonathan may have kept a horse at his grandparents' stable a few blocks away in order to visit his parents, whose house was about two-and-a-half miles outside of Canonsburg.[19]

College tuition totaled $30 a year. Student housing costs ranged from $1.25 to $2.50 per week. Some landlords charged extra for coal to heat tenants' rooms, typically about three cents per bushel. Overall, parents anticipated their child's annual college expenses to be less than $100.[20]

Letterman and others typically arose at 5:30 a.m. Breakfast was served at 6:00 a.m. and classes ran from 8:30 a.m. to noon. In his first year at Jefferson, Letterman took classes in Roman and Grecian Antiquities, Cicero's *Orations*, Algebra, and Latin Composition.

As a freshman, Letterman cofounded Jefferson College's chapter of the Beta Theta Pi fraternity. It soon became known as an elitist fraternity, and the founders readily acknowledged that they emphasized membership quality over quantity. Beta Theta Pi initiated about five students per year. Members tended to regard themselves the best of the student body. Once their organization became known, other students referred to them as Betas, but membership remained a tightly held secret.[21]

Many of Letterman's fraternity brothers built successful careers after graduating from Jefferson. Joseph Calvin, Alonzo Linn, and Enos Barnett all became college professors. James Beaver was elected governor of Pennsylvania and became a justice on its supreme court. Milton Latham was elected governor of California, while Ulysses Mercur served in Congress for twenty years. William West became attorney general in Ohio before serving on its state supreme court as well.[22]

Literary societies also were a major source of extracurricular activity. Letterman joined the Philomathean Society. The stated goal of the "Philos" was to educate future leaders by emphasizing rhetoric, oratory, and writing skills. Letterman and others wrote essays, debated different points of view, and competed for the annual honor of making a speech on graduation day. The keynote speeches reflected the lofty goals of Philos. "For the sake of our country, blessed with wise political institutions, we stand in need of all the light that can be shed over it by education. Your relative duties of this Republic, of which you are favored citizens, are of the highest importance. You, whom I address, are the future freeman, or rather the sovereigns of your country; and knowledge will be as necessary to enable you to perform those high duties, as it is to the monarch on the throne," opined one Philo.[23]

The curriculum in Letterman's second year included Geometry, Odes and Satires of Horace, Geography, Surveying and Navigation, and Elements of Rhetoric.[24] In his final two years, his education shifted away from the classics and toward a more contemporary curriculum. His classes in 1844 included Natural Philosophy (as the study of the natural world was known), Nautical Astronomy, Analytic Geometry, Chemistry, and Physiology.[25] The four-year curriculum's courses began in October and concluded in March.

By that point in his college career, Letterman either had decided to become a physician or, at the very least, his father intended that his son attend medical school. The elder Letterman had written to Jefferson Medical College in Philadelphia in the spring of 1844, asking that his son be admitted following his graduation from Jefferson College in 1845. Leatherman may have written the letter in advance of his son's graduation because he knew he was ill. Shortly after he wrote it, the elder Jonathan Leatherman died, on April 11, 1844. He was fifty-eight years old.

At nineteen years of age, Jonathan became the senior male of the family. His mother, Anna, had three sons to care for, the youngest being William, who was eleven.[26] An opportunity to train with his father while finishing his undergraduate work had been lost. If Letterman decided to pursue a medical education, he would have to leave his widowed mother and his family to attend a medical school in Philadelphia or elsewhere. He had reached the first major fork in his life's path: stay in Canonsburg or leave to become a physician? He would have to decide in less than a year when he completed his undergraduate studies.

In his senior year, Letterman took Differential & Integral Calculus, Mental Philosophy, Political Economy, and Paley's Natural Theology.[27] By that time, he had made an impression upon other students. "[He is] one of the noblest spirits of our class, a diligent student cheerful and hopeful, he was always prepared for class and his friends admired his open-hearted frankness."[28] Upon graduation in the spring of 1845, he moved to Philadelphia to begin studying at one of the nation's foremost medical schools, an institution whose roots led directly back to Letterman's college campus in Canonsburg.

The same year Jonathan Letterman had been born, Jefferson Medical College was established as the medical department of Canonsburg's Jefferson College. The founder was George

McClellan, a bold, twenty-eight-year-old physician who had graduated from medical school five years earlier in 1819. McClellan became one of the four original professors when the school opened on January 1, 1825, in a former cotton warehouse. McClellan took a clinical approach to the medical school's curriculum, treating poor patients as case studies for medical student observation. That was atypical at the time, as most medical colleges emphasized lectures and reading over clinical involvement.[29] McClellan became the medical school's most noted professor, famous for lecturing without notes and involving his students in his presentations.

The trustees of Jefferson College bore no responsibility for the financial health of the affiliated medical school in Philadelphia. The college received $15 for each degree issued by the medical school. Medical school professors paid rent to the college and in turn charged fees for their lectures. The more noted the professor, the higher the fee he charged his students. In the early years of Jefferson Medical College, class fees ranged from $14 for Anatomy, Surgery, or Chemistry to $12 for the Practice of Medicine or Midwifery and Diseases of Women and Children.[30] By the time Letterman entered medical school, the fees had been standardized at $15 per course, payable in advance, plus $30 for the diploma.[31]

By 1838, Jefferson Medical College had become so popular that it needed to expand, but it lacked the resources to finance enhanced facilities to accommodate a growing student body. When the state legislature granted an independent charter to the medical school that year, it acquired the legal authority to acquire property and finance construction. By that time, it was one of twenty-eight medical schools in the country but had lost much of its early luster.[32]

The medical faculty had become fractured with camps aligned with and against McClellan and his oversized personality.

The school's board of trustees opted to fire the entire faculty, including McClellan, on June 10, 1839, because ". . . there were too many inharmonious elements, too many conflicting interests, too much friction in the operation of the machinery, too much selfishness on the part of some members."[33] The firing carried a proviso that the professors could apply for reinstatement. Although trustees rehired some professors, they rejected McClellan's application for reinstatement. The founder of Jefferson Medical College, in effect, had been fired by his school.

Shortly after Letterman arrived in the fall of 1845, the school underwent a major expansion project, for it had become the largest medical school in the country. A widely recognized architect, Napoleon LeBrun, redesigned the façade of the single, multistory building so that it resembled a Roman temple. Six massive columns across the school's entrance each sat on a base that rose seven feet above street level.[34] The lecture hall on the first floor accommodated six hundred students. The two floors above formed an amphitheater, called "the pit," complete with a skylight to help hundreds of students look down on the surgeries taking place. A museum at the rear of the second floor held medical specimens; illustrations and engravings of fractures, dislocations, tumors, and diseased organs; and a diseased bone collection.[35]

Although McClellan was no longer a member of the medical staff (he established a competing medical school in Philadelphia after leaving Jefferson), the emphasis on student interaction through lectures over reading textbooks continued. School administrators also hired some of the nation's foremost physicians as professors. They lectured about six hours a day, four days a week. Students not only observed their professors treating patients but also had the opportunity to provide follow-up care.

The strength of Letterman's medical education lay in the quality of the faculty, regarded at the time as one of the finest in the country. Letterman learned from the doctors who wrote many of the textbooks used by other medical schools. Dr. Robley Dunglison was a prolific writer who later came to be known as "the Father of American Physiology." Dr. Robert Huston taught therapeutics and had served as an assistant surgeon in the War of 1812. Dr. John Mitchell taught the practice of medicine and was an entertaining lecturer, research chemist, and published poet. Dr. Charles Meigs taught obstetrics and childhood diseases and was a devoted translator of French medical literature. Dr. Thomas Mutter taught surgery, relying on diagrams and specimens from the medical school's growing museum.[36]

The school year spanned two four-month semesters with the second term a repeat of the same courses of the first term. Students were not graded throughout their coursework. They passed most courses based on an oral quiz at the end of the semester. The curriculum covered eight principal areas: anatomy, physiology and pathology, pharmacology, therapeutics and pharmacy, chemistry and medical jurisprudence, theory and practice of medicine, principles and practice of surgery, and obstetrics and diseases of women and children.[37]

Apart from taking classes, Letterman worked as a physician's apprentice in the community. The city was perhaps the most cultured and dynamic metropolitan area in America, with a cosmopolitan population. Nearly four hundred thousand residents in the Philadelphia area reflected the nation's changing demographics, for famine as well as political and social discontent in Europe had provoked waves of immigration, sparking anti-Catholic, -Irish, -German, and -African protests.[38] The poor newcomers settled in overcrowded neighborhoods where malaria, cholera, smallpox, and tuberculosis were common and where the wooden frame houses were vulnerable to devastating fires.

Letterman studied medicine near the end of an era that some historians have characterized as "the darkest in the history of medicine in the United States."[39] Many medical schools were little more than diploma factories available to those who could afford the tuition. Some states prohibited students from dissecting cadavers, and some schools dawdled in accepting the relatively few medical advances of the period. Harvard reportedly did not offer its medical students a stethoscope until 1868, nearly thirty years after its invention.[40] In some respects, military outpost physicians were less qualified than many of the doctors during the Revolutionary War who had been educated in Europe.

Physicians in the eighteenth and early nineteenth centuries dogmatically believed nearly all diseases could be explained by one or two principles. They often cited decaying vegetable or animal matter as a principal cause of disease.[41] Many considered fever to be a disease rather than a symptom. No one knew conclusively what caused cholera, malaria, and tuberculosis, diseases that ravaged overcrowded cities and military camps. Few could distinguish between malaria and yellow fever with their similar symptoms.

Physicians often diagnosed ailing patients as having what they called an imbalanced system. That led to widespread use of massive amounts of purgatives in the belief that they restored a patient's physiological balance. Many doctors believed mercury cleansed the cardiovascular and digestive systems. Heavy doses of calomel mercury to treat pneumonia, dysentery, typhus, tuberculosis, and yellow fever led to patient poisoning. Bloodletting to drain "impure" blood to restore a patient's balance was declining in popularity but still practiced.

Physicians also were nearly powerless against infection. In the late 1840s, surgeries on wounds, abscesses, tumors, and fractures nearly always led to infected wounds that oozed pus. Physicians considered pus a positive sign of healing. It would be nearly twenty years before Joseph Lister discovered that bacteria were the source of infection and that using bandages soaked with antibacterial carbolic acid reduced the incidence of infection.

Medicine had not yet become a learned profession. The proliferation of profit-making medical schools in the early 1800s led to modest admission and graduation standards. American medical education trailed that of leading institutions in Europe, most notably the Paris Medical School. State licensing of physicians did not exist. As a result, public distrust of physicians grew while interest in homeopathic medicine increased. Medical charlatans thrived, and the army began requiring examinations of physician candidates to confirm their qualifications.

Although army doctor examinations were instituted beginning in 1832, for nearly sixty years the military had considered medical care almost as an afterthought. In 1775, Congress authorized the army hospital department, drawing on a modest civilian medical profession that numbered approximately 3,500 doctors throughout the colonies. Only about 10 percent of those doctors had attended medical school.[42]

As had been the case in every war to that time, disease proved to be more deadly than enemy fire. Only 2 percent of the wounded soldiers died on the Revolutionary War's battlefields, but the mortality rate in military field hospitals was nearly 25 percent. Soldiers carried straw and empty sacks so they could make their own hospital beds.[43] Although smallpox inoculation became a significant medical innovation of the Revolutionary War and would carry far-reaching ramifications, the overall mortality rate of disease was ten times greater than the death rate from enemy fire.[44]

There were no major advances in the relatively primitive practice of medicine in the early 1800s. Lay healers competed with unlicensed physicians who may have studied in Europe or served for a brief time as an apprentice to another unlicensed doctor, or who had no training at all. Most medicines were herbal and unregulated.

Battlefield medicine, like medicine for the general population, had remained stagnant since the end of the Revolutionary War. America had disbanded its army and in 1802 had only two military surgeons and twenty-five assistants. In the War of 1812 between America and Britain, organized battlefield care did not exist. In the absence of an ambulance service, wagons patrolled the battlefield after the guns fell silent, searching for the wounded. There were no organized military hospitals, so physicians placed the wounded in temporary shelters, often called "Indian houses," constructed after each battle.[45]

Throughout most of the early 1800s, many military doctors practiced outpost medicine. Some were responsible for more than one outpost, making rounds with their meager supplies that amounted to little more than a first-aid kit, with a limited number of pharmacological concoctions and almost no equipment in a medical era that predated syringes and thermometers. Most practiced a holistic style of medicine that favored herbal remedies.

It wasn't until 1818, in the aftermath of the war, that Congress authorized the establishment of a surgeon general for the army. The first was Joseph Lovell, an uncommonly well-educated physician. He had graduated from Harvard College in 1807 and was a member of Harvard's first medical school graduation class in 1811. Curly hair, narrow eyes, and a small, thin lip gave him an academic look. A year after graduation he demonstrated his leadership skills as a hospital administrator in the War of 1812.

He assumed his post as surgeon general on April 18, 1818, at the age of twenty-nine, and moved quickly to consolidate authority, although his was a small department. In 1821, it numbered only eight surgeons and forty-five assistant surgeons. Lovell established an esprit de corps and took great personal pride in establishing the rudiments of a professional medical corps. One of his pioneering standards of professional conduct required quarterly reports from his outpost surgeons that included not only disease statistics but standardized weather observations.

He led the abolition of the daily whiskey ration that had long caused problems in the army. He also was instrumental in establishing procedures that enabled boards of officers to remove incompetents among the surgeons. Both subordinates and superior officers held Lovell in high esteem. He reigned over an embryonic military medical corps in an era of unlicensed and unregulated civilian doctors.

Between 1812 and 1839, the number of military outposts from New Hampshire to Florida ranged between forty and seventy-five. Military doctors remained in chronically short supply. In 1821, there were only forty-four doctors available for the army's fifty-four posts and stations.[46] The shortage produced horrific working conditions. In 1829, Surgeon General Lovell wrote his medical corps was "barely sufficient to supply the several posts, they are seldom permitted to leave their stations, as no one else can perform their duties; and they are thus sometimes compelled in urgent cases to hire a substitute at their own expense, while at most of the interior posts even this is impracticable, and hence some have been on daily duty for ten years; whereas an officer of the line can be at once relieved by the next in command, or his place be supplied by one of the same grade."[47]

Six years later, Lovell issued a similarly dire report to Secretary of War Lewis Cass, focusing the lack of facilities for the sick: "Many of the military posts are entirely destitute of suitable accommodations for the sick. A large portion of the buildings appropriated to that purpose have been erected a long time and were built with perishable materials in a hasty manner to meet the exigencies of the occasion, while at most of the works recently completed, no provision is made for the sick, who are necessarily placed in damp casements, or in temporary buildings entirely unfit to protect them from the inclemencies of the weather, or to preserve the property under the charge of the medical officers."[48]

In 1839, the 8,950-man army of the United States reported 22,248 cases of disease. On average, a soldier reported sick every five months.

While Letterman attended medical school classes in early 1846, negotiations were taking place between the United States and Mexico over America's expansionist intent to annex the Southwest, from Texas to California. That summer less than seventy-five medical officers supported General Zachary Taylor's 8,000 soldiers when they marched into Mexico-controlled South Texas. As it had been at the outset of the War of 1812, the military medical corps was unprepared and understaffed. Scurvy, measles, mumps, and malaria overwhelmed the medical staff. Volunteer soldiers from rural areas who had not been exposed to childhood diseases proved particularly vulnerable.[49]

As the war extended into Mexico and America's army grew twelvefold, Congress authorized a medical staff increase to only 115 medical officers and 135 medical staff volunteers.[50] Staff shortages plagued the medical department. The absence of an ambulance corps forced medical officers to sometimes beg quartermasters for wagons to transport the wounded and sick. The army's regimental hospitals amounted to little more than a collection of tents that lacked nurses and stewards.[51] Wounds quickly became infected and infested with maggots as hospital gangrene swept through rows of patients.

Mortality rates became appalling. In 1847, the overall yellow fever mortality rate totaled 28 percent, and spiked to 66 percent in August of that year.[52] The supply of quinine to treat malaria was insufficient. Some of the troops had not been inoculated against smallpox, although General George Washington had proved the vaccine's effectiveness when he became the first general to have his army inoculated seventy years earlier.

By the time the Treaty of Guadalupe Hidalgo was signed on February 2, 1848, more than 100,000 troops had been sent to Mexico. Enemy fire killed 1,500 while more than 10,000 died from disease. Statistically, it became America's most deadly war with one in ten men dying of disease. The disease rate was ten times that of the civilian population, not counting the thousands of soldiers who returned home permanently debilitated by chronic dysentery.[53] An undermanned and unprepared military medical corps had stood nearly powerless in its war against disease and the enemy.

Jonathan Letterman graduated from Jefferson Medical College in March 1849. He had completed two sets of lectures, studied as a physician's apprentice for three years, and wrote a medical paper that he submitted to the school's dean. His final-year thesis was entitled "Influence of Sects in Medicine on the Science."[54] After passing an oral examination by the entire medical school faculty, Letterman became part of a graduating class of 188 new doctors.

Letterman could have returned to Canonsburg and established a medical practice. His mother's side of the family remained well connected, and his father had built a respected family medical reputation prior to his death. It presumably would not have been too difficult to become a successful leading citizen in his hometown, where there were few physicians, and to help his mother raise his two younger brothers. But perhaps life's horizon beckoned to the young man who had been away from home for the first time in his life. A strong work ethic and powerful drive for achievement had propelled him to an elevated status in the student body. Perhaps that had spawned a desire for a career greater than small-town medicine. The army needed physicians and offered medical school graduates immediate responsibility for hundreds of men. Remote outposts in

California, Kansas, New Mexico, Florida, Minnesota, Arizona, and elsewhere carried the scent of adventure.

Jonathan Letterman traveled to New York City to face a military examination board. As one of fifty-two U.S. Army physician applicants, he had to demonstrate "knowledge of Latin, of physics or natural philosophy, of a given amount of practical anatomy in the form of dissection and a certain amount of clinic instruction." Eighteen withdrew during the review, seven failed the physical examination, and one was not a U.S. citizen. The U.S. Army accepted Letterman and twenty-five others. One of those accepted, medical school graduate William Hammond, later would form a far-reaching alliance with Letterman. On June 29, 1849, Hammond and Jonathan Letterman joined the U.S. Army as assistant surgeons.[55]

America had grown to encompass thirty states. A vast territory from Colorado's Rockies to California's Sierra Nevada had been added to the country. Gold had been discovered in California. Waves of immigrants reached both coasts. A railroad network had begun to connect the major cities of the East. Westward expansion into remote and barely explored territories took place in wagons and on foot. Territories from Florida to Minnesota required security that only an undermanned U.S. Army and its skeletal medical department could provide. The need for hundreds of army outposts, most of them staffed by a single medical officer, provided unique opportunities for medical school graduates eager to practice their craft, including Jonathan Letterman. Upon passing his exam by the army medical board of examiners in New York City in 1849, he received orders to report to a remote outpost in Florida where he would be responsible for the health of up to two hundred men.[56] He was twenty-four years old.

2

OUTPOST MEDICINE

"We had no bandages."

Summer swarms of mosquitoes greeted Letterman when he arrived at Fort Meade in the heart of southern Florida's swamps in late summer 1849. Nearly all of the army's outposts were located in remote regions of America's expanding frontier. Here, as in many far-flung outposts, hasty construction in an unsuitable site based on real and perceived threats made duty rigorous and oftentimes debilitating.

Although the brutal, seven-year war against the Seminoles had ended in 1842, tension between settlers and the Seminoles in southern Florida persisted when Letterman arrived seven years later. Isolated Indian attacks against white settlers in 1848 prompted the army to build a two-hundred-mile, all-weather road from Tampa on the west coast across to Fort Pearce on the east coast, reinforced by military outposts about every ten miles along its route. The line of defense was intended to keep Florida's Indians penned inside 26,000 square miles of extreme South Florida.[1] Lieutenant George Meade surveyed a portion of road's route in late 1849 and identified the location for a new fort alongside Peace River about fifty miles east of present-day Tampa.

Endless swamps surrounded the location. When senior officers approved his plan, they named the outpost Fort Meade.[2]

Within a few months, a half-mile square bluff overlooking the river had been converted into a hardscrabble military outpost. A bridge, ferry, barracks, officers' quarters, and one-room hospital were constructed. During the first summer's operation in 1850, Letterman faced widespread malaria among the troops. Nearly a third of the detachment of two hundred men fell victim in one ninety-day period.[3]

Because of the army's chronic shortage of medical officers, Letterman also became responsible for the troops at a nearby outpost, Fort Chokonikla. They, too, suffered horribly at the onset of summer. In June, approximately 70 percent of the troops had fallen sick. Letterman's diagnosis on July 1 concluded that the "prevailing sickness is caused by malarious exhalations, and is chiefly in the form of Intermittent and Remittent fevers, which are in a majority of cases, irregular, and accompanied, frequently with excessive vomiting, owing to an inflammation of the inner coat of the stomach." In a second letter, Letterman recommended the fort, surrounded by marsh on three sides, be abandoned, noting, "a day but seldom passes without some men, varying from one to four or five, being taken sick, who were, apparently, in perfect health in the morning."[4]

Letterman apparently wasn't pleased with his first army assignment. In July 1850, he wrote Surgeon General Thomas Lawson, asking if a medical officer had been assigned to a military expedition to map the relatively new border between the United States and Mexico. Lawson had been named the army's second surgeon general in 1836, a few months after Joseph Lovell died at the age of forty-seven. His eighteen-year tenure as surgeon general had been marked by increased professionalism among the medical corps and widespread support for his policies within the corps. His successor, Lawson, was nearly the polar opposite of the genial Lovell.

Lawson had begun his military career by enlisting in the navy and then resigning after two years' service, before joining the army as a garrison's surgeon's mate in 1811. Lawson shared his predecessor's ambition to increase the standing and role of the medical corps. In 1839, his office published a twenty-year compilation of army medical statistics summarizing illness and mortality rates, military outpost weather reports, and medical officer reports on the physical condition of army outposts.

Yet Lawson's leadership style contrasted sharply with the Lovell's. He often clashed with superior officers, was considered relentless to a fault by those who knew him, and unhesitatingly removed subordinate medical officers deemed incompetent. A lifelong bachelor, he lacked Lovell's charm, a weakness that hampered his efforts in a political position that required tactful advocacy, coalition building, and the cultivation of powerful allies.

Lawson was sympathetic to Letterman's plight. In 1839, he had written: "The service in Florida to most of the medical officers employed there, has been, indeed, not only irksome but exceedingly laborious and hazardous, many of them having from the very dispersed state of the troops to give their attention to two, three, or more posts and stands; frequently passing from one station to another without an escort, and occasionally under fire of the enemy."[5] Nevertheless, Lawson denied Letterman's request. Four months later, Letterman sought reassignment to Oregon. That, too, was rejected. Letterman remained at Fort Meade, treating the sickly garrison.

In December 1851, the soldiers dismantled the outpost and reconstructed it at a new site on a ridge one mile west of the river.[6] It remained in an extremely remote area of Florida. The nearest civilian settlers lived more than ten miles from Fort Meade.[7] The move came during one of southern Florida's coldest winters on record. "Officers and men suffered much from the cold ... the quarters being entirely inadequate for their protection. The buildings are very inferior; those of the men are no more than sheds, which afford but little protection from the rain or cold. Being placed upon posts several feet high, and situated upon the highest ground in the vicinity, and no trees of any size near, they are necessarily much exposed to the winds, which frequently, during the winter, blow strong and cold," wrote Letterman.[8]

As the threat of Indian attacks faded following Fort Meade's relocation, the garrison's troop level shrank to less than seventy-five. On at least one occasion Letterman and the outpost's commanding officer were the sole officers present.[9]

When Congress approved an increase in the army's size during wars and conflicts, as they had done during the Mexican-American War of 1846–48, the medical department often lagged behind in the authorization of additional medical officers. In 1848, the army listed ninety-four surgeons and assistant surgeons. After accounting for illness or incapacity, certainly fewer than that were available at any given time, which left some of the army's eighty-nine outposts without a medical officer and none nearby in the event of an emergency. The shortage was not new. In 1842, the army had only seventy doctors for its seventy-five outposts.[10]

The shortage forced Surgeon General Lawson to restrict leaves of absence and to rely on contract surgeons. A civilian doctor with a private practice could make as much as $50 a month from the army by treating its soldiers. He received additional pay if he provided his own medicine, and his compensation could reach as much as $100 monthly if he had to leave his private practice behind when accompanying troops on an expedition. Some army doctors desiring personal leave reportedly had to pay for their own replacement contract surgeons if the army refused to provide funding.[11]

Army and contract doctors often faced major outbreaks of disease at isolated military outposts like Fort Meade. Yellow fever periodically raged in military ports along the Eastern seaboard and in remote outposts plagued by hordes of mosquitoes. Doctors did not understand the cause and treatment of many diseases, and some debated when and under what conditions it was necessary to place sick and dying patients in quarantine. Meanwhile, soldiers dreaded the progression of yellow fever. "In its progress, the eyes and skin became gradually yellow, until the whole body was of an intensely yellow hue; black vomit came on; tongue became black, and there was hemorrhage from the mouth and nostrils; hiccough; delirium, or coma; and death closed the scene," wrote surgeon J. B. Porter in 1841.[12]

Malaria was a near constant companion in some forts, including Fort Meade. On occasion doctors had difficulty diagnosing malaria. A soldier's jaundice could stem from spleen or liver problems. His diet could be deficient. A flushed face, rash, red eyes, and headaches resembled typhoid. Cholera produced similar diarrhea, vomiting, and stomach pain symptoms.[13]

Although doctors knew the benefits of quinine, Letterman and others sought additional treatments to ease the agony of the ill. Letterman believed ten to thirty drops of chloroform mixed with water helped soothe the stomachs of soldiers stricken with malaria. However, Letterman also briefly mentioned that such a treatment wasn't advisable for patients with inflamed stomachs.[14]

At times, Letterman dealt with inflamed egos as well as raging bowels. On December 18, 1850, William French reported to Fort Meade as the commanding officer. The same day Thomas J. Jackson reported as the quartermaster officer. Both held brevet major rank and had served together in the Mexican War. Within a few months, their friendship disintegrated, beginning with a dispute over who had responsibility for outpost construction, the commanding officer or the quartermaster.

Letterman became the unlikeliest and probably least qualified go-between in the dispute. The outpost's medical officer
had little use for interpersonal politics. He related to people
more on an intellectual than an emotional level. Yet involvement in the rapidly escalating feud between the commanding
officer and quartermaster proved unavoidable for the medical
school graduate, who had been in the military less than eighteen
months.

The disagreement became so personal that, on February 13,
French placed Jackson under arrest briefly for conduct unbecoming an officer. For his part, Jackson refused to speak to
French except when his duties required it. Jackson received a
reprimand from the commanding officer of the troops in Florida
for his behavior but remained openly defiant. On April 12, he
began interviewing soldiers about a rumor of improper conduct
between French and a nurse who cared for his bedridden, sick
wife.

Letterman had developed a moderately close relationship
with French and tried to talk Jackson out of pursuing what had
become a personal vendetta. He also didn't want French's wife,
Caroline, to learn of the rumors.[15] Jackson pressed ahead by
reporting his findings to Winfield Scott, the commanding general of the U.S. Army, but received another reprimand for insubordination. On May 21, he left Fort Meade for a philosophy
and artillery tactics teaching post at Virginia Military Institute.
French, however, was not mollified.

On July 22, French pressed charges of improper conduct
against Letterman and another officer, apparently for their
role in attempting to mediate the feud with Jackson. Senior
command saw no merit in the charges and did not convene a
court-martial hearing. Again, on August 22 and September 29,
French wrote letters to Adjutant General Roger Jones
criticizing Letterman. Again, senior officers declined to hold a

court-martial hearing. Finally, in October 1851, the army transferred French out of Fort Meade, leaving Letterman to focus
on troop health.[16] Thomas J. Jackson later became famous in the
Civil War as Stonewall Jackson.

Three years in the swamps of Florida took its toll on Letterman. On July 4, 1852, he applied for a leave of absence due
to "very disagreeable and unhealthy stations . . . harmful effects
of the climate . . . (and) matters of a private character of much
importance to me." However, he remained in Florida, and the
following March he renewed his campaign for reassignment,
requesting orders to join a survey party planning to chart a
new railroad route to the Pacific Ocean.[17] This marked his third
request for transfer, and this too was denied. Instead, Letterman
received four months' leave. He visited his mother and family
in Canonsburg before reporting for a new assignment at Fort
Ripley, Minnesota, in August 1853.

Fort Ripley had been established in 1848 by General George
M. Brooke. The Winnebago Indians had been relocated from
Iowa to an approximately ninety-square-mile reservation near
the Crow Wing and Mississippi Rivers in Minnesota. The troops
at Fort Ripley, about 150 miles northwest of St. Paul, monitored
the Winnebago as well as the Chippewa and Dakota tribes, who
were at odds.[18]

Brooke had selected a location on the western bank of the
Mississippi, even though the sole road leading to St. Cloud ran
on the opposite side of the 180-yard-wide river. The outpost
sat on a one-square-mile plateau overlooking the Mississippi.
It comprised a collection of one-and-a-half story, wood-
frame buildings that formed three sides of a square. The north
side consisted in housing for officers, a chapel, and Letterman's hospital. The south row of buildings contained additional officers' quarters, chaplain's quarters, and a sutler's store,
while the west side held the enlisted men's barracks. On the

east, the fort opened to the Mississippi.[19] As with many remote forts, river marshes lay nearby. Hills covered with dense stands of birch, pine, maple, and elms rose up near the swampy ground that extended from the river's bank.[20]

Letterman had traded the suffocating summers and one uncommonly cold winter in Florida for the biting winters of Minnesota. On January 23, 1854, some mercury was taken from a thermometer at Fort Ripley and placed in a charcoal cup. It froze in fifteen minutes. The next day the mercury congealed in the thermometer bulb. Temperatures recorded elsewhere in the region that morning consistently read more than thirty degrees below zero, making it the coldest stretch of weather in fourteen years.[21] Besides severely impacting the health of the troops in Letterman's charge, the harsh living conditions produced a different kind of hazard: the risk of losing control of the fires that were kept burning in poorly constructed wood barracks in order to stay warm.

Letterman's medical duties at Fort Ripley were typical of military outpost medicine in the 1850s. He examined newly arrived recruits, managed the one-room cabin called a hospital, and recorded weather and geographical features of the region at the direction of the surgeon general. Weather observations had been standardized among all outposts. Letterman kept a weather log filled with daily readings taken at sunrise, 9:00 a.m., 3:00 p.m., and 9:00 p.m.[22]

He treated disease with limited resources under primitive conditions, which led to relapses and sometimes permanent disability. Every army outpost doctor faced the same. "Intermittent fever is a subject of much interest to the army medical officer, inasmuch it is encountered at every step of the progress. He has to deal with the disease under circumstances hostile to his remedial means; for his patients have frequently only the shelter of a tent from the chill night air and the burning sun, and their continuance in unhealthy positions, which for military reasons, cannot be abandoned, subjects them to the continued influence of the cause of the very disease he is attempting to cure; hence the liability to relapses and fresh attacks, which prove so harassing to the surgeon, and, occasionally, so ruinous to the health of the soldier," wrote Assistant Surgeon Robert Southgate in 1853. "Soldiers, as a class are proverbially reckless. Although warned, when returned to duty, against throwing themselves into currents of fresh air after having been heated by drill or other military duty, I have known relapses repeatedly induced by such exposure. An hour's exposure in the ardent rays of the sun, in the passive amusement of fishing, has repeatedly brought back to the hospital soldiers who, a few days before, were returned to duty in perfect health."[23]

Letterman spent one winter at Fort Ripley before the army transferred him to the Department of New Mexico. He traveled down the Mississippi by steamer in April 1854 and disembarked at St. Louis. He then took an overland route to Fort Leavenworth, Kansas, where, on July 1, he joined troops on a march toward the southwest, and reported for duty in Albuquerque on September 6. There he received orders for Fort Defiance in northeastern Arizona. He reported for duty there on September 20.[24]

Letterman had never seen anything like the region of Fort Defiance. A high, desert sun baked the soil chalk dry. Naked, red ridges and crumbling mesas alternated with deep arroyos and canyons. Dense stands of trees in sandy riverbed bottoms revealed a reachable subsurface water table and the course of seasonal flash floods. Ancient lava flows hundreds of feet thick and sometimes nearly a mile wide sat frozen on a long-ago course of their choice. Dry, bone-chilling winter cold gave way to dusty spring winds. Summer baked everything to the horizon, briefly punctuated by towering, smoke-gray thunderstorms that pounded the parched desert along their paths.

At the outbreak of the Mexican War in 1846, the army had
sent a detachment from Fort Leavenworth to seize control of
the New Mexico territory. Colonel Stephen Kearny met no
meaningful resistance. Following the war, the army established
Fort Union near Santa Fe in 1851, and in the same year Colonel
Edwin Sumner founded Fort Defiance in the heart of territory
long occupied by the Navajo. The outpost had been built on
the southern slope of the Chuska Mountains at an elevation of
nearly seven thousand feet, about one mile west of the present
Arizona–New Mexico border and about eighty miles south of
the Four Corners region.[25]

When Letterman arrived in 1854, a rough collection of buildings formed Fort Defiance, at the mouth to Quartzite Canyon.
Five enlisted men's barracks on the east and west sides of the
parade ground each measured one hundred long by twenty feet
wide. Officers on the north side lived in two-room quarters that
included a small kitchen. The post also comprised storerooms, a
guard house, a shop, and a hospital the same size as an enlisted
barrack. Log buildings with sod roofs failed to block northeastern Arizona's cold winds.[26]

Once again Letterman found harsh conditions. During the
heat of summer, monsoon rains from late June to September
made all but a few well-worn paths impassable. Pine, pinon,
scrub oak, and scrub cedar were in sparse supply, and there
was little grazing for the horses. The troops lived in poorly
ventilated barracks and suffered from a variety of respira-
tory ailments. A deficient diet often led to additional medical
issues. Scurvy, a preventable vitamin C deficiency, sickened
many men.

Scurvy surfaced seasonally at many military outposts in locations where the soil was too poor for vegetable gardens and
too remote for a steady supply of fresh produce from regional
supply depots. The symptoms included fatigue, nausea, bleeding

gums, loosened teeth, generalized aches, slow-healing wounds, and internal bleeding into muscles and joints.

Long before Letterman had joined the army, its first surgeon general, Joseph Lovell, had considered the army-sanctioned diet that emphasized meat to be a major cause for concern. The daily food ration included twenty ounces of beef and twelve ounces of pork, about a third of a pint of whiskey, and no daily requirement for fruits or vegetables. Usually soldiers found themselves cooking for the first time in their lives. They tended to overboil the beef, which destroyed its nutrients, while the salt pork was eaten raw. Some soldiers drank diluted whiskey with meals for weeks at a time instead of water or coffee. Lovell had advocated less meat and more vegetables (in soups), molasses or beer instead of liquor, and more bread. Attempts at supplying barely edible dried vegetables were met with disdain by the troops. In the Southwest, edible native plants rich in vitamin C offered an alternative. They included pokeweed, prickly pear cactus, and wild onion.[27]

Other outposts were less fortunate. When Fort Laramie assistant surgeon Edward Jones requisitioned vegetables, the army's commissary department replied, "Attempts have on several occasions have been made by this department to forward potatoes, fresh, to Fort Laramie from Fort Leavenworth, but the loss and decay has been so great as to make the expense for the benefit conferred, very heavy. On this occasion it was deemed less necessary, as that post was liberally supplied with desiccated mixed vegetables, and desiccated potatoes."[28]

While Letterman monitored his troops' diet at Fort Defiance, his former medical school classmate, William Hammond, conducted dietary experiments on himself while stationed at Fort Riley, Kansas. Hammond published a paper on the results that received an award from the American Medical Association. The deleterious effects of self-experimentation and national recognition earned him a leave of absence to recuperate and study with one of the nation's leading medical scientists, Silas Wier Mitchell, in Philadelphia.[29] Hammond, a physician of insatiable curiosity, boundless ego, and a willingness to challenge conventional thought, had taken the first step on a path that would lead him to becoming the army's surgeon general and to a close relationship with Letterman during the Civil War.

The variable desert weather affected troop health as well. January sunrise temperatures in the twenties were common, while summer heat routinely rose into the nineties. For the third consecutive post, Letterman's troops suffered from record-breaking winter cold. On December 25, 1855, the temperature sank to thirty-two degrees below zero, and the winter of 1855–1856 became one of the most severe in recent memory, according to the Navajos who lived in huts made of branches and twigs or in caves among the rocky outcrops.[30]

The Navajos did not impress Letterman. As at all military outposts, medical officer responsibilities included written reports on the region's local population. Although the Navajos got along well with the Fort Defiance troops, selling them peaches in August, "Like all Indians, they will not work more than is necessary for subsistence. . . . They are, however, industrious beggars," wrote Letterman. "Theft and mendacity are common vices. The habit of stealing is so common, that they will appropriate to themselves whatever they can lay their hands on, whether of any use or not, such as door-knobs and keys."[31]

In May 1857, Letterman marched with Colonel William Loring on an expedition into the Mogollon Mountains in southwestern New Mexico to capture renegade Mogollon Apaches who were suspected of kidnapping Indian agent Henry Dodge. Originally educated as a lawyer (he had practiced law in Florida), Loring had been wounded three times in the Mexican-American War and had lost an arm. During the California gold rush, he had taken command of the Oregon Territory before being assigned to a series of military outposts, including Fort Union. He favored long hair that curled over his ears and a mustache wrapping around his mouth and merging into a narrow beard covering his chin and hanging down in front of his throat. The one-armed veteran had become noted for his aggressive attacks against an enemy. The year before, at the age of thirty-eight, Loring had become the youngest colonel in the army.

Loring's expedition could not find the Mogollon Apaches but crossed paths with a band of Mimbres Apaches who were herding two thousand stolen sheep into deep canyons formed by vertical red cliffs. Loring tracked them into a particularly rocky canyon. Rifle fire echoed between the canyon's walls when Loring's soldiers ambushed the Indians on May 24, 1857. A number of Indians fell dead as warriors launched arrows up into the expedition's elevated positions. Several soldiers were wounded before the Indians abandoned the herd, leaving their chief, Cuchillo Negro, and six others lying dead among the scattered sheep.

Letterman treated the soldiers who suffered arrow wounds in the battle. The procedure was usually as follows: the surgeon would stick his finger into the wound along the shaft to find the arrowhead and then use long forceps to yank the arrowhead out. While that procedure might avoid blood poisoning, an infected wound almost inevitably resulted. Wound treatment at the time generally left the wounds open, which extended the healing process.

The Loring expedition returned in September to Fort Union, New Mexico, where Letterman became that post's medical officer. Loring was so impressed with him that in a letter to a friend years later he described him as responsive and professional, qualities that endeared him to fellow soldiers, and wrote: "I never knew an officer who was all the time more ready to act at the call of duty; full of many sympathies, he was ever ready to render timely aid to the suffering, whether at the summons of an officer or the call of a private soldier." He concluded that Letterman was "an ardent student" in quest of "the highest knowledge in the scientific advancement of his profession."[32]

Once more Letterman confronted the challenge of maintaining the health of soldiers stationed at a poorly built, exposed, and crumbling military outpost. Fort Union was located in the barren Mora Valley east of Santa Fe, near the junction of the Cimarron and Mountain branches of the Santa Fe Trail. It sat at the edge of the plains in a sea of gamma grass at an elevation of nearly 6,700 feet. The nearest source of timber was seven miles away, and the Mora River flowed five miles from the outpost.[33] Its singular strategic value lay in protecting caravans on the Santa Fe Trail as they passed through Southern Ute and Apache land in the north as well as Comanche and Kiowa land on the plains.

The assistant surgeon wasn't surprised by Fort Union's dilapidated condition. A year earlier, in 1856, Letterman had inspected the collection of more than two dozen buildings made of pine and adobe. He had submitted a particularly critical sanitary report on the outpost, which had been built five years earlier and housed a fighting force of about 160 men. "Unseasoned, unhewn, and unbarked pine logs, placed upright in some and horizontally in other houses . . . and as a necessary consequence are rapidly decaying. . . . The unbarked logs afford excellent hiding places for that annoying and disgusting insect the *cimex lectaularius* (bedbug), so common in this country . . . the men almost universally sleep in the open air when the weather will permit." The hospital was in worse condition. "The building at present used as a hospital, having a dirt roof, has not a room which remained dry during the rain in the later part of September last, and I was obliged to use tents and canvas to protect the property from damage." Letterman recommended that the entire military post be rebuilt.[34]

Fort Union was another post where the troops' diet concerned him. Lack of reliable irrigation and grasshopper infestations that ravaged the prairie limited the post's ability to grow vegetables and other crops. "Extra issues of pickles, etc., from time to time, were deemed necessary for the health of the troops who were liable at any time to be called upon for hard service," wrote Letterman.[35]

He left Fort Union on September 15, 1858, when he accompanied the outpost's sick commanding officer, Brigadier General John Garland, to St. Louis along with a small contingent of officers and five mounted riflemen. For the second time in eight years' service Letterman received a leave of absence for several months. He visited colleagues in Baltimore and Philadelphia. Two years later the army assigned one thousand men to demolish and rebuild Fort Union.

Letterman reported for duty at Fort Monroe, Virginia, on March 24, 1859. A few months short of his tenth anniversary in the military, in mid-April, the army promoted him major at a fort that later would play a prominent role during the Civil War, in the region bounded by the Confederacy's capital in Richmond and Washington. Its strategic location on the Virginia peninsula where the James and York Rivers empty into the Atlantic made it an ideal staging area for the Union's Army of the Potomac to guard against Confederate incursions toward Chesapeake Bay and attacks against Washington. Surrounded by a moat, it was the largest fort in the country. Many called it the "Gibraltar of the Chesapeake."[36]

Letterman spent a few months at Fort Monroe before he was transferred to the army's medical purveyor's office in New York City. That assignment lasted only four months, and at the end of the year Letterman again rode west, this time to California. In February 1860, he reported for duty at Fort Tejon, a military outpost in the foothills north of Los Angeles.

The collection of adobe buildings that formed Fort Tejon was located near Tejon Pass in Southern California's Tehachapi Mountains at the top of Grapevine Canyon. It had been built in 1854 in the heart of territory occupied by Chumash Indians. Poppies, lupines, and goldfields carpeted rolling hillsides in the spring, while native grasses and dense copses of oak dominated the landscape. Despite the semi-arid climate, bears prowled Fort Tejon's reliable mountain-fed stream. Its benign climate was considerably more pleasant than Florida's summers and Minnesota's winters. It was by far Letterman's most comfortable assignment after more than ten years of military service.

Like many of the posts where Letterman had served as the sole medical officer, Fort Tejon was relatively small, typically housing about two hundred men. In 1858, Fort Tejon had become a stop on an overland stage route stretching from California to St. Louis. It also was located along a major trail used by gold prospectors headed for the Sierras. Telegraph lines soon reached Fort Tejon, connecting the fort to the East Coast. Fort Tejon was one of the least-isolated outposts in Letterman's pre–Civil War career.

Two months after Letterman's arrival, Major James Henry Carleton mounted an expedition to the east against the Paiute Indians in California's Mojave Desert. The son of a ship captain had joined the army in 1838. After serving at a number of Great Plains outposts, he arrived at Fort Tejon in early 1858 with several hundred new recruits. His eyes radiated intensity, matching his zealous disciplinary demeanor. Carleton had demonstrated a particular brutality against Native Americans, and he intended to punish the Indians who allegedly had been attacking travelers on the road between Salt Lake and Los Angeles.

Widely scattered apricot mallow, lilac sunbonnet, and prickly poppy blooms dotted the Mojave Desert when Letterman accompanied Carleton's troops on the weeklong,

170-mile march to the Mojave River, near present-day Bar-
stow.[37] Fine dust floating in their wake marked the progress of
their column of horses and wagons along the nomadic Indian
trails that connected the Colorado River and the Pacific Ocean.
Letterman crossed salt marshes and skirted low hills dotted
with sagebrush, creosote bush, and yucca as the desert grew
more barren as the expedition headed east. Cottonwoods and
clouds of insects marked where the river cut between heavy
sand and gravel ridges that stretched to the horizon.

Upon arrival, the expedition built a crude camp, mostly
comprised of dugouts carved out of the desert sand and
covered with brush and wet mud that passed for adobe. A
square five-foot-high perimeter wall, forty feet long on each
side, protected the temporary camp. Shortly afterward, Carleton
dispatched patrols in search of Paiutes in the area, apparently with
little regard to whether they had been involved in the reported
attacks. On April 19, Second Lieutenant B. F. Davis's patrol
found two Paiutes hunting game. On orders by Davis, the troops
charged, firing their weapons. The Paiutes' meager return fire
of arrows wounded two soldiers. Soldiers carried the wounded
men twelve miles back to Camp Cady for Letterman's treatment. "In the affray, two men were seriously wounded, one in
the neck and one in the abdomen, by Indians. . . . Both were
doing well, but the one wounded in the abdomen is not out of
danger yet," wrote Letterman.[38] It became the last documented
instance in which Letterman treated "combat" casualties before
the outbreak of the Civil War.

Carleton's patrols searching for the Paiutes continued for
weeks, sometimes covering as much as thirty miles a day in the
Mojave Desert whose summer temperatures routinely stayed
above one hundred degrees. One group covered more than
three hundred miles of desert before returning to the camp. By
the end of June, Carleton convinced himself the road to Los

Angeles had become safe. His troops left Camp Cady on July 3 and returned to Fort Tejon.

Letterman spent an uneventful eleven months at Fort Tejon before transferring on June 21, 1861, to Camp Fitzgerald, a training post in present-day Los Angeles that was hampered by too little water or forage for the army's horses. He arrived in a time of uncertainty within the military medical corps. One month earlier Surgeon General Thomas Lawson had died. By the time the Confederates attacked and seized Fort Sumter in the Charleston, South Carolina, harbor on April 12, 1861, he was old and sick. He succumbed less than six weeks after the start of the Civil War.

Lawson's twenty-five-year tenure had been marked by isolated medical corps accomplishments. Infamous for his impatience, aggressiveness, and jealous stewardship of his authority, Lawson on his death bequeathed his department many of the same issues that had confronted his predecessor a generation earlier: inadequate staffing, a pressing need for medical qualification standards, and adequate authority over medical supply logistics.

Part of his legacy was an army medical corps trained in outpost medicine, but that knew little more. Four decades of Indian wars resulted in small, mobile military outposts and self-reliant medical officers whose standing orders included treating soldiers, observing the local population and topography, and recording each day's weather.

Some American military officers had been sent to Europe in the 1850s to study the medical corps of other armies and their equipment and procedures. Yet, although medical officers had examined such things as alternative designs for an improved carriage for battlefield evacuation, no decisive action had been taken prior to the Civil War. Nearly eighty years old by the time of his death, Lawson had become so parsimonious that he considered medical textbooks and extra surgical instruments an extravagance.

He spent nearly a third of his budget on contract physicians. Citing a lack of medical office replacements, he had kept some of his medical officers at their posts up to ten years before granting them a two-month leave of absence. His departmental budget on the eve of the Civil War was $115,000, an inadequate sum to staff dozens of outposts and treat 30,300 disease cases annually (which represented about two illnesses per man). After the outbreak of the Civil War, his department's budget would skyrocket to a congressionally authorized $241,000 in the first year, mostly for supplies.[39] Yet stagnation, not innovation, had become the defining characteristic of his administration.

While America's military medical corps remained focused on outpost medicine, elsewhere in the world the changing face of warfare assailed and overwhelmed military medicine. In the late eighteenth century, the chief surgeon for Napoleon, Baron Dominique-Jean Larrey, had developed a rudimentary mobile field hospital concept comprised of surgeons and supplies in modified horse-drawn carriages. The carriages moved with the flow of fighting on the battlefield. The usefulness of this concept was proven in the Napoleonic Wars that followed, and by the 1830s it had become a standard component of the French army.

Conversely, the British medical corps largely had failed the 83,000 troops sent to fight in Russia in the Crimean War of 1854–1856. About one in four of the troops died, the vast majority succumbing to disease. The horrific conditions aboard patient transport ships bound for Turkey, where wounded soldiers lay on open decks, precipitated a massive public outcry. Thanks to this, a sanitary commission was eventually established to monitor and support the British medical corps.

After the fall of Fort Sumter in April 1861, war loomed in America. President Lincoln called for volunteers, and by April 27 several states had responded, with the rolls of volunteers ranging from 1,000 from Rhode Island to 30,000 from New York, and to as many as 100,000 from Pennsylvania.[40] State volunteer regiments included surgeons who lacked battlefield experience and some who had never operated on a patient. The state regiments' civilian doctors, who had almost no relevant experience and had no understanding of the unique challenges of military medicine, marginally augmented the undermanned and ill-prepared army medical corps.

Equally challenging, volunteer physicians often differed in their approach to patient care. Some, considered "irregular doctors," were not necessarily medical school graduates. Irregulars included eclectic practitioners who blended family herbal medications, botanical medicine, and sometimes Native American remedies. Some were homeopaths who believed small doses of substances that caused symptoms in healthy patients could cure sick patients who exhibited those same symptoms. Unlike the eclectic and homeopathic doctors, the army's "regulars" favored massive doses of purgatives as well as mercury- and opium-based compounds as medications.

By mid-July, tens of thousands of soldiers sat idle in suffocating humidity among hundreds of white conical tents in army camps around Washington, waiting for orders. Army doctors checked their supplies and requisitioned more while President Lincoln pressed Brigadier Irvin McDowell of the Army of Northeastern Virginia, to attack the Confederates in Virginia. Twenty-five miles away, near Manassas Junction, Confederate generals Joseph E. Johnston and P. G. T. Beauregard prepared their 30,000 troops for battle. McDowell lacked confidence in his untested army, which was comprised mostly of new volunteers, but he developed a plan to make a diversionary attack at Manassas and then flank the Confederates' position to cut off their retreat to Richmond.

On July 16, McDowell's army, the largest army assembled in the history of the nation to that point, left Washington to confront the Confederates. The lumbering, undisciplined, and poorly coordinated march toward the enemy squandered McDowell's manpower advantage. And while his army took two days to reach Centreville, the medical corps lost critical supplies when many of its wagons were left behind to hasten the march toward the enemy. Then, during the two days the Union army spent in the Centreville area, "no hospital arrangements were made . . .; no plan was made for transporting the wounded; everything was left to take care of itself, haphazard."[41] The disorganized battle preparation gave Johnston and Beauregard invaluable time to marshal their Confederate forces, since they knew where McDowell's troops were positioned.

Before dawn on July 21, more than 30,000 Union soldiers marched toward Manassas Junction followed by hundreds of Washington residents in private carriages, eager to watch the first major battle of the war. Most had yet to set out picnic blankets atop ridges when the first artillery exchange started a little after 5:00 a.m.

Once the battle began, Union artillery proved particularly lethal as the fighting intensified throughout the morning. But the frequently timid McDowell held two of his five divisions in reserve and allowed a lull in the fighting to take hold about midday. As the Confederates regrouped, hundreds of soldiers wounded after a few hours' fighting confronted McDowell's medical officers.

The medical department's lack of preparedness and cohesive authority became evident as the casualties mounted. Some state regiments had gone into battle with almost no field medical support. The First Connecticut Volunteers, numbering nearly 700 men, "had one two-horse ambulance and two wall tents for hospital use; no hospital supplies and apparently no litters. There were no men to use this equipment except the band men."[42] There were few places to evacuate the most seriously wounded. Medical officers set up treatment stations in commandeered houses, churches, and dry creek beds where necessary.

Once the aid stations became operational, the fragmented nature of a Union army comprised of federal troops and state volunteer regiments became evident. Army medical director William S. King reported that "a hospital established by one regiment, refused to receive certain wounded men because they belonged to other regiments."[43]

The fighting resumed at mid-afternoon after the Confederates had fallen back and regrouped. The battle turned in the Confederates' favor when one of their Virginia units, dressed in blue uniforms similar to the Union army, advanced to within seventy yards of the Union's deadly hilltop artillery. Their sneak attack devastated the artillery troops and enabled the Confederates to take control of the strategic position. Although McDowell's forces assigned to the hill outnumbered Confederate forces by an almost two-to-one margin, he engaged just three of his five divisions at any one time, neutralizing his advantage for lack of nearby reinforcements in the midst of battle.

Carnage in the Union army mounted under withering Confederate fire. Nurse Emma Edmonds recorded the destruction in her diary. "Still the battle continues without cessation; the grape and canister fill the air as they go screaming on their fearful errand; the sight of that field is perfectly appalling; men tossing their arms wildly calling for help; there they lie bleeding, torn, and mangled; legs, arms and bodies are crushed and broken as if smitten by thunder-bolts; the ground is crimson with blood; it is terrible to witness."[44]

Without artillery protection, the poorly disciplined Union army disintegrated. By 4:00 p.m. full and chaotic retreat had begun, leaving hundreds of wounded lying on the battlefield and at makeshift aid stations. Wagons that could have evacuated some of the wounded had been commandeered for a more rapid retreat. In some cases, medical officers abandoned their patients to the enemy, while others stayed at their posts.

As the Union army fell back, some medical officers reassigned to makeshift hospitals in the rear at Centreville found conditions little better than those on the front line. "We had no bandages, no lint, no sponges, no cerate, and but very little water, and I think only one basin. . . . Three or four (patients) had balls (pass) through their bodies, and had walked two or three miles to the village . . . one was brought up with a wound in his thigh, who had lain on the field since the Thursday preceding (a casualty from a pre-battle skirmish)," wrote New York volunteer surgeon Frank H. Hamilton.[45] The army's retreat continued into the night as a handful of doctors frantically sought to stem the bleeding of the wounded.

The handful of ambulances available had no field hospitals to which they could transport wounded. Three hundred wounded were deposited at Sudley Church and in nearby stands of trees. Surgeons gathered there as well, in the absence of clear orders to treat the wounded at specific locations. The bulk of the battle's wounded were left to either walk off the battlefield or lie abandoned in the field of fire.

The following day, when the weather turned cold and wet, Hamilton and other surgeons left their most severely wounded patients at Centreville to the Confederates and returned to Washington. "I could not tell them I was about to leave them, and I trust in leaving them so I did them no wrong. I could be of no more service to them until morning, and then I presumed they would be in the hands of a civilized and humane enemy who would care for them better than we could."[46] A few surgeons voluntarily stayed with approximately 500 wounded army soldiers in the Sudley Church area, where the wounded and doctors were eventually taken prisoner and shipped to Richmond as a blanket of shock settled on the defeated Union army.

The shock wave reached Washington the following morning, when residents rose to a ghastly sight. "I awoke from a deep sleep this morning, about six o'clock. The rain was falling in torrents and beat with a dull, thudding sound on the leads outside my window; but, louder than all, came a strange sound, as if of a tread of men, a confused stamp and splashing, and a murmuring of voices. . . . I saw a steady stream of men covered in mud, soaked through with rain, who were pouring irregularly, without any semblance of order, up Pennsylvania Avenue towards the Capitol. . . . Many of them were without knapsacks, crossbelts, and firelocks. Some had neither great-coats nor shoes, others were covered with blankets. . . . I ran down stairs and asked an officer . . . where the men were coming from. 'Where from? Well, sir, I guess we're all coming out of Verginny as far as we can, and pretty well whipped, too . . . I know I'm going home. I've had enough of fighting to last a lifetime.'"[47]

That soldier had reached Washington after a retreat that had become mired in "the dust of the turnpike, between Centreville and Fairfax, raised by our soldiers and wagons passing, floating over the road like a thick fog . . . in this passage, horse, foot, and vehicles were jammed in great confusion; upturned wagons and their contents blocked the way at short intervals . . . so slow was our progress that we did not reach Fairfax, a distance of only seven miles, till two o'clock the next morning," wrote King.[48]

For days in the battle's aftermath, the walking wounded wandered the streets of Washington, waiting for space in one of the city's four hospitals. More than 1,500 casualties had over-whelmed an inexperienced medical corps that had no medical battle plan, suffered from a significantly fractured organiza-tion, and had endured a paucity of resources. Hundreds more casualties remained on the battlefield, enduring two days of cold and rain. The last of the wounded were removed from the bat-tlefield a week after the battle.

Reports from regimental surgeons horrified the general pub-lic. W. W. Keen of the 5th Massachusetts stated that his ambulance drivers and hospital stewards were members of the regiment's drum corps. John Foye of the 11th Massachusetts wrote that his regiment was supplied with a single ambulance well stocked with stimulants and medical implements but devoid of medicine and tents.

Yet the Army of Northeastern Virginia's medical director William S. King painted a different picture five days after the battle when he wrote, "It is due to the ambulance drivers to say that they performed their duties efficiently, and the results of their operations also show how absolutely necessary these means of conveyance are to the comfort and relief of the wounded, in giving them shelter and water when ready to perish with heat and thirst." He claimed regiment medical staff "discharged their duties satisfactorily" but acknowledged that "The impossibility of making a careful survey of the field after the battle had ceased must be my apology for the briefness and want of detail in this report."[49]

Regardless of King's claims, reports of how the wounded suf-fered and lay unattended horrified the North. President Lincoln, political leaders, and civilians in Washington looked out their windows at homeless, wounded soldiers in search of shelter. Many had walked more than twenty miles back to the city. One soldier hiked back to the city after an arm had been shot off. Another made it after having been shot through his cheeks, jaw and tongue. One soldier hiked back to the city after being shot through both thighs and the scrotum. The dehydrated, walking wounded reached a city whose hospitals were already full. A report issued after the battle by a civilian organization formed to assist the military's medical department stated dimly: "The Sanitary Commission was unable to learn of a single wounded man having reached the capital in an ambulance."[50]

The Union had suffered a crushing defeat on a battlefield almost within sight of the nation's capital. The debacle revealed a fundamentally flawed and unprepared Union army incapable of ending the war in a few months, as many had formerly expected. Its medical department needed new leadership, organization, resources, and perhaps most importantly, the authority to adequately prepare, deploy and treat the wounded in battle. Worse, the battle at Manassas Junction (which was also called Bull Run) would become a harbinger of far larger and deadlier battles. Ultimately the 2.2 million–man Union army would become a fighting force more than twenty times larger than the army that had been assembled in the Mexican–American War thirteen years earlier. Those soldiers would depend on a meager medical corps that would have to hone its medical skills and leadership ability under fire.

3

THE HAMMOND ALLIANCE

"Their wounds, as yet, undressed"

The disaster that ripped through the Union troops at Bull Run should not have been a surprise. Brigadier General Irvin McDowell had taken command of the Army of Northeastern Virginia only two months earlier, over the objections of the Union army's general in chief, Winfield Scott. A surprise appointment by President Lincoln, the forty-two-year-old West Point graduate from Ohio had never commanded troops in battle. Oddly proportioned with a large body atop short legs, he had a huge appetite, spoke French, and had a fondness for waltzes, landscape gardening, and architecture. McDowell had been inspecting volunteer regiments at the time of his appointment. Scott considered other officers better qualified to lead troops into the first major battle of the war.

McDowell's medical director, William S. King, had much less time to prepare for war. He had arrived at McDowell's headquarters a few days before the army began its march toward Bull Run. King had only seventy-two hours to make preparations for a major campaign by 30,000 soldiers. The quartermaster corps, responsible for providing medical transportation, denied his request for twenty medical wagons, an omen of the medical-supply shortages he would face under fire. During the battle, King's medical corps was hamstrung by an inventory of only approximately fifty ambulances manned not by teamsters but by the army's musicians. The army's line officers, anxious to engage the enemy, had ignored King's counsel to feed the troops before embarking on a double-quick march hours before sunrise on the day of battle.

Bull Run confirmed the worst fears of many in the civilian medical community. Early in 1861, with war on the horizon, several private humanitarian organizations had been established, mostly to provide supplies and technical assistance to the Union army. Chapters were established in various states that were forming more than three dozen volunteer regiments.

One such organization was the United States Sanitary Commission. A few days after the attack on Fort Sumter, Dr. Henry Bellows, a prominent Unitarian minister, and Dr. Elisha Harris, the superintendent of a New York City hospital, began forming a humanitarian organization. They feared Union soldiers could suffer as horribly as British soldiers had during the Crimean War five years earlier. Massive armies around the world with increasingly lethal weaponry produced unimagined numbers of wounded in the mid-nineteenth century. Few had confidence that the Union army's medical department had kept pace.

They marshaled commitments from other newly formed relief societies and sent a delegation to Washington. On May 18, they asked acting Surgeon General R. C. Wood to recommend establishment of a Sanitary Commission representing their interests that would investigate and advise on standards of soldier care. They sought no federal funds or legal authority. Wood clung to the belief that imminent war with the South would be "only the Florida or Mexican war on a large scale, and that the existing machinery was capable of such expansion as fully to provide for every possible contingency . . . and any attempt from outside to interfere with its methods, could produce only confusion, embarrassment, and all those evils which destroy an army by introducing into it loose notions of military discipline and responsibility."[1]

Despite the medical department's blinkered, provincial attitude, on June 13 President Lincoln approved Secretary of War Cameron's recommendation to create the United States Sanitary Commission. Its charge was to advise military medical officers on the health inspections of recruit, military camp sanitation, preventive health care, military diet, and medical supplies and logistics. It could provide donated medical supplies, clothing, and other personal items for soldiers. Although limited in its influence, the commission took an active interest in the leadership of the army's medical department when Surgeon General Lawson died on May 15, at the age of seventy-two.

The commission lobbied for any of several much younger and highly qualified surgeons to replace Lawson. One was William Hammond, the intellectual surgeon-scientist who had entered the military with Letterman and later attracted national military medicine attention with the diet studies he conducted early in his career. President Lincoln instead appointed another elderly surgeon, Clement Alexander Finley, as surgeon general. His decision infuriated the commission. "It is criminal weakness to intrust such responsibilities of the surgeon-general to a self-satisfied, supercilious, bigoted blockhead, merely because he is the oldest of the old mess-room doctors of the frontier-guard of the country. . . . He knows nothing, and does nothing, and is capable of knowing nothing and doing nothing but quibble about matters of form and precedent," wrote the commission's executive secretary, Frederick Law Olmstead.[2]

Clement Alexander Finley, age of sixty-four, had served as a medical officer since 1818 in a string of routine garrison assignments. His single substantial opportunity to develop combat medical experience was during the Mexican-American War, but twice his service had been cut short by illness and transfer back to the United States. At the time of his appointment, much of his duties had been to examine military surgeon candidates. To many, it appeared he was appointed by President Lincoln over the acting Surgeon General Wood because Wood was the brother-in-law of the Confederate president, Jefferson Davis.

Finley was an unremarkable military surgeon who became surgeon general at a time when most line officers held the medical department in low regard. That lack of respect placed a premium on resolute and collaborative leadership by the new medical commander. Finley failed on both counts. Shortly after Finley took office, Major General Benjamin Butler's troops suffered a number of casualties while attacking a Confederate battery near Fort Monroe. Rather than rely on his medical director, John Cuyler, and Cuyler's staff as it coped with a measles outbreak, Butler commandeered a local hotel as his command hospital for fifty-three wounded. To treat them, he asked his family's physician, Gilman Kimball, to leave an army hospital in Annapolis where he was a contract surgeon. Although Kimball violated Finley's direct orders not to abandon Annapolis, the surgeon general did nothing about that act of insubordination and later Kimball became a brigade surgeon.[3] Cuyler wasn't the only medical director whom the surgeon general failed to strongly support.

While Letterman and other veteran medical officers continued to serve in isolated military outposts thousands of miles from the war, the build-up of a massive army filled with incompetent civilian doctors and unqualified soldiers tested the leadership deficit in the medical department even further. In the months preceding Bull Run in 1861, newly formed state volunteer regiments poured into the nation's capital, some of them arriving in cattle cars. Many of the troops were sick, some were dehydrated, and few had the requisite equipment a soldier needed to wage war or take care of himself.

The recruits supposedly had been screened prior to arrival. But lax army regulations led to haphazard inspections based mostly on a cursory visual inspection. "In passing a recruit, the medical officer is to examine him stripped; to see that he has free use of all his limbs; that his chest is ample; that his hearing, vision and speech are perfect; that he has no tumors, or ulcerated or cicatrized legs; no rupture or chronic cutaneous affection; that he has not received any contusion, or wound of the head, that may impair his faculties; that he is not subject to convulsions; and has no infectious disorder that may unfit him for military service."[4]

As undemanding as the screening standards were, many of those responsible for the screenings were unqualified to conduct them. In Indiana, the governor suggested a medical staff appointee who had been a hospital steward and had read materials in a doctor's office. While Ohio, Vermont, and Massachusetts regiments had rigorous examinations by qualified medical personnel, in Wisconsin regiment colonels "examined" medical staff volunteers[5]—a medical degree was not required at the time.

Many marginally qualified doctors in the volunteer regiments thus became responsible for the health and hygiene of thousands of vulnerable young men away from home for the first time. Many volunteers had not developed immunity to childhood diseases and had been used to mothers or servants washing their clothes, cleaning their quarters, and cooking their food. The military camp hygiene of these men was deplorable. Meanwhile, civilian doctors had to learn the army's way of ordering food and medical supplies, securing transportation from the quartermaster, obtaining horses and forage, erecting and maintaining hospital tents, and protecting medicines in the field.[6]

Although the regular army too had a critical need to replace the surgeons who had resigned to join the Confederacy, the dearth of qualified candidates crippled its efforts to recruit them. On the day in May when Finley took over as surgeon general, the medical department accepted 62 of 116 candidates. The shortage forced the army to hire civilian doctors, many of whom were more interested in field duty so they could develop operating experience than in the routine, daily health care of soldiers.

Army quartermasters, many of whom were equally new to the army, failed to adequately prepare for the proliferating needs of the newly arrived combat units. Soldiers stood in midsummer lines for hours, waiting to be issued rations and shelter assignments where, noted one observer, "At last, utterly worn out and disgusted . . . they reached their camps, where they received rations as unwholesome as distasteful to them, and endeavored to recruit their wasted energies while lying upon rotten straw, wrapped in a shoddy blanket."[7]

The quartermaster corps was similarly ill-prepared to provide the horses and wagons needed by the medical department. The competing priorities of carrying out officers' orders, filling troop needs in supplies and ammunition, and outfitting the medical department compounded the problem of a shortage of horses, feed, supplies, and wagons.

In July 1861 came the first significant change that would lead to Jonathan Letterman joining the Civil War. The day after the Bull Run disaster, President Lincoln decided that General McDowell had to be relieved of his command. The same day a charming and magnetic general in Ohio received a telegram. George B. McClellan, the son of the man who founded the medical school that Letterman had attended, was summoned east.

After enrolling at West Point at the age of fifteen, he had graduated second in his class of fifty-nine cadets, where aristocratic Southerners were his closest friends. After graduation, McClellan had proven to be a charismatic leader. He traveled to Europe in 1855, as part of the Delafield Commission to study the military lessons of the Crimean War. At a time when the American army had no established ambulance system, minimal hospital capacity, and moribund medical leadership, McClellan had seen firsthand how a poorly managed and inadequately equipped medical department could ravage an army.

Part of the Delafield Commission's report read, "The requisites for an ambulance should be such to adapt it to the battlefield, among the dead, wounded and dying; in the plowed fields, on hill-tops, mountain slopes, in siege batteries and trenches, and in a variety of places inaccessible to wheel carriages, of which woods, thick brush, and rocky ground are frequently the localities most obstinately defended, and where most soldiers are left for the care of surgeons."[8]

McClellan had resigned his commission in 1857 to become a railroad engineer. He rejoined the army on May 3, 1861. Among several states that sought him to command their regiments, McClellan became the commanding officer of Ohio's militia. Short, handsome, and broad-shouldered, "Little Mac" valued the pomp and circumstance of the military. His subordinates praised his organizational ability, work ethic, and general affability. McClellan had little use for civilian involvement in military matters and generally held his tongue in the presence of politicians. He did not support immediate abolition of slavery, instead favoring gradual emancipation, but confessed "to a prejudice in favor of my own race & can't learn to like the odor of either Billy goats or niggers."[9]

For all his charisma, the diminutive McClellan also had a darker side. An enormous ego led to his belief that most men were his intellectual inferior and a conviction that he was the man to save the Union on the battlefield. Others held him in high regard as well. Eleven days after reentering the service, he was promoted to major general in the Union army. At the age of thirty-four, he became the second most senior officer in the army. McClellan's presence and intellect led to his appointment in July as the commanding officer of the Military Division of the Potomac. It was one of the more prestigious and pressure-filled commands within the Union army. His primary mission was to defend the nation's capital and take the fight to the Confederates' capital, Richmond. He wasted no time in calming the chaos and organizing the post–Bull Run remnants of the highest-profile army in the Union.

McClellan demonstrated his respect for the medical department in August 1861, when he appointed Charles Tripler to replace King as medical director. Amiable but sometimes grumpy, Tripler was a highly regarded surgeon. Not only had he gained combat experience in the Mexican War at Cerro Gordo, Contrera, Churubusco, Mexico City, and Chapultepec, he had published the widely adopted *Manual of the Medical Officer of the Army of the United States* in 1858. Three years later, he published *Handbook of the Military Surgeon* with a colleague, and he had been among the candidates recommended for the post of surgeon general by the Sanitary Commission. He was lecturing on military surgery at Cincinnati Medical College at the time of his appointment.

Tripler inherited a medical department whose infrastructure had broken down. Hotels, seminaries, and other Washington buildings had been converted to makeshift hospitals, he discovered. Regimental surgeons had transferred patients to the capital without knowing if hospitals there had open beds. Hundreds of wounded and diseased soldiers were confined to their cots waiting for care in overcrowded spaces with inadequate staffing. "My friend, Lieut. M. is extremely weak and nervous, and the wild ravings of J.C. (another patient) disturb him exceedingly. I requested Surg. P. to have him removed to a more quiet ward, and received the reply, 'This is the most quiet ward in the whole building.' There are five hundred patients here who require constant attention, and not half enough nurses to take care of them.... While I write there are three being carried past the window to the dead room," wrote nurse Emma Edmonds.[10]

The lieutenant wasn't alone in his suffering. Disease rates among the various Union armies in August 1861 averaged about 30 percent, as thousands suffered from diarrhea, severe dysentery, and malaria. Army medical directors complained of a lack of tents, as most had been allotted for soldier quarters and storage. A shortage of canvas that summer made matters worse, forcing medical directors to build patient shelters from materials they scrounged in the immediate vicinity.

Yet steps were being taken after the Bull Run debacle that would later prove important for Letterman when he implemented his battlefield care reforms. On August 20, McClellan's determination to convert Union armies from a bureaucratic-style organization led to the merger of the Departments of West Virginia, Northeastern Virginia, and Shenandoah into the Army of the Potomac. McClellan now had a massive army firmly under his control and told President Lincoln that Virginia would be the primary battlefield of the war. He sought to nearly triple the size of his army to more than 250,000 men, largely based on what proved to be inaccurate reports of enemy strength developed by his intelligence officer, the detective Allan Pinkerton, who used the alias E. J. Allen.[11]

By this time, the War Department had endorsed more rigorous examination of military doctors and an investigation into complaints of poor medical care. For the first time, the army began screening military doctors when they joined the army, promoted them on merit, and held each of them accountable for his conduct. While McClellan lobbied for a larger army, his medical director now had clear authority to hold his surgeons to account for the quality of their care. But everywhere Tripler turned he saw poor organization and substandard hygiene.

Tripler took action in several areas. He became critical of the physical condition of many recruits. Faced with a disease rate of 33 percent among some regiments, he ordered the relocation of camps away from vermin- and insect-infested marshes. He also thought the long wait between reveille and breakfast contributed to malarial fevers and secured an order ensuring soldiers had coffee available shortly after sunrise reveille. He ordered vaccinations for Confederate prisoners and allowed them exercise.

Within two months, Finley grew jealous of Tripler's early success in organizing the Army of the Potomac's medical department. When Tripler met with the surgeon general in the fall of 1861, a violent argument erupted. Finley berated Tripler. Although Finley had command of all hospitals in the Washington area that served the Army of the Potomac, Tripler had opened new hospitals in the area to relieve overcrowding without informing him. The surgeon general grew so irate at what he considered insubordination that he ordered Tripler out of the room. Tripler, in turn, was so offended by Finley's conduct that he filed charges of conduct unbecoming an officer against his superior. The two settled their differences before the court martial hearing that had been scheduled for early December 1861.

By that time, Jonathan Letterman had been transferred from Los Angeles to an assignment in New York City. He had spent more than a decade rotating from one isolated military outpost to another. He had been responsible for the health and welfare of hundreds of men at a time, with no nearby medical support, and had been accountable for their health, disease and wound treatment, diet, and personal hygiene habits. Having unsuccessfully sought transfers, he had endured assignments to a series of remote postings that seemed to coincide with some of the severest regional winters in recent memory.

Letterman's duty in New York City was as a medical purveyor, whose job was to purchase supplies for the medical department. This assignment became his first experience in considering the health and material needs of thousands of soldiers rather than a few hundred. He also learned the nuances of supplying a medical corps comprised of both professional military doctors intent on spending their careers in military service as well as civilian physicians in volunteer regiments whose primary purpose was to beat the Confederates and return home as soon as possible.

In some cases, the regiments' surgeons saw the battlefield care problems more clearly than the stodgy surgeon general's office in late 1861. For example, a surgeon with the 89th New York volunteers, T. H. Squire, published a detailed battlefield evacuation plan in the *Boston Medical and Surgical Journal*. Other civilian doctors, including J. O. Bronson and Pennsylvania's surgeon general, H. H. Smith, also developed plans to speed the treatment of the wounded on the battlefield. Finley adopted none of the proposals on the grounds they had not been submitted through the chain of command and that supplies and equipment were not available to implement them.[12] At the end of 1861, Tripler and other army medical directors grew increasingly frustrated with a system where an army general commanded the military operation, the Secretary of War controlled medical supplies and logistics, and a surgeon general in a time of war was rigidly territorial rather than flexible and innovative.

While Tripler remained at odds with Finley, the Sanitary Commission became critical of Tripler. The medical director resented what he saw as intrusiveness by the Sanitary Commission and other relief organizations, writing: "I may mention here that a great deal of presumptuous intermeddling with the Medical department of this army occurred from time to time. . . . Sensation

preachers, village doctors, and strong-minded women, suddenly
smitten with a more intimate knowledge and thorough perception of the duties and administration of the medical department
of an army that I had been able to acquire in more than thirty
years' experience and study, obtruded their crude suggestions,
and marring when they could not make, and paralyzing when
they attempted to quicken, succeeded by their uniformed zeal,
innocently enough, perhaps, but no less the unfortunately on
that account, in defeating measures I had much at heart."[13]

About a month before Tripler took medical command of
the Army of the Potomac, the commission had issued detailed
recommendations of *Rules for Preserving the Health of the Soldier*
that called for short haircuts, ten-to-fifteen-minute breaks every
hour during marches in the field, and a "quick time" marching
pace of ninety to one hundred paces of twenty-eight inches per
minute. This precise standard for the soldiers' stride and speed
enabled the army to maintain a sustainable advance of about
two-and-a-half miles per hour.[14] The Union army had suffered
thousands of casualties in the early months of the war and everyone, it seemed, had an idea about how to keep soldiers healthy
and how to improve the care of those who fell on the battlefield.

The Sanitary Commission's lack of confidence in Tripler in
late 1861 matched its dedication to orchestrating the removal
of Finley as surgeon general. Tripler and Finley had held their
posts less than six months before coming under public fire.
The commission also advocated that the commanding officer
of each army, instead of the surgeon general, should select his
army's medical director. The commission went further, calling for the establishment of an ambulance regiment, given
the "utter want of experience, neglect, and even the posi-
tively inhumanity of the soldiers detailed as nurses, as well as
in order to secure the services of all enlisted men in the discharge of their ordinary military duties a corps of nurses, men

and women also, if deemed expedient, should be engaged for the special care of the sick and wounded."[15]

On October 13, the Sanitary Commission intensified its anti-Finley campaign. Several commissioners had become impressed with William Hammond's scientific credentials, military experience, and robust leadership. They recommended that Hammond, previously thought to be a worthy Tripler replacement as medical director of the Army of the Potomac, in fact should replace the surgeon general. Additional concerns over the shortage of supplies and medicines faced by Union army surgeons prompted the commission to construct large supply depots in Wheeling, Cincinnati, Philadelphia, New York City, and Washington. The commission also distributed a circular addressed to "the Loyal Women of America," calling on them to form relief societies and go door to door "in sacred service to their country" to collect donations for their men in uniform.[16] Dozens of relief societies across the North collected donations, ranging from bandages to pillows to food that were amassed by the Sanitary Commission for delivery to the battlefield by rail and wagon.

The Sanitary Commission climbed far onto a political limb when it also recommended that the surgeon general be required to respond to the Sanitary Commission in writing when he declined its recommendations. The commission campaign to oust Finley and Tripler, as well as to establish a more professional field army medical corps, initially failed in both respects. However, it heightened public awareness of the medical shortcomings on the battlefield that would lead to a number of changes the following year.

The political intrigue escalated in December 1861 after the Army of the Potomac had settled into its quarters for the winter. Although no significant fighting would take place until March, reports of still rampant disease, inadequate hospital quality and capacity, and appalling military camp living conditions persisted. Nearly one in four soldiers remained ill in December. McClellan apparently had lost faith in his medical director, prompting the general to appoint a board of inquiry to investigate the cause of fevers that plagued his troops. Meanwhile, his soldiers faced a daily routine of mud, rain, snow, and boredom. They griped about their food, soaked their hardtack in coffee for days at a time to render it edible, and bought fruit from sutlers for curing in jars of whiskey.

That month, the Sanitary Commission began lobbying Congress to establish a corps of medical inspectors. When Finley overruled one of his medical officers who planned to establish a military hospital in Union-held territory in South Carolina, because Finley believed the state's mild climate made a hospital unnecessary, a vociferous public outcry resulted. Public pressure for fundamental change in military medicine mounted.

On December 10, Senator Henry Wilson introduced a medical department reform bill. The legislation called for promotion of medical officers based on merit rather than seniority, a younger and more vigorous surgeon general, a hospital inspector corps, construction of military hospitals based on more advanced European hospitals, responsibility for medical transportation transferred from the quartermaster corps to the medical department, and the establishment of medical supply depots. Reform dominated the headlines in New York City's *The World* and *The Times* newspapers as some called for Finley's removal while others criticized the meddling of the Sanitary Commission. At about the same time, the Sanitary Commission met with General McClellan and presented a long list of complaints. McClellan appeared sympathetic, and indicated he would push for Hammond as Finley's replacement if Congress passed the reform bill and it became law.

Correspondents' reports, editorials, and published soldiers' letters filled newspapers with frustration, resentment, and anger in the latter half of 1861. Bull Run had demonstrated that America faced a long, bloody war beyond the scope of anyone's imagination or preparation. McClellan commanded a sickly army largely comprised of undisciplined volunteer regiments unfamiliar with the demands of military life. He had been locked in a feud with the army's general in chief, Winfield Scott, before Scott retired and McClellan became general in chief on November 1 as well as commander of the Army of the Potomac. But by the end of 1861, President Lincoln had grown weary of McClellan's demands for an ever-increasing troop level in the absence of an announced battle plan. McClellan's egotistic attitude had further soured his relationship with the president on November 13, when Lincoln waited half an hour for a meeting with his general before being told that McClellan had retired for the night and would not be awakened for the president.

Tripler, meanwhile, had demonstrated a certain organizational ability after four months on the job, but mounting frustration over a fragmented command structure, the quality of army recruits, inadequate equipment, and what he saw as interference from non-military organizations had produced a paralysis that had cost him the confidence of McClellan, the Sanitary Commission, and others.[17] Public pressure weighed on both Tripler and McClellan. The Army of the Potomac had grown into a massive force of more than 170,000 men, but with a leadership that was sharply and publicly questioned. When spring arrived in 1862, the first full year of Civil War campaigns would begin, and the Union army would be supported by a military medical structure that lacked foresight, innovation, and the ability to adapt. Generals leading those armies endured immense public pressure to produce victories, but that would require a healthier fighting force and far better care of the wounded.

In January 1862, two devoted career military surgeons arrived at the same command on the western edge of the Civil War. After thirteen years' military service, the quiet and thoughtful Jonathan Letterman became medical director in the Department of West Virginia, under the command of General William Stark Rosecrans. The same month Hammond, the high-profile, widely traveled, and prolific surgeon who now counted the Sanitary Commission among his most powerful supporters in Washington, became Rosecrans's medical purveyor.

The gaunt-thin and reflective Letterman cut a far different figure than the oversized Hammond, who stood six feet two inches, weighed two hundred fifty pounds, and sported a full, bushy beard that surrounded a round, soft face. Yet they shared many qualities. Neither lacked self-confidence. Both enjoyed tackling complex problems and developing carefully analyzed, multifaceted solutions. The army's early war experience had revealed a number of unprecedented medical department issues and shortcomings that demanded such intelligent medical officers, who intuitively and independently sought solutions to seemingly insurmountable issues. Now, within the limits of a divided military and medical command system, Letterman and Hammond largely controlled an army's medical personnel, supplies, hospital construction and operations, hygiene-standard inspections, and battlefield care. They were in a position to make meaningful changes with Rosecrans's support, and in the face of continued political turmoil at the top of the Union army's leadership they formed a professional alliance.

As commander in chief, President Lincoln's dissatisfaction extended beyond his general in chief, McClellan, to his War Department. In January 1862, Lincoln replaced Secretary of War

Simon Cameron ten months after appointing him to the post the previous March. Cameron's administration had been plagued by charges of corruption, indefensible patronage, and incompetence. To many, Cameron appeared more interested in making money than prosecuting the war. Besides this, Cameron's annual report in 1861 had proposed the emancipation of slaves, which caused a maelstrom for a president not yet ready to make the same pronouncement.

While the Sanitary Commission and leading members of Congress publicly campaigned for the replacement of what they believed was President Lincoln's antiquated and overmatched surgeon general, the president sought to restore order at the top of the War Department. His choice, Edwin Stanton, became a surprising appointment.

Stanton held an unconcealed low opinion of Lincoln, which stemmed from their participation in a legal case in 1857. A Democrat, Stanton had been a reporter for the Ohio Supreme Court, built a successful law practice, and had been appointed attorney general by President James Buchanan in 1860. Opinionated, sometimes belligerent, and extremely intense, the new secretary of war could be as dismissive of those he considered unworthy as he could be deferential to others when it served his purpose. But Stanton had the backbone and organizational acumen that the president's War Department desperately needed, and to secure them Lincoln was willing to live with his appointee's personal disdain.

Upon his appointment as medical purveyor in the Department of West Virginia, Hammond traveled to New York and Washington to personally procure badly needed supplies, ranging from operating equipment to mattresses and books for Letterman. Hammond then turned his attention to the crude state of midwinter military hospitals in West Virginia and Maryland. He called one hospital "disgusting" and considered it unfit for patients, given the lack of supplies, inexperienced surgeons, bad diet, filthy conditions, and absence of records. Another hospital, he wrote, "defies description. It is simply disgusting. The outhouses are filled with dirty clothes, such as sheets, bed sacks, shirts, etc., which have been soiled by discharges from sick men. The privy is fifty yards from the house, and is filthy and offensive, ad nauseam. It consists of a shed built over two trenches. No seats; simply a pole, passing along each trench for men to sit on. . . . I do not hesitate to say that such condition of affairs does not exist in any other hospital in the civilized world."[18]

His scathing report recommended replacement hospitals comprised of small buildings of fifty patients each that emphasized proper ventilation and that conformed to the prevailing medical community thought. It led to Hammond's appointment as hospital inspector in March. Working with Letterman, he was now in a position to apply years of European military medical study to the massive medical challenges presented by the Civil War. He had seen little to praise in American military hospitals. "The permanent military hospitals of the United States are . . . of little importance as models. None of them are built after the plans which have been adopted by hygienists as best coming up to the standard required by sanitary science," he wrote.[19]

Hammond considered adequate ventilation and efficient operation vital to military hospitals. His pavilion-hospital design featured an elevated ridge at the top of the roof lines to vent the interior space. Holes along the sides of the wards under the beds provided intakes of fresh air. He wrote that a hospital ward should be confined to no more than two rows of beds and ideally should be no taller than one story. His precise calculations called for 1,205 cubic feet of space for each patient bed, and he claimed that an oblong patient ward of no more than fifty patients was ideal.

Letterman used Hammond's design to build one of the first military pavilion hospitals in the United States in Parkersburg, West Virginia, featuring an administrative building and two detached patient wards. Soon thereafter, Letterman supervised the construction of a similar pavilion-style military hospital in Grafton, West Virginia. Both were completed in the spring, at a time when the Sanitary Commission also employed Hammond's pavilion philosophy to build several large military hospitals in advance of the coming combat season.

Letterman and Hammond also collaborated with General Rosecrans, brigade surgeon William Hayes, and assistant surgeon Edward Dunster on a new ambulance design after early war models had proved inadequate or unreliable. They designed a 750-pound wagon that was drawn by two horses and could carry between two and six patients. Compartments held medical supplies, stretchers, and five gallons of water. The interior benches and seats could be removed to accommodate specific patient needs. Their design struck a balance between earlier models that had been too light or too heavy. The "Wheeling Wagon" became the army's standard ambulance wagon until an improved model was adopted in 1864.

This first collaboration between Letterman and Hammond was cut short by an act of Congress. On April 18, 1862, the Sanitary Commission's six-month lobbying campaign resulted in passage of legislation that overhauled the surgeon general's office and army's medical department. The commission had specifically campaigned for "a Surgeon General who should have some adequate conception of the real wants to the army, and capacity and energy enough to carry into execution a liberal system of providing those wants . . . a thorough inspection and enforced by official authority."[20] The law not only called for a new surgeon general, it authorized promotion based on merit rather than seniority and the addition of eight medical inspectors.[21] On the eve of 1862's battles, the way had been cleared for bright, young surgeons to take control of the army's medical department.

On April 25, at thirty-three years of age, Hammond became the new surgeon general as a brigadier general. He replaced Finley after the latter had been reprimanded for trying to bar the Sanitary Commission from military hospitals, relieved his surgeon general duties, and sent to Boston to await further orders. Finley elected to resign.[22] Hammond had leaped over more senior medical officers, including Letterman, but his military experience, nutrition research, medical school teaching experience, hospital expertise, and imposing presence made him the ideal choice. McClellan, too, was an ally. When McClellan spotted Hammond's name on a list of medical officers he said, "He is our man. He is the only one of a whole corps, who has any just conception of the duties of such a position, and sufficient energy, faithfully to perform them."[23]

Hammond took possession of a hollow office comprised of four rooms and a meager staff responsible for hundreds of thousands of men in the field and more than one hundred military hospitals. The year before Hammond took over, Finley proudly noted the medical department did not spend all of its allocated $2.445 million budget. In his first year in office, Hammond's budget would total more than $10.1 million and he would exceed that by nearly $1.5 million.[24]

Hammond tested hospital stewards applying for jobs on his staff on their verbal, written, and penmanship skills and laid the groundwork for a far more activist department. He also turned to colleagues he knew, respected, and trusted. Jonathan Letterman was one. Hammond recommended to Secretary of War Stanton that Letterman be transferred to Washington and become responsible for that city's hospitals. Hammond wanted medical inspectors assigned to major cities with large concentrations of

THE HAMMOND ALLIANCE

69

military hospitals.[25] However, the egos of Stanton and Hammond clashed almost immediately, delaying implementation of some of his recommendations. As the drama between the surgeon general and the secretary of war grew heated, the fighting on the battle-field had already resumed.

In March, the Army of the Potomac finally began its long-awaited campaign aimed at the Confederate capital of Richmond. General McClellan had envisioned a grand strat-egy. First, assemble the largest army in the history of the United States. Next, flank the Confederate troops threatening Washington by making an unprecedented amphibious landing at Fort Monroe on the southeastern tip of the Virginia pen-insula, followed by a fifty-mile overland campaign across the peninsula west to capture Richmond. To the sound of blaring bugles and bands, ships departed from Washington filled with men, destined for a large meadow at Fort Monroe. Hundreds of barges were moored there along the shore as tons of ord-nance, supplies, and matériel were unloaded and stacked in massive piles. Temporary shelters were carved out of the for-est. In approximately one month, an estimated 100,000 Union soldiers filled the temporary military camp.

Disease inevitably followed. Tripler discovered rampant scurvy among some units whose soldiers refused to eat the nearly inedible desiccated vegetables. Hygiene in a tempo-rary camp built in swampy spring mud was deplorable. As McClellan's army assembled in Virginia, Tripler thought it inevitable that he would be faced with 50,000 cases of diar-rhea.[26] He also desperately sought 250 four-wheeled ambu-lances prior to the start of battle, but received only 177.[27] It took nearly a month before McClellan had marshaled his troops and supplies and felt ready to march toward Yorktown, about twenty miles away. The Confederates waited.

They established three lines of defense, stretching north to south from the York River on the north down to the James River, which formed the southern edge of the peninsula. As McClellan's army moved west, it encountered the Confederates' first line of defense at Yorktown, where artful tactics by the Confederates confounded McClellan and stalled his poorly disciplined troops. Badly outnumbered, the Confederates had painted logs to look like cannon and made show as though their military force was far greater than it was. McClellan's attack on Yorktown turned into a siege that lasted nearly a month before the Confederates withdrew to the west.

Spring rains soaked the Union soldiers, who had carried too much gear on the march and slept in the open. Roads became quagmires that bogged down the army's renewed advance. Soon "Chickahominy Fever" took hold. So many soldiers fell sick that Tripler decided to evacuate them to Washington, Annapolis, and Baltimore. When malingerers swamped patient boats headed north, Tripler reversed course and kept thousands of sick patients on the peninsula, despite a critical shortage of medical tents.

Meanwhile, Hammond and Stanton settled their differences enough that Letterman was transferred to his new inspector's post in Washington. Upon his arrival, he discovered his hospitals had no room for the Peninsula Campaign's flow of casualties. Letterman made arrangements for patient transfers to Philadelphia, Annapolis, Alexandria, New York City, and Baltimore while instructing an Alexandria surgeon to "put the men in churches and make the best disposition possible. It is not possible to take them here."[28]

As McClellan's army slogged westward across the Virginia peninsula in May, Surgeon General Hammond had already become testy with Tripler's pleas for more supplies. On April 14, during the Yorktown siege, Tripler had complained to Hammond's predecessor that his medical supplies were nearly exhausted. He renewed his complaint to Hammond on May 18, as he grew impatient with delayed medical supply deliveries. In telegrams he pleaded his case for supplies again on May 20 and May 29, begging for more quinine after receiving 100 ounces instead of the 2,000 he had requested.[29] Hammond told Tripler to stop complaining and take command of the local situation, as Tripler had the authority to do so. Two days after Tripler's latest plea, the Confederates attacked McClellan's forces at Seven Pines in hopes of avoiding a siege of Richmond.

Feints, counterassaults, and flank attacks by the Confederates stopped the Union advance. After two days' fighting, Tripler faced nearly 3,600 wounded soldiers. The shorthanded medical department required more than a week to transport all the wounded to nearby ports where hospital ships awaited. The smell of putrid flesh announced the arrival of boxcars filled with wounded at White House on the James River.

The plight of the wounded four days after the end of fighting shocked Sanitary Commission observers. "Some (wounded) were just as they had been left by the fortune of war; their wounds, as yet, undressed, smeared with filth and blood, and all their wants unsupplied. Others had had their wounds dressed, one, two, or three days before. Others, still, were under the surgeon's hands, receiving such care as could be given them by men overburdened by the number of their patients, worn out by excessive and long-continued labor," the observers wrote.[30] Many of those patients arrived in Washington on barges and ships that lacked food, water, and sanitation facilities. Some had lain in the early summer sun for days, suffering at the hands of their army that still did not have an organized battlefield care and evacuation system in place.

Shaken by the damage inflicted by the Confederates, McClellan halted his assault for more than three weeks to draw reinforcements and supplies. The delay gave Confederate General Robert E. Lee valuable time to strengthen Richmond's defenses and construct a line of defense that stretched thirty miles across McClellan's path. Fearful of a siege of Richmond by the Army of the Potomac, Lee took the initiative with attacks on June 25, which became the start of the Seven Days Battle. McClellan had lost the initiative and relentless attacks by Lee broke the Union army's spirit, forcing McClellan to order withdrawal to the James River, about thirty miles southeast of Richmond.

Six major engagements in seven days produced more than 8,000 wounded men. Although McClellan never overextended his army, railroads remained available, and the Union navy controlled waterways, McClellan's medical department had been overwhelmed by the flood of the wounded and dying almost from the outset of the Peninsula Campaign. Although Tripler never received the logistical support he believed necessary, public outrage at the plight of the wounded during the Peninsula Campaign destroyed any credibility he had held with Surgeon General Hammond and the Sanitary Commission.

Tripler had failed to earn the respect of McClellan too. He had not known that some of his army's patients had been shipped to a Cumberland, Maryland hospital when a public controversy erupted over its filthy condition. He had been unable to overcome the shortage of support staff and hospital inspectors, incompetent volunteer regiment doctors, and the fact that he lacked authority over line officers. He had become so desperate that he had asked for fifty runaway slaves from the quartermaster corps.[31] Tripler had taken to pleading for supplies more than taking action. Circumstance and lack of leadership had defeated the medical director just as his army had been beaten back by the Confederates.

Between the end of the Battle of Seven Pines and the start of the Seven Days Battle, Tripler had already been replaced. On June 19, Tripler conceded professional defeat when he asked for reassignment to Detroit Barracks, Michigan, a post where he had served prior to the war. Hammond approved Tripler's request and on the same day appointed a man he knew and respected, Jonathan Letterman, as the new medical director of the Army of the Potomac. For Letterman the assignment included a promotion to surgeon and the military rank of major.

In many ways, Letterman's experience did not qualify him for the medical responsibility of more than 50,000 men. Outpost medicine bore little resemblance to supervising hundreds of physicians and their assistants; managing the flow of tons of medical supplies; planning tactical medical plans in concert with battle plans for more than fifty regiments; and ensuring thousands of wounded men could be treated promptly and ultimately transported to hospitals more than fifty miles away. At the same time, he had to earn the respect and trust of his commanding general and, to a lesser extent, the commanders of the various corps as well as the quartermasters.

Who could manage the mountain of logistical considerations without losing sight of the fundamental compassion essential to caring for each wounded soldier? Who could piece together the mosaic of military medicine at the army-command level, knowing that ultimate success rested in the hands of hundreds of anonymous surgeons and stretcher bearers? Who could assimilate, process, reorganize, and act with alacrity when unexpected enemy fire shredded men and anticipated battle plans? It would take a man whose self-confidence left little room for conscious doubt. Someone who was as intuitive as he was analytical. A system builder who instinctively questioned existing procedures and protocols in the face of unprecedented challenges. Surgeon General Hammond believed Letterman was that man.

Letterman arrived at Harrison's Landing on July 1, surveyed the carnage, and met with McClellan, who later recorded his first impression of Letterman, writing: "I saw immediately that

Letterman was the man for the occasion, and at once gave him my unbounded confidence. In our long and frequent interviews upon the subject of his duties, I was most strongly impressed by his accurate knowledge of his work—the clear and perfectly practical nature of his views and the thorough unselfishness of his character. He had but one thing in view—the best possible organization of his department—and that, not that he might gain credit or promotion by the results of his work, but that he might do all in his power to diminish the inevitable sufferings of the soldiers and increase the efficiency of the Army. . . . I never met with his superior in power of organization and executive ability."[32] From his perspective, McClellan had both a surgeon general and now a medical director worthy of his support.

The thousands of men who had fallen wounded across eastern Virginia desperately needed both of them.

4

TAKING MEDICAL COMMAND

"I found it in a deplorable condition."

Chaos greeted Jonathan Letterman when he transferred to an army that regularly fought in major battles. The Army of the Potomac had been bloodied and defeated and was exhausted after three months' battle. The long-awaited assault to take Richmond had foundered on the outskirts of the city. The Seven Days Battle, which ended on July 1, had broken McClellan's army nearly within sight of Richmond, resulting in another humiliating Union army retreat, stinging criticism by the Sanitary Commission, and outrage in leading newspapers of the North. Thousands of wounded men lay unprotected along the James River, waiting for treatment and evacuation.

America had been at war for a year. Frequent reports of filthy hospitals, the wounded lying on battlefields, rampant disease, and horrific loss of life had fueled public outrage. Approximately five years earlier, Americans had read similar reports of suffering in the Crimean War between Russia, France, and Britain. The British in particular had been indignant over how poorly their wounded and sick soldiers had been treated. In the first six months of the Crimean War, the British illness rate exceeded 100 percent. In one month, one in ten British soldiers died of disease, with illness killing three times as many men as the enemy.[1] The American military medical establishment had clearly learned little from the British experience. The American public demanded improvement both on the battlefield and in the hospital.

When Letterman officially took over from Tripler on July 4, he faced the evacuation of nearly 13,000 casualties to Fort Monroe on the peninsula and aboard steamers to hospitals in the North. Worse, "[t]he nature of the military operations had also unavoidably placed the Medical Department in a very unsatisfactory condition. Supplies had been almost exhausted or necessarily abandoned; hospital tents abandoned or destroyed, and the medical officers deficient in numbers or broken down by fatigue," wrote McClellan.[2]

Letterman hadn't known exactly what he would face. "It was impossible to obtain proper reports of the number of sick in the army when it reached Harrison's Landing. . . . The data on which to base the precise percentage of sick and wounded could not then be obtained but from the most careful estimate which I could make, the sickness amounted to at least twenty percent," wrote Letterman.[3] The army of which he took medical command was also ravaged by scurvy. Letterman's experience in the West told him that thousands more, in addition to those diagnosed with the vitamin deficiency, "do not feel sick, and yet their energy, their powers of endurance, and their willingness to undergo hardship, are in a great degree gone, and they know not why. In this way the fighting strength of the army was affected to a much greater degree than was indicated by the number of those who reported sick."[4]

For all that he confronted, Letterman had unparalleled authority from Surgeon General Hammond, who had broken his predecessors' habit of micromanaging medical directors. Hammond's letter of appointment gave Letterman widespread authority, coupled with autonomy moderated solely by the requirement that Letterman keep him advised of actions taken and submit requests for necessary supplies.

Hammond specifically told Letterman that he carried the authority to hold medical officers accountable for inadequate supplies. At the same time Letterman had authority to draw supplies at his sole discretion from large depots in the North, regardless of whether they were authorized by the surgeon general's office. Letterman also had authority to report deficient medical officers to the commanding general of the army. Further, he did not have to wait for additional medical officers to be sent by the surgeon general. "You will hire such physicians, nurses, etc., as you may require, and as you can obtain on the spot, making known to me immediately your deficiencies in that respect at the earliest possible moment, so I can supply you," wrote Hammond.[5]

No medical director in the history of the United States Army had been given such widespread authority. Hammond placed the health of the Union army's highest profile command in the hands of a man he had grown to trust, despite Letterman's lack of battlefield experience. Letterman followed suit when he brought assistant surgeon Edward Dunster from West Virginia to become his director of transportation.

Letterman's initial evacuation of wounded soldiers took place on steamers recently taken over by the surgeon general's office and that had earlier been operated by the Sanitary Commission. The commission continued to work with army medical directors, including Letterman. Its relationship with Letterman was strained at best. The Unitarian minister who had founded the Sanitary Commission, Dr. Henry Bellows, held a grudging respect for the Army of the Potomac's new medical director. While Bellows characterized Letterman as having a "strong professional ambition and zeal," he resented what he viewed as Letterman's intent to keep the commission in its place and subservient to the medical department, and he thought Letterman difficult to work with due to a lack of "personal humanity." Bellows found him to be an incessant smoker and "dry, taciturn, and impenetrable." Yet, "[o]ut of confusion ... (Letterman) fashioned order and a system. Never again would the commission have to serve as the (medical) bureau's crutch," wrote Bellows.[6]

As Letterman dealt with thousands who needed evacuation and thousands more who required treatment, a devastated General McClellan resolutely asked President Lincoln for more troops to replenish the Army of the Potomac's fighting strength. Lincoln called the general's request for 50,000 men "absurd." Letterman found himself answering to a general who believed his army remained undermanned and felt unappreciated by his president, at a time when public debate over the Army of the Potomac's defeat turned caustic and partisan.

Some editorials thought McClellan had offered a dishonest explanation for his army's retreat, while others characterized the same retreat as bold. The polarizing general was painted as either the architect of failure in the Peninsula assault or the victim of a president who didn't provide the necessary personnel and equipment that he needed to achieve success. Conspiracy theories abounded. Some felt Secretary of War Stanton had withheld troops to force a McClellan defeat, while others suspected strict abolitionists in the Lincoln administration worked behind the scenes to hamstring the general because he favored gradual emancipation. The withering criticism wasn't lost on McClellan, who described Stanton as an "unmitigated scoundrel" in a letter to his wife and admitted he had lost all respect for Lincoln.[7] His troops, too, remained divided. Some were bitter over the lack of reinforcements while others thought McClellan had been outwitted by the Confederate generals.

As newspaper headlines battled for supremacy in the post-battle campaign, Letterman wasted no time in resurrecting what had become a gutted army medical department. He asked Hammond for 1,000 tents to shelter the sick, so patients could remain with the army and return to duty sooner. He also sought 200 ambulances to speed the pace of evacuation of others.

Deplorable sanitation and rising rates of disease at Harrison's Landing also demanded his immediate attention. Disease had always been the foremost enemy of armies at war. Dysentery, caused by parasites in contaminated water or food, was the scourge of many military camps. Far more soldiers died of disease than from enemy fire in the Mexican War. The British lost eight times as many men to disease as to the enemy in the Napoleonic Wars. A lack of sanitation was a principal cause of a sickly army. An army could be smelled before it appeared. Soldiers bathed infrequently and warm water was a rarity. Dead animals, butchered livestock, open sewers, and raging infections of open wounds gagged hospital stewards. Preventive medicine was not a core element of medical school curriculum, and no state had a health department at the start of the Civil War.[8]

Letterman found such chaos unacceptable. He drafted medical orders for consideration by McClellan so radical that only a commanding general who had complete faith in his medical director would entertain them. In addition, Letterman could forge a massive overhaul of army health care because he had unfettered authority granted by a surgeon general who embraced new approaches based on experience, considered study, and analysis. Hammond, Letterman, and McClellan had come together at a critical juncture in the war. Rampant disease and the neglect of the wounded no longer could be tolerated.

McClellan needed Letterman. The egotistical general fumed over the failed Peninsula Campaign and the stinging criticism that followed. Regardless, he needed a much stronger and healthier army for his grand plans to take the fight to General Lee. Less than a week after his arrival, Letterman presented McClellan with a plan that would become the first step in recasting battlefield medicine.

On July 8, McClellan issued Special Order No. 197 and later General Orders No. 139 and 150 to establish fundamental medical department organization and to mount a campaign against disease. Together, the three orders required Letterman's approval for a soldier's admission to a hospital on the peninsula or to be evacuated north; sanitary inspections, with reports sent to senior officers; and a regular supply of fresh vegetables to prevent scurvy. Bathing and human waste disposal policies were established. McClellan also endorsed a letter by Letterman on how to cook food properly for the troops. The series of orders centralized fundamental army health responsibility by taking it out of the regiments and placing it in army headquarters. Letterman laid a foundation of standardization, enforcement, and accountability that would become the cornerstones of the battlefield care overhaul he was about to implement.

Within a few weeks of his arrival in Virginia, Letterman's impact became apparent. The medical department was no longer paralyzed by a fractured chain of command. By the third week of July, hundreds of tents had arrived. Tons of potatoes, onions, cabbage, tomatoes, squash, and fresh bread arrived in quantities that outstripped the army's ability to transfer it to the troops in the field. As a result, some produce rotted on the dock.

Army morale improved along with army health. A long proven army command axiom held that there were three essentials to good troop morale: a soldier had to believe he would be taken care of if he was wounded on the battlefield; he had to have generally good health; and he had to know he could rely on a steady and edible food supply.

Letterman's first priority had been the overall health of the army, starting with diet and extending to camp routine and sanitation. Within two weeks of assuming medical command, he also submitted specific recommendations to McClellan that fundamentally would change the organization and operation of military camps in the Army of the Potomac. Letterman wanted two men in each company designated as permanent cooks, who would follow instructions in making nutritious soups and other meals. Experience had shown that inexperienced soldiers overcooked their personal food and suffered from malnutrition. Summer rains in Virginia that turned military camps into muddy quagmires led Letterman to recommend that tents be relocated every week onto new ground covered with freshly cut pine boughs to avoid sleeping directly on the ground. He also believed the troops should be limited to two forty-five-minute drills per day, be allowed to sleep until sunrise and then have breakfast, and be required to take one fifteen-minute bath per week in a nearby river.

Refuse and waste also were a priority, in Letterman's view. He specified how to cover outhouse trenches with six inches of earth daily and that, when they filled to within two feet of the surface, they be moved to a new location. He also addressed the disposal of kitchen refuse in freshly dug pits, and how the remains of slaughtered cows and other livestock should be buried at least four feet deep; and he recommended that regimental commanders be held accountable for heightened camp sanitation standards. "I think if these suggestions be carried into effect that we may with reason expect the health of this army to be in as good a state as that of any army in the field," wrote Letterman.[9]

Widely publicized filthy military camp conditions and chronic army malnutrition in the first year of the war were ample evidence in support of Letterman's initiatives. Union troops were chronically underequipped and often hungry or thirsty. A soldier counted himself lucky if he owned a tin dipper, plate, knife, fork, and spoon. Few men washed utensils and

plates after a meal, other than with a swipe of a piece of bread
or clump of straw. When on the march, a soldier's daily ration
consisted of sixteen ounces of hard bread, twenty ounces of
fresh meat (or twelve ounces of salt pork), plus sugar, coffee, and
salt. When in camp, the meat ration remained the same, plus a
prorated share per 100 men of beans, rice, coffee, tea, sugar, salt,
pepper, and, when available, potatoes.[10]

Hardtack and meat of varying quality were a soldier's staples.
Neither was particularly nutritious. Soldiers considered hardtack
biscuits too hard to chew and nearly inedible. Porous hardtack
boxes stored outside at supply depots leaked rainwater, turning
soldiers' food moldy. Maggots and weevils commonly riddled
the biscuits. Insects' webs covered some biscuits and disappeared
when soldiers crumbled biscuits into their coffee to serve as
a breakfast or supper. Some added hardtack to thicken soups,
fried the crumbs in fat (called "skillygalee"), or toasted hardtack
over a fire. It was often eaten with salt pork, the most common
meat available. Boiled or fried, salt pork sandwiched between
two pieces of hardtack made a quick meal that could be eaten
on the march.[11]

Most soldiers derided army-issued dried vegetables. A concoction of dried carrots, turnips, beans, onions, and sometimes
roots, twigs and pebbles were molded into square cakes about
one inch thick. Thorough boiling rendered them borderline
edible but void of most vitamins. Letterman, however, considered them useful if used as a soup base.

"The desiccated vegetables should be steeped in water for
two hours and boiled with the soup for three hours ... and a half
ration of desiccated vegetables previously soaked in cold water
for an hour, with a few small pieces of pork, adding salt and
pepper, with water sufficient to cover well the ingredients, and
stewed slowly for three hours, will make an excellent dish. . . .
The secret in using the desiccated vegetables is in having them

thoroughly cooked. The want of this has given rise to a prejudice against them which is unfounded; it is the fault of the cooking, and not of the vegetables," he wrote.[12]

Hospital patients were at the mercy of sporadically available medical supplies and unappetizing food. They couldn't forage in the countryside for fresh meat and produce as healthy soldiers did. Nor could they buy food from the sutlers, private merchants who followed the paymasters when they visited armies on payday. At a pay rate of about $13 monthly, soldiers were hard-pressed to pay the going rates of fifty cents for a pound of cheese, seventy-five cents for a can of condensed milk or a dollar for a pound of butter.[13]

Consequently, patients cherished donations from private relief societies, which typically spiked following newspaper reports of horrific battle casualties. Soldiers prized lemon and blackberry syrup as flavor additives to a bland diet. Valuable sources of seasonal nutrition included pickles, onions, sauerkraut, potatoes, horseradish, and cabbage.

Soldiers slept where they could on the march and built primitive huts when establishing semi-permanent winter quarters. Six or eight men often shared a single hut, hollowed out of the ground with short side walls made of logs or hardtack boxes. Beds were little more than pine saplings or grain sacks on the ground. A few boxes at the head of the hut contained soldiers' personal belongings. Sometimes soldiers built a makeshift fireplace, but that often resulted in huts burning to the ground. Men endured the long winters at night in the dim light of a candle stuck on the end of an upright bayonet or in a hollowed-out potato. Warm clothes and blankets were always in demand. In 1861, Sanitary Commission inspectors surveyed 200 regiments and found that one in four lacked one good blanket per man and 5 percent had no blankets at all.[14]

Impossibly cramped, damp, and poorly ventilated quarters spawned all manner of disease, infection, and infestation. Just as Letterman had experienced insect infestations in the poorly built military outposts of the West, the Army of the Potomac's soldiers were plagued by similar misery. Lice proliferated by the millions in thousands of rarely washed uniforms. Adult lice thrived in the seams of uniforms and reproduced prolifically, and their larva began sucking soldiers' blood almost immediately upon emerging. A soldier could pick dozens of lice off a single shirt. If a man couldn't boil his clothing to kill the infestation, he suffered until he received a new uniform and then he burned his old clothes as soon as possible.[15]

Although Letterman had never been in medical command of an assemblage of men the size of the Army of the Potomac, he understood the measures necessary to protect the health of tens of thousands of soldiers living shoulder to shoulder for months at a time, exposed to the elements. General McClellan codified his camp sanitation recommendations in General Orders No. 50. The effect was immediate and profound. By August, the Army of the Potomac disease rate declined by one-third in Letterman's first month of medical command.[16]

While military camp hygiene remained a priority, the early Civil War horrors on the battlefield also had made it clear that the army's medical department had to reinvent itself to cope with thousands of wounded and possibly dying men after a few hours' fighting. Advances in weaponry had outpaced both an army's tactical battle plan and its medical department's organization, neither of which had changed in more than half a century. The first year of the war had hardly done anything to change that.

Both generals and their medical directors were unprepared for the weaponry available at the start of the Civil War. For more than one hundred years military tactics had been built around the short-range, highly inaccurate musket. It was lethal to about fifty yards. It took a soldier nearly half a minute to reload as he bit open a paper cartridge, poured gunpowder down the barrel, tamped the paper cartridge down onto the powder, rammed a bullet onto the paper, inserted a firing cap above the trigger, cocked the weapon, aimed, and then fired.

As a result, commanders had crammed their troops together, shoulder to shoulder, often three rows deep. When the front row fired in unison, it dropped back to reload as the next row moved up to fire. Rigid ranks of attackers mounted frontal assaults against defensive lines similarly assembled in order to consolidate their limited firepower. It was effective when bullets flew only 100 yards. It became suicidal in the Civil War, when soldiers on both sides had rifles that were deadly at nearly 1,700 yards and reliably accurate to 250 yards.

The Civil War's .58 caliber Springfield musket and .69 caliber Harpers Ferry rifle made condensed, frontal assaults obsolete. Both weapons had rifled barrels that greatly increased their accuracy by spinning the bullet as it left the barrel. Improved range and accuracy were matched by greater lethality inflicted by new ammunition, called the Minie ball. It had been invented near the end of the Mexican War, in 1848, by a French army captain. It was smaller than previous bullets, so the soldier could ram it into the bore faster. When fired, the half-inch hollow bullet expanded up against the rifling that spun it as it traveled through the barrel, producing greater range and accuracy. It also tended to yaw and then tumble as its speed decreased.

When the Minie ball slammed into a human body, often at an angle, it flattened and obliterated the surrounding tissue. It splintered bone and sent shock waves through the victim. It produced massive and complicated wounds never before seen by most doctors at the outset of the war. "One poor fellow . . . was wounded in four places, namely: in the neck, breast, shoulder, and right arm—all the wounds having been made by a single ball."[17] A volunteer doctor typically had limited general health-care experience, and most military doctors like Letterman were more familiar with arrow wounds than gunshot injuries.

Artillery also produced far greater injuries than previously experienced. The U.S. military adopted a small, relatively por-table piece of artillery, the "Napoleon," four years prior to the outbreak of the Civil War. The smoothbore, muzzle-loading cannon fired a twelve-pound projectile that terrorized troops tightly positioned for either assault or defense. It functioned as a massive sawed-off shotgun. It fired canisters that exploded, freeing hundreds of small iron balls to tear through groups of men. An accurate artillery fusillade could vaporize a group of soldiers clustered together along the enemy line. Although its maximum range extended to nearly a mile, it was particularly lethal inside 250 yards, the typical spread of many Civil War fire exchanges.

Early in the war, outdated military tactics in the face of far more lethal weaponry produced horrific numbers of dead and wounded. Despite the unexpected casualty rates, taking care of the wounded remained a secondary priority for many gener-als. Winning the battle at hand took precedence. Some generals considered their army's medical department little more than a nuisance, and assigned slackers and sick soldiers to care for the wounded. Several generals abandoned medical supplies in their rush to engage the enemy. Battlefield evacuation remained as haphazardly organized as it was left to circumstance.

The world's armies had no organization for battlefield evacu-ation. Some had tried, such as the French, who in 1859 relied on military musicians as stretcher bearers. In America, the con-cept of corpsmen and medics didn't exist. A soldier relied on his comrades to possibly drop their rifles and staunch his bleeding or push his intestines back into his lacerated abdomen. Frequently, a handful of soldiers who had no stomach for the fighting carried him off the battlefield, and then the rescuers somehow "got lost" on their return to the field of fire. On occasion, the regiment's band members carried him away from the most intense fighting. More likely, he lay on the battlefield until the fighting had ended and then yelled for help as survivors searched the cratered and shredded landscape for the wounded. He couldn't be sure if his rescuers would be from his army or the enemy. His survival typically depended on a pain-wracked return to friendly territory and a makeshift hospital in a barn, under a tree, in a cluster of tents, or perhaps a brutal ride in a suffocating boxcar, destined for an enemy prisoner-of-war camp.

Letterman knew the existing fragmented approach to battle-field care could no longer be tolerated in the face of thousands of casualties in a single day. An effective ambulance system could not remain the province of both the medical staff and the supply corps. "Medical officers and quartermasters had charge of (ambulances), and as a natural consequence little care was exercised over them and they could not be depended upon during an action or on the march. . . . It seemed to me necessary that whilst medical officers should not have the care of the horses, harness, etc., belonging to the ambulances, the system should be such as to enable them at all times to procure them with facility when wanted for the purposes for which they were designed, and to be kept under the general control of the medical department. Neither the kind nor the number of ambulances required were in the army at that time, but it nevertheless remained necessary to devise a system that would render as available as possible the material on the spot, particularly as the army might move at any time, and not wait for the arrival of such as had been asked for, only a portion of which ever came," wrote Letterman.[18]

Within a few weeks after taking medical command, Letterman devised a coordinated and centralized approach that would redefine the realities of battlefield care under fire. In clear, direct language, Letterman forged a philosophy and organization for battlefield evacuation whose premise underlay many Letterman achievements: organization and accountability. On August 2, General McClellan issued General Orders No. 147, the latest in a series of orders stemming from the medical department and grounded in those principles.

The sixteen provisions of General Orders No. 147 became the foundation of battlefield evacuation as a subspecialty of the medical department, eliminating it as an afterthought among many line officers. For the first time an ambulance corps was created that carried the command and authority of the Army of the Potomac's headquarters. Letterman now commanded a new ambulance structure that extended from army's medical director down through divisions and to the regiment level. He consolidated authority of all ambulances by establishing a defined chain of command. A captain was designated as commander of all ambulances in each army corps. His new duties were clear. "He will pay special attention to the ambulances, horses, harness, etc., requiring daily inspections to be made by the commanders of the division ambulances, and reports thereof to be made to him by these officers. He will make a personal inspection once a week of all the ambulances, transport carts, horses, harness, etc., whether they have been used for any other purpose than the transportation of the sick and wounded and medical supplies, reports of which will be transmitted, through the Medical Director of the Army Corps, to the Medical Director of the Army every Sunday morning."[19]

In addition, each division had a first lieutenant responsible for its ambulance service. A second lieutenant had similar duties at the brigade level, and each regiment had a sergeant in charge of ambulances. Each officer had a prescribed number of two-horse and four-horse ambulances and transport carts for which he was responsible. All were required to regularly inspect and report on the status of both equipment and the men assigned to the ambulance corps.

Chronic shortages and often the absence of ambulances on the day of battle would no longer be tolerated. Letterman attached ambulances to specific units and prohibited their use by non-medical officers. No longer could they be used at the whim and convenience of line officers. Ambulances were parked together when in camp and kept under supervision. Officers responsible for them had to remain with the ambulances in the army train when on the march to ward off unapproved use.

For the first time, each ambulance was staffed by two men and a driver. Fully trained soldiers would be assigned to ambulance duty, subject to approval by each ambulance corps commanding officer. Line officers could not transfer derelict soldiers to ambulance duty. Each ambulance crew also had to be trained in the proper way to load and unload patients from an ambulance. Letterman also forbade non-ambulance corps soldiers from evacuating wounded men. Letterman believed that disciplined men from the same unit, trained as ambulance crews, were more motivated to evacuate wounded men from their own unit and return to battle than the undisciplined, volunteers, contract civilians, and army musicians who had evacuated the wounded in the Civil War's early battles. No longer would half a dozen spirit-broken men "help" a soldier off the battlefield and then fail to return to battle.[20]

In the space of a single order, Letterman redefined battlefield evacuation from a post-battle scavenger hunt to one marked by military discipline. Too, he integrated the battlefield medical service into military operations. A line officer could be arrested for non-authorized use of an ambulance. Weekly reports up the medical command hierarchy instilled accountability. Each ambulance corps officer now was as responsible for the ambulances, crews, and supplies in his charge just as the line officers held responsibility for the conduct and efficiency of the soldiers under their command.

Letterman's philosophy became the first step toward battlefield medical specialization. His medical officers could now focus on the care of thousands of wounded men, while others were responsible for the efficient operation of the ambulance service. He had created a central authority and chain of command similar to that which had been the hallmark of combat troops for centuries. Similarly, he created a sense of unity by prescribing a green band and chevrons to be worn only by the ambulance service. He applied a basic military principle: uniforms foster identity and cohesiveness.

Yet the day the Army of the Potomac adopted his plan, the army's new general in chief, Major General Henry Halleck, ordered McClellan back to Washington and to send his army's Third, Fifth, and parts of the Ninth Corps to reinforce General John Pope's Army of Virginia. Disheartened by his military defeat and his army's recall, McClellan delayed his return, giving Letterman valuable time to begin implementing the army's medical department reorganization.

But there wasn't enough time before the fighting resumed. Letterman received copies of his orders from the printer for distribution to units a few days before the Army of the Potomac was broken apart, some departing for General Pope's forces and the remainder bound for Washington. As a practical matter, the Army of the Potomac ceased to exist when Letterman prepared to fully implement his plan. On August 23, General McClellan boarded a steamer at the city of Hudson. His departure marked the end of the Peninsula Campaign, fourteen weeks of fighting that cost thousands of lives and ended in a defeat that made it clear battlefield care no longer could be entrusted to amateurs.

The chaos that confronted Letterman when he arrived in Virginia extended beyond the Army of the Potomac. A feud had developed between Surgeon General Hammond and the quartermaster general, Montgomery C. Meigs. Meigs's father and brother were physicians in Philadelphia. But that didn't help Meigs and Hammond reach an agreement over control of medical department ambulances and supplies. Although the Sanitary Commission agreed with Hammond that he should control the ambulances, Meigs refused to cede his authority, resulting in a persistent split of command and control at the army's top level when it came to its ambulances.

Hammond also stumbled when he sought Union army–wide adoption of Letterman's ambulance system. The surgeon general pressed for an independent organization premised on providing six ambulances with trained crews for each regiment. McClellan agreed, but on August 21 Stanton rejected the proposal, believing it would "increase the expenses and immobility of our army . . . without any corresponding advantages."[21] General in Chief Halleck also opposed army-wide adoption. A dedicated ambulance corps would remain the exclusive province of the Army of the Potomac, a fighting force that now had been split into two groups, one of which was bound for the Second Battle of Bull Run eight days later.

The Confederates' General Robert E. Lee saw an opportunity following the defeat of McClellan in the Peninsula Campaign. McClellan's Army of the Potomac had been shredded and demoralized, leaving it undermanned and undersupplied on the eastern tip of Virginia. Not far away, General John Pope's Army of Virginia near the Rapidan and Rappahannock Rivers appeared vulnerable. Lee's Army of Northern Virginia near

Manassas needed to attack Pope before McClellan could reinforce his army. As McClellan executed Halleck's order and
commanded that two of his corps join Pope thirteen months
after the first Union army defeat at Bull Run, Lee positioned his
army for a second assault against a Union army over the same
ground.

Confederate strategy again forced the Union army to react
rather than attack. On August 28, approximately 25,000 Confederate soldiers under the command of General Thomas
"Stonewall" Jackson completed a fifty-four-mile march that
flanked Pope's army and cut off his supply and communications lines. Pope reacted, marching his force in search of Jackson. On the night of August 28, Jackson had his troops ready
to ambush Pope's force, while a second Confederate force of
25,000 commanded by General John Longstreet was poised to
attack the Union army as well.

The armies collided near dusk. Thousands of soldiers
unleashed artillery and small arms fire sometimes only seventy
yards apart. Lead tore into men, producing horrific casualties.
When darkness stilled the fighting, one brigade had lost 40 percent of its men and another, the 2nd Wisconsin, lost 50 percent.

The following day the Confederates' firepower, coupled with
General Pope's poor strategy and vague communications, proved
deadly for the Union army. Pope's plan to launch a pincer attack
on the Confederates dissolved into chaos when Union army
units were placed in the wrong position, flanking attacks failed
to materialize, and the Confederates launched furious, continu-
ous fire for more than nine hours. A massive flanking attack
by Pope in late afternoon proved disastrous by leaving some
of his troops unprotected. General Longstreet counterattacked
with 30,000 fresh men, destroying exposed Union army units.
In ten minutes of fighting, the 5th New York lost nearly half
its men. By midnight, the Union army had again retreated at

Bull Run, heading back to the familiar defensive line near Washington. They had left nearly 10,000 men dead, wounded, or captured by the Confederates.

Only the Army of the Potomac's corps that had been briefly trained by Letterman had any sense of battlefield care at Bull Run. While its level of battlefield evacuation was superior to the remainder of Pope's medical department, they, too, were crippled by minimal supplies and poor medical department leadership. Some of the Army of the Potomac's divisions had no ambulances, and the entire corps had about one-fourth of the 170 needed ambulances: "the ambulances with their equipments (sic) were left behind to be sent after the troops as vessels could be spared for that purpose. A large portion of the medical supplies were also left behind, and, in some cases, everything but the hospital knapsacks, by orders of colonels of regiments, quartermasters, and others; in some instances without the knowledge of the medical officers, in others notwithstanding their protest. It would appear that many officers consider medical supplies to be the least important in an army; the transportation of their baggage is of much more pressing necessity than the supplies for the wounded," a frustrated Letterman later wrote.[22]

Army of Virginia medical director Thomas McParlin's decision to establish the main military hospital seven miles away from the worst fighting exacerbated the lack of ambulances.[23] Too few supplies, not enough ambulances, and the remoteness of the battle's principal hospital forced army surgeons to leave thousands of wounded men on the battlefield.

Meanwhile, Letterman had returned to Washington and to new sources of frustration: a paucity of surgeons and inadequate hospital capacity. Fully occupied city hospitals had no room for the torrent of Bull Run casualties that would flow into Washington. As reports from Bull Run arrived, he searched

for surgeons to ride the bloody battlefield that remained littered
with nearly 3,000 wounded men three days after the fighting had
stopped. Meanwhile, Surgeon General Hammond procured 200
private carriages and wagons to ferry critically needed medical
supplies to Bull Run. But that proved bittersweet, as many private contractors driving the wagons stole the supplies, refused to
pick up some of the wounded, and sometimes stole from those
they loaded onto their wagons.[24] One wagon train departed
Washington with 200 vehicles. "About daybreak on Sunday
Fairfax Courthouse was reached, in a heavy rain. The road from
here on was filled with troops, artillery, wagons, ambulances,
and stragglers. When the column struggled up the Centreville
hill there remained but sixteen of the vehicles that had started.
Some had broken down, the horses of others had given out,
many had escaped from the line and returned to Washington on
Monday."[25]

Frustration and anger mounted in the days following the battle as rumors of patient care that bordered on neglect for lack of
advance preparation. Dispassionate reports from medical officers
bore witness to the suffering. "I was not attached to any organization and nobody gave me orders; but as I found in the little
church in Centreville one hundred wounded men who needed
attention, I saw my duty well marked out. All these men were
severely wounded, for slightly wounded marched away with the
army. Upon a few mattresses, and with almost no other conve-
niences or comforts, the men were laid in rows upon the floor.
Most of them had, in fact, not even a mattress, but only a little
straw under them," wrote medical officer W. W. Keen. "The third
day after the battle I passed such a night as I had never before
experienced in my life. Long trains of ambulances arrived, carrying wounded men from the field of battle back to Washington,
and there were but four surgeons to look after them and their

many imperious needs. Fifty poor thirsty fellows were crying for water; fifty more were crying with the pain from a jolting ride of nine miles over a corduroy road. Most of them had had nothing to eat for one, two, or three days, save for what they had obtained from haversacks of the dead," wrote another surgeon.[26]

Hammond grew livid with Secretary of War Stanton, writing, "Up to this date (Sept. 3), six hundred wounded men still remain on the battlefield, in consequence of an insufficiency of ambulances and the want of a proper system of regulating their removal in the Army of the Virginia. Many have died of starvation; many more will die in consequence of exhaustion, and all have endured torments which might have been avoided."[27] It wasn't until September 7, a week after the fighting had ended, that the last of the wounded Union soldiers had been evacuated off the battlefield. Jonathan Letterman's barely established ambulance system saved hundreds of wounded soldiers in the two corps that had been transferred from the Army of the Potomac to Pope's command. It came too late to save thousands more who were left stranded on the battlefield and then faced a primitive, undersupplied field hospital organization that, in fact, was not organized at all.

By that time, President Lincoln had fired General Pope and returned command of the once again consolidated Army of the Potomac to McClellan, over the objections of some of his cabinet members, including Secretary of War Stanton. McClellan's popularity with his troops made him the president's choice. But the selection left Lincoln with an army's commanding general who didn't have the confidence of the cabinet or the War Department. His surgeon general bickered with both the quartermaster general and the secretary of war. Meanwhile, a highly visible Sanitary Commission pressed its public campaign for continued reform of battlefield care. The Union army command lacked cohesion at a time when rumors of a Confederate invasion into Maryland and a possible attack on Washington abounded.

Letterman took medical command at what some historians consider the Union's low point in the Civil War. Crushing early defeats had destroyed any illusions of a hasty end to the fighting. There had already been more battlefield casualties than those suffered in the entire history of the nation up until the attack on Fort Sumter. Reports of abandonment, neglect, and near-starvation suffered by wounded soldiers horrified civilians. No one had imagined such human devastation. Few had the intellectual capacity to determine how to cope with the new battlefield reality. Military outpost medicine had to be abandoned and an entirely new approach to combat care had to be forged simultaneously on the march, at the highest levels of government, and within the civilian community. It had to be completed almost immediately, as massive clashes of armies on the battlefield would not wait for thoughtful deliberation, discussion, and then implementation.

Against this backdrop, Jonathan Letterman resumed medical command of the Army of the Potomac on September 2. He wrote: "I found it in a deplorable condition. The officers were worn out by the excessive and harassing labors they had undergone during the time they were attached to the Army of Virginia. A large portion of their supplies had been left behind, as I have said, at Fortress Monroe, and even much of what they had brought was thrown away by commanding officers when on the way to join General Pope. The labor expended at Harrison's Landing in rendering this Department efficient for active service, seemed to have been expended in vain, and required to be completely refitted before it would be again in proper condition."[28]

Beginning in July, Letterman had begun to fundamentally overhaul battlefield care and had laid that foundation in less than a month. But in the ensuing thirty-one days that he and

McClellan did not have command of the Army of the Potomac, much of the progress had been gutted.

Only three days after they returned to command, the Army of the Potomac marched out of Washington toward new army headquarters at Rockville, Maryland, fifteen miles northwest of the capital. The army's mission again was to stop a feared invasion of the north by General Lee, an assault that some thought could reach as far as Philadelphia, Boston, or New York City. For hours the army's march out of the city passed the front door of General McClellan's house, instead of following a route past the White House according to common practice. While McClellan once again propped up his command at the expense of his commander in chief, Letterman prepared for battle by ordering ambulances from Alexandria. He also ordered supplies from the medical purveyor in Baltimore, although "[i]t was impossible at that time to know where the proper place to direct them to be sent."[29] Those decisions would have to be made in a two-story brick farmhouse in the rolling hills of Maryland.

5

ANTIETAM

"I pray God may stop such infernal work."

Lieutenant Thomas Jefferson Spurr's legs seemed to evaporate when the Minie ball slammed into his thigh. He fell in the shadow of where he stood, exposed to the enemy on a small hill overlooking a fenced cornfield. Initial numbness gave way to searing pain. As his blood soaked the ground, he waved off his rescuers. "Do not stay for me," he told them. "Take care of yourselves."[1]

The 15th Massachusetts Volunteers retreated as the Confederates advanced on Spurr. Gunfire and artillery ripped through men as they sought cover among the cornstalks and in shredded stands of nearby trees. More than 300 men fell wounded or dead. Within twenty minutes, enemy fire destroyed more than half of Spurr's regiment.

For more than three hours, bitter fighting had raged on September 17, pitting more than 90,000 Confederate and Union soldiers against each other in rolling western Maryland farm country, bordered by the Potomac River in the west and South Mountain to the east. Jonathan Letterman had been given two weeks to prepare for the first major battle of his military career and one of the most horrific battles of the Civil

War. Thomas Spurr became one of thousands of wounded men whose lives depended on a fledgling battlefield medicine system Letterman had yet to complete.

Letterman had been as shocked as he was discouraged when he had resumed medical command of the Army of the Potomac on September 2. The progress he had made in his first two months as medical director—when he began to fundamentally overhaul battlefield care with an ambulance system that replaced the former haphazard approach—had been largely gutted. He barely had time to assess the damage before the Army of the Potomac received new orders. Four days later, on September 6, lead elements of the Army of the Potomac marched out of Washington. They headed for Frederick, Maryland, a regional hub of 8,000 residents, that advance units of General Lee's invading Army of Northern Virginia had already reached.

The Frederick residents, some of them sympathetic to the South, had known for two days that Lee's troops were approaching. They evacuated 398 patients to hospitals in York, Pennsylvania, and in the streets burned bulk supplies that could not be moved out of town. The fires still smoldered when 5,000 men commanded by General Stonewall Jackson marched down Patrick Street in Frederick.

As Letterman confronted a disorganized medical department on the march, he also had to assimilate the medical personnel of thirty-six newly formed state regiments of volunteers that were now part of the Army of the Potomac. Those regiments' medical personnel were wholly untrained in military medicine, and many held a "my state" philosophy of treating their regiment's wounded first and sometimes exclusively. Making matters worse, McClellan's army moved northwest across a twenty-mile front toward Lee's troops. Warm, dry weather created a hot, dusty march and stragglers, especially in the new regiments, soon became a major problem. By September 11, the army was within six miles of Frederick.

Letterman could not train an expanded medical department on the move. Nor was it possible to scout and establish hospitals in the absence of a known battlefield. That left one priority that he could address: supplies. He wasted no time. "I had ordered a number of 'hospital wagons' from Alexandria, Virginia, which reached me after we left Washington, and were at once distributed to different corps. While at Rockville, Maryland, I directed the Medical Purveyor at Baltimore to put up certain supplies and have them ready to send to such place as I should indicate. It was impossible at that time to know where the proper place to direct them to be sent," Letterman wrote.[2] Meanwhile, he was hamstrung by the illness of McClellan's chief quartermaster, Rufus Ingalls, which delayed the arrival of nearly 5,000 horses, more than 200 wagons, and 100 ambulances.[3] The sole good news he received on the march was the arrival of 200 wagons after he reached Rockville.

As Letterman assembled supplies for an unidentified battlefield, his commanding general did him no favor with his estimate of enemy strength and, by extrapolation, potential numbers of Union wounded. As a matter of routine, McClellan vastly overestimated the strength of his foe. Some officers derisively commented that McClellan "tended to see double." McClellan thought his 80,000-man army was marching toward a Confederate force of nearly 125,000. Based on casualty rates in earlier battles, if McClellan's estimate proved accurate Letterman had to plan for an unprecedented number of wounded men. The high end of McClellan's estimate envisioned a massive clash of perhaps 200,000 soldiers from both sides.

As the Army of the Potomac neared Frederick, Lee ordered a withdrawal from the town, ceding the strategic location to McClellan. Frederick was located along Monocacy River, a generally shallow creek lined with trees. The national pike and a railroad made it a natural army headquarters location. Recognizing that, the Rebels destroyed the railroad bridge over Monocacy River before they departed, severing the critical railroad supply line from Frederick east to Baltimore. Unbeknownst to Letterman at the time, that single act nearly a week before battle would prove to be a tremendously complicating factor in his plan to treat the wounded.

When the Army of the Potomac reached Frederick on September 12, Letterman brought medical supplies forward. The bulk of Lee's troops remained less than twenty miles away in Hagerstown, near Harpers Ferry and on South Mountain, still in Maryland, and generally northeast of the meandering Potomac River, which separated Maryland from the South. Battle loomed. It became clear that Frederick would be a central staging area, regardless of where the battle took place.

"I directed the establishment of hospitals in that city (Frederick) for the wounded in battles which were imminent— ordered the supplies to be sent from Baltimore, and sent for a large amount of articles, in addition, for the field and hospitals," wrote Letterman.[4] He ordered the conversion of thirty-four buildings, often redbrick churches and inns, into hospitals. Most featured wide, double doors that provided good access for the wounded, open space on the ground floor for maximum capacity, and tall windows for added light to help with surgeries and treatment.

They were organized into seven general hospitals, augmented by some homes that would be used for patient care and two tent hospitals. In Frederick, many were concentrated along and near Church Street. All were within a town about twelve blocks wide, making it easier for Letterman to efficiently supply them.

McClellan arrived in Frederick at 9:00 a.m. on September 13. Although frequently faulty intelligence plagued the general and affected Letterman's plans, about two hours after McClellan's arrival he received irrefutable evidence of his enemy's intent. Corporal Baron Mitchell had found an envelope in a meadow. It held an official-looking document wrapped around three cigars. The heading read "Hd Qrs Army of Northern VA Special Orders No 191." General Lee's chief of staff had signed it. Although it did not detail troop strength, it contained his army's plan to capture nearby Harpers Ferry and seize its supplies. It was a remarkable find that gave McClellan invaluable intelligence on Lee's intentions as well as his troop deployment in western Maryland.

Letterman's attention, however, was directed to the rear. A massive traffic jam had developed on the railroad line that stopped at the destroyed bridge south of Frederick. Everything had to be loaded into wagons for the final four miles. In some cases, medical supplies were near the rear of a twenty-mile backup of railroad cars, more than a third of the distance back to Baltimore. While Letterman prepared for the medical needs of an 80,000-man army about to engage in battle, critical supplies languished in trapped railroad cars.

"A great deal of confusion and delay was the consequence, which greatly embarrassed the Medical Department; and this embarrassment was increased by the fact that cars loaded with supplies were, on some occasions, 'switched off' and left for some time (when their arrival was all-important) on the side of the road, to make way for other stores. Some of the articles ordered, I have been informed, never left the railroad depot in Baltimore; they certainly never reached Frederick," wrote Letterman.[5] The scarcity of supplies reaching Letterman alarmed Sanitary Commission agents. One estimated Letterman had less than one-tenth the amount of supplies he judged necessary for battle.[6]

To the west of McClellan's force, South Mountain separated the two armies. More a ridgeline running north and south than a single mountain, it was largely barren. The trees had been stripped to feed nearby foundries. Scattered "wood lots" remained, relatively small stands of trees that farmers carefully harvested for fuel, fencing, and building material. Few trees were more than ten inches in diameter (the ideal size for fence-rail splitting), and most of the undergrowth had been eaten by grazing livestock. A dry summer that year had produced brittle vegetation and many of the seasonal creeks had little water flowing in them.

The Army of the Potomac had to cross South Mountain at several points, principally through Turner's, Fox's, and Crampton's Gaps, about seven miles apart. The army then would drop down into Pleasant Valley, cross Antietam Creek, and attack Lee at Sharpsburg. Lee's first line of defense stood at the gaps in South Mountain. Behind it Lee had positioned 15,000 troops in the Sharpsburg area, and commanded another 15,000 attacking a Union garrison at Harpers Ferry on the Potomac River, about a day's march from Sharpsburg.

On September 14, twelve days after McClellan and Letterman had resumed their commands, three corps of the Army of the Potomac attacked Confederate positions on South Mountain. Battles in the three gaps stretched into the night as Union troops fought up a 300-foot barren and rocky slope toward Confederate positions on high ground. Confederate troops, hunkered down behind roadside and property-line stone walls, could see and hear the Union troops approach across farm fields and up the slopes long before they were within range. One assault wave followed another as Union soldiers fell dead or wounded until sunset. As Union forces finally neared the crest, their casualties mounted. Each side totaled nearly 2,000 casualties after a single day's fighting that stretched into one of the few night battles of the Civil War.

Letterman had ordered the medical directors of the three engaged corps to secure hospitals in Middletown, a small town four miles from the battle. As he often demonstrated, he remained mindful of war's impact on civilians, noting "churches and other buildings were taken as far as was necessary, and as little inconvenience as possible to the citizens."[7] He particularly favored the large barns that proliferated in the region, noting greater ventilation had a direct effect on patient health. Straw and water supplies also were critical.

Letterman monitored South Mountain battle reports from his surgeons at Middletown, Crampton's Gap, and from Burkittsville where many patients had been taken after first being treated in barns and buildings closer to the battlefield. As darkness fell, he met with McClellan and received a battlefield status report in what became his first full day of combat after thirteen years in the army.

It was the first day of a new life for Jonathan Letterman. He no longer had direct control over the wounded in his charge. The vast scale of the Army of the Potomac required dependence on a long chain of medical officers, beginning with each corps's medical director, extending through surgeons in field hospitals, and reaching the stretcher bearer who first made contact with a wounded man. He became dependent on reports from line officers on the battlefield and surgeons in field hospitals that sometimes required instant reassessment and new orders as the enemy continued firing. The test of every officer came when the strength or surprise of the enemy forced unexpected changes to battle plans carefully crafted before the first shot was fired.

By midnight, the Union army had taken control of Turner's Gap to the north and stood poised to overrun Crampton's Gap at dawn. Letterman had watched some of the fighting from a hospital. Although responsible for dozens of aid stations and makeshift hospitals treating hundreds of wounded men with more probably not yet found on the mountain, he found beauty in what he saw. "And when the sun went down, the continual flashing of musketry from General Gibbon's brigade (as it pushed up the valley leading to the pass from which we wished to dislodge the enemy), making darkness visible, adding greatly to the beauty of the scene."[8]

If Letterman was inspired by night fighting, General Lee had to be disappointed. His troops had lost control of Turner's Gap. Retreat from Maryland might be necessary. Then he learned Crampton's Gap in the south appeared ready to fall. If that happened, advancing Union troops would be in a position to threaten his 15,000 men at Harpers Ferry a few miles further south as well. But when General Stonewall Jackson informed Lee that he believed he could take Harpers Ferry the next day, Lee decided to remain in Sharpsburg, await Jackson's reinforcements from Harpers Ferry, and confront the Army of the Potomac. With Potomac River nearby, Lee was narrowing his limited retreat options by deciding to stay in Sharpsburg. If McClellan attacked in earnest the morning of September 15, his troops might not be able to hold long enough for Jackson's reinforcements to arrive.

The next morning, Union forces poured through the mountain gaps and into Pleasant Valley. They reached the east side of Antietam Creek and stopped. Across the river, Lee had deployed his 10,000 men in three concentrations on the eastern edge of Sharpsburg. One concentration was in the north near a drought-stunted cornfield surrounded by small woodlots. Another was positioned near the Dunker Church in the center. A third was directly opposite a bridge that crossed Antietam Creek slightly south of Sharpsburg. Union troops were positioned to the east, on the far side of farm fields, rolling hills, small groves, and thickets. By late afternoon both armies had settled on either side of Antietam Creek, across a six-mile front.

The afternoon breeze carried the smell of imminent battle. The trees whispered as leaves lost their grip on summer and rode the warm, late-summer wind to the ground. Confederate troops were located in stands of trees, behind five- and six-rail farmers' fences, along sunken roads that separated farm fields, and among the trees that snaked atop seasonal creek beds. They could hear tens of thousands of unseen Union soldiers preparing for battle, less than a mile away.

A few miles to the east, Letterman stood on the crest of a hill that overlooked Antietam Creek and the battlefield further to the west. He finally knew where men would fall wounded. He could finally calculate how they would have to be evacuated from the battlefield and where hospitals would have to be established in nearby hamlets and on farms. Surgeons and personnel had to be assigned, ambulance units had to be dispersed along anticipated routes of travel, and supplies had to be brought forward to the churches, farmhouses, mills, and barns that were being converted into aid stations and hospitals. All this had to be accomplished within the day and in a region Letterman had never seen before.

Letterman passed through Boonsboro in the morning and Keedysville in the afternoon, two small towns at or near farm-country crossroads. Both were less than five miles from the likely battlefield. He identified hospital sites, reliable supplies of water, and assigned personnel for their establishment. He ordered them to "choose barns well provided with hay and straw, as preferable to houses, since they were better ventilated, and enabled Medical officers to attend a greater number of wounded—to place the wounded in the open air near the barns, rather than in badly constructed houses—and to have the medical supplies taken to the points indicated. These directions were generally carried into effect, but the hospitals were not always beyond the reach of the enemy's guns."[9]

He was short of tents but wasn't overly worried due to the warm weather. Mid-September weather in Maryland typically reached the upper seventies during the day and often settled in the fifties at night.

In search of additional intelligence, McClellan dallied a second day on September 16, as early morning fog blanketed the area, allowing the lead elements of Lee's force from Harpers Ferry to arrive in Sharpsburg. Although McClellan had lost the initiative his men had earned by crossing South Mountain, his forces still outnumbered Lee's by a factor of two to one. McClellan's battle plan called for committing approximately 50,000 men and holding 30,000 in reserve. Letterman spent the day riding throughout Pleasant Valley in search of additional hospital sites. He skirted wheat fields nearly ready for harvest, orchards, and herds of grazing cattle. Hilltop farmhouses offered sweeping views and improved ventilation but also were inviting targets for the enemy's artillery corps. Rolling hills afforded convenient aid station locations on the lee side, close to the fighting. Deeply rutted roads made patient transport to hospital barns painful but possible.

Late in the day, Letterman returned to McClellan's headquarters at the Pry House, a two-story brick farmhouse built in 1844 on a large farm east of Antietam Creek. Owned by Phillip and Elizabeth Pry, the redbrick hilltop farmhouse was a tall, narrow landmark. Staircases at both ends of the narrow, two-room-wide home creaked under every user. Ten windows on the west and east sides provided panoramic views and access to afternoon breezes.

A few paces west from the house to the western edge of the hill provided a distant, nearly level view of the elevated farming landscape between Antietam Creek's west bank and Sharpsburg. Letterman and McClellan could see Dunker Church, which would become the center of the battlefield, but could not see

Lee's troops deployed on the far side of ridges. They would have to rely on couriers and the signal corps with reports of fighting in the cornfield to the north and what became known as Burnside Bridge to the south.

Letterman established an operating room on the ground floor for officers and recovery rooms upstairs. His staff converted a massive barn slightly down the hill into the position's main hospital for enlisted men. If its 3,200 square feet proved inadequate, Letterman's staff could erect tents on the farm's 140 sloping acres.

The ambulance system Letterman had first organized two months earlier had effectively evacuated the wounded out of Turner's, Fox's, and Crampton's Gaps on September 14. With the Army of the Potomac set for the attack on Sharpsburg, Letterman deployed his resources accordingly. With 300 medical department wagons available as ambulances and for supplies (one per 200 men) he was relatively well supplied. He had overcome a lack of hospital organization by decentralizing his medical command and relying on professional military doctors he trusted. "We were practically quite free from control, in the sense of direction," assistant surgeon Alfred Woodhull later wrote of Antietam. "At first it depended upon the lack of organization . . . later it followed because we were regulars . . . I do think it was assumed that, as we were intelligent men who had been carefully selected and were living in an atmosphere of discipline, we could be depended on to look out for the services in a matter-of-fact way; while the volunteers, even after a year's life under canvas, required supervision and direction."[10]

Letterman had used McClellan's delay to organize a vast network of nearly 100 hospitals in barns, farmhouses, stands of trees, churches, and large public buildings that supported the three commands that McClellan had positioned for attack. General Joseph Hooker commanded approximately 8,000 men in the north and would attack through the woods and cornfield. He had hospitals at White House, the Middlekauf house, the Joseph Poffenberger house, and other farms to the rear. General Edwin Sumner in the center had approximately 15,000 men on the front line in his command. He would launch an attack toward Dunker Church on the east side of Sharpsburg and had hospitals at Keedysville, Letterman's Pry House, and in other farmhouses in support. In the South, General Ambrose Burnside engaged approximately 9,000 soldiers. Burnside had the only command east of Antietam Creek, so he faced the prospect of taking a heavily defended, narrow bridge. Hospitals in nearby farmhouses and at Locust Springs in the hills to the rear would handle the inevitable casualties.[11]

Drizzle dampened the Pry House as Letterman prepared for battle at dawn on September 17. As the sky lightened, it faded to a steady mist. At 5:00 a.m. the Confederates heard General Hooker's men moving south through the North Woods toward a thirty-acre cornfield, where many of General Stonewall Jackson's 7,000 men waited on the far side. The cornfield, sunken roads between farm fields, and farmers' woodlots gave the Rebels secure cover. The cornfield provided illusionary safety to advancing Union troops. Although the undulating ground and sparse rock outcrops provided some shelter, when Hooker's men entered the field enemy musket and artillery fire erupted. Approximately 15,000 soldiers blended into a chaotic mosaic of gunfire, explosions, and screams.

Artillery fire, called "death missiles" by some, rained down on the Union troops from Confederate artillery positions on Nicodemus Heights, less than half a mile to the west. The savagery shredded cornstalks, tree trunks, and soldiers. Confederate and Union soldiers fell by the hundreds, sometimes a few yards apart, while the cacophony of gunfire swallowed the cries of the wounded. In one hour, more than half of General Jackson's command was killed or wounded.[12] Both sides reinforced units that had been decimated in a few hours' fighting. At about 8:00 a.m. Hooker suffered a severe foot wound. His command's losses mounted by the thousands with each passing hour. Many lay stranded in the cornfield and nearby woods. After three hours' fighting, Letterman faced 8,700 casualties on the battlefield.

At 9:00 a.m. one of the deadliest few minutes in American history unfolded. The cornfield changed hands several times as Union soldiers pushed south and then were repulsed by advancing Confederates as bodies fell upon each other. When Major General John Sedgwick led his men into a deadly trap, the "West Woods Massacre" bloodied the soil. In twenty minutes' time, 2,000 men fell dead or wounded. After four hours' fighting, Jonathan Letterman had become responsible for more than 10,000 casualties.

The intensely private Letterman never revealed his personal reaction to knowing 10,000 bleeding men depended upon how and when he might make his next decision—a decision that could determine whether a soldier had a chance at survival. A surgeon might be hoping that the next shipment of medical supplies would be sent to his hospital. A wounded soldier might be wondering whether enough stretcher bearers would be sent into his stand of trees so that he would be found in his nest of rocks before he bled to death. A stretcher bearer might wonder if he'd have to search for wounded through the night, his lantern making him an easy target for enemy sharpshooters. Nearly all of them depended on a medical director they had never met and who had never endured the heat of battle command.

By 10:00 a.m. spotters at Pry House and couriers from the battlefield reported the massive losses to Letterman. Assistant Surgeon Benjamin Howard rode from one field hospital to the next, assessing the damage and giving messages to McClellan's couriers as they rode back to the Pry House. Letterman faced thousands of wounded, some being treated at aid stations in gullies and in stands of trees, with hundreds more screaming for help while lying on barren ground and alongside farm roads. As the battlefield became a mile wide, Letterman knew some of the medical reports he received were at least an hour old. Regardless, he ordered some of the ambulances he had assembled at Pry House down the hill, across Antietam Creek, and north toward the field hospitals that were already filled with wounded from the cornfield. He had to get hundreds of wounded men out of frontline aid stations and hospitals if the stations were to be able to receive thousands more patients later in the day. Soon fighting would erupt in the center of the front line, near Dunker Church and along Sunken Road.

Confederate generals James Longstreet and D. H. Hill had positioned troops along one of the area's many farm roads that sometimes were up to eight feet below the farm fields on either side. The equivalent of a broad, flat-bottom trench, they provided ideal protection for Confederate troops as exposed Union soldiers advanced toward them over the crest of barren farm fields. Unfettered Confederate fields of crossfire would make it nearly impossible to miss the vulnerable attackers who would be tightly bunched with both flanks exposed. Thousands of attackers and defenders would collide along a 1,000-yard stretch of what became known as the Sunken Road in the center of the Antietam battlefield.

Second corps division commander William French led more than 5,000 men onto a slaughter field. Several waves of attacks proved futile, producing 1,700 battlefield casualties. In twenty minutes of wicked crossfire, the 15th Massachusetts Volunteers lost 330 men, more than half of its fighting force. In less than half an hour, Letterman's aid stations nearby faced another 298 wounded soldiers, most of whom had to be evacuated off the

battlefield under enemy fire. By the time the attacks and counterattacks ebbed, McClellan had lost 3,000 more men in the area
surrounding Sunken Road, a blood-soaked path that became
known as Bloody Lane.

At midday, the Confederate forces were running low on
ammunition. Union army units that had attacked Sunken Road
from an elevated position had achieved a minimal advance after
losing thousands of men to deafening volleys of enemy fire.
Smoke hung in the morning air. Shortly after noon, the Confederates withdrew from Sunken Road, now a stretch of barren
dirt covered with dead and twitching bodies. The retreat created a gap in the center of the Confederate defense. But again
McClellan failed to take advantage of an opportunity that had
come at the cost of thousands of lives. He ordered his exhausted
and shell-shocked men to hold their position.

By 1:00 p.m. fighting between 13,000 troops in the cornfield's
vicinity had produced 2,900 dead and wounded Union soldiers.
The pressure on Letterman's ambulance system and network
of aid stations had become relentless after a half-day's fighting.
Meanwhile, the Union and Confederate positions along Sunken
Road tactically remained unchanged.

While Sumner's troops had bogged down along Sunken
Road, General Ambrose Burnside launched an attack in the
south. About 500 Confederate troops defended the bridge
across Antietam Creek that Ambrose's Ninth Corps sought.
They were outnumbered by more than ten to one, but had dug
in on a hill directly overlooking the narrow stone bridge. The
creek and bridge at the foot of the hill, gave Burnside's troops
no room to assemble once they crossed the bridge. Confederate troops, in effect, held a hillside "castle" that was protected
by a creek "moat" and single bridge that crossed it. Confederate troops fired almost straight down on exposed men as they
raced across the bridge.

McClellan grew impatient with Burnside's lack of progress. He sent senior aides to Burnside ordering him to take the bridge, no matter the cost. Waves of Union soldiers followed each other to the foot of the Confederate-held hill before being turned back. Hundreds lay wounded. Only a few could be carried back across the bridge to aid stations hidden in stands of trees.

At 1:30 p.m., Union soldiers reached the far side of the bridge or creek. It took another two hours before the bulk of Burnside's men crossed the bridge and established a threat to Sharpsburg from the southeast. Still furious with the lack of advance, McClellan ordered Burnside's exhausted troops to press their attack up the hill and open a route toward Sharpsburg. As Burnside's units launched a late-afternoon advance toward Sharpsburg, Confederate forces unexpectedly appeared on the Union flank. General A. G. Hill had led 3,200 men on a ten-hour march across seventeen miles of countryside from Harpers Ferry to attack Burnside's left flank and stall his advance. The costly assault ground to a halt. More than two thousand Union soldiers were killed or wounded during their river crossing and assault toward Sharpsburg.[13] Shortly before dark they pulled back to the bridge with the Confederates back in control of the hillside. As the sun set on September 17, more than 23,000 Union and Confederate soldiers had become casualties, the bloodiest day in American history.

During a lull in the day's fighting, Lieutenant Spurr had been moved to a safer location and placed on a bed of straw. Alongside him lay Union and Confederate soldiers, waiting for care. Thousands of dead and wounded littered the open battlefield. Nearly 8,000 bodies remained on the thirty-acre cornfield that had changed hands six times that day.[14] The carpet of death horrified Union surgeon George Stevens, moving him to write, "At one point in our own front, for more than half a mile, the rebels lay so thickly as to almost touch each other.

On the field where Hooker's men had won and lost the field, the dead and dying were scattered thickly among the broken cornstalks, their eyes protruding and their faces blackened by the sun. Wherever the lines of battle had surged to and fro, these vestiges of the terrible work were left. . . . Some were shot while attempting to get over the fence; and their remains hung upon the boards. A more fearful picture than we saw here, could not be conceived."[15]

America's bloodiest day had ended at sunset. The early morning attacks had cost the Union army 7,300 wounded and killed. The midday phase produced nearly 2,900 casualties. All told, 11,600 Union troops had been killed or wounded. The Confederate toll stood at more than 9,000 killed or wounded. The equivalent of every resident of Atlanta, Georgia, and Alexandria, Virginia, had been killed or wounded in one day at Antietam.[16]

Soldiers had fallen wounded or dead at the rate of 2,000 per hour. Every two seconds, for twelve consecutive hours, a Union or Confederate soldier fell wounded or killed along the battlefront. Lee's grand plan of driving deep into the heart of the North had been foiled. The cost in suffering, though, had been brutal. Jonathan Letterman's battle at Antietam, however, had just begun.

The following day hundreds of wounded men lay on the battlefield as the two armies held their positions, Lee in Sharpsburg and McClellan along Antietam Creek. Neither army had the strength to fight a second day. Already the wounded packed Letterman's hospitals, testimony to the previous day's carnage. Located close to the battlefront, the hospitals had filled quickly on the previous night as one wagon arrived after another, loaded with wounded, "Indeed there was not a barn or farmhouse, or store, or church, or schoolhouse, between Boonsboro and Keedysville, Sharpsburg and Smoketown that was not gorged with wounded—Rebel and Union. Even the corncribs, and in many instances the cow stables, and in one place the mangers were filled," wrote the Sanitary Commission's Dr. Cornelius Agnew.[17]

Two large general hospitals established by Letterman, one at Smoketown able to treat 600 and another at Locust Springs able to treat up to 400 were at capacity. They reflected the reality that the seriously wounded could not withstand a long trip to a distant city for hospital care. Thousands of men wounded in a major battle could not be patched up and sent back to the front line or put on a train for a long trip to Baltimore, New York City, or Philadelphia. For the first time, general hospitals near the battlefield were established as the next logical link in Letterman's emerging concept of battlefield care that moved seriously wounded soldiers from aid station to an intermediate makeshift field hospital and, when strong enough, to a general hospital as expeditiously as possible. It formed a concept Letterman would codify less than two months later, building on his crucial first step of establishing an ambulance corps.

The homes of area residents not designated as potential hospitals before the battle were commandeered on September 18, as Letterman's staff desperately coped with legions of wounded. After telegraphing for more supplies on the night of the battle, Letterman searched for more as the magnitude of the previous day's human destruction became clearer. The supply logjam at Monocacy River persisted as frustration mounted among underequipped doctors at the hospitals. It was worse for volunteer regimental surgeons, who were given a small allowance to purchase food instead of being provided Army food. "I am sometimes almost famished for want of something to eat," wrote surgeon Daniel Holt of the 121st New York regiment. "As we have no camp or cooking utensils, and no means of carrying provisions we are all the while upon short allowance and every often upon no allowance at all. . . . Were it not for peaches and tomatoes with an occasional onion to eat with my ginger cakes it would go hard enough I assure you."[18]

Many were unaware of Letterman's efforts to get tons of supplies off the boxcars, loaded into wagons, and driven either to the supply depot at Frederick or further west into the rural constellation of hospitals. At 9:00 a.m. on the 18th he gratefully accepted a wagonload of medical supplies from the Sanitary Commission at Keedysville. He decided to use most of the supplies at Keedysville and nearby aid stations. A few hours later, he rode to Middletown to check on its hospital. There, another wagonload of Sanitary Commission supplies arrived for his distribution.[19]

Surgeons who had been operating on the most seriously wounded at the outset of the battle were still operating the following day as Letterman focused on supplies and the ongoing battlefield evacuation. In a letter to his wife, Union surgeon William Child wrote, "The days after the battle are a thousand times worse than the day of the battle—the physical pain is not the greatest pain suffered. . . . The dead appear sickening but they suffer no pain. But the poor wounded mutilated soldiers that yet have life and sensation make a most horrid picture. I pray God may stop such infernal work, though perhaps he has sent it upon us for our sins. Great indeed must have been our sins if such is our punishment."[20]

There would be no more fighting at Antietam after Lee withdrew from Sharpsburg the night of September 18 and crossed the Potomac the following day. Fortified by the bulk of the Sixth Corps that had been held in reserve on the day of the battle, McClellan allowed Lee an unchallenged retreat. By the time Lee began his withdrawal, within twenty-four hours after the battle had ended, Letterman's ambulance system had evacuated nearly all of the wounded off the battlefield, a landmark accomplishment in the evolution of battlefield care.[21] Letterman toured the hospitals and battlefield, giving orders, overseeing the evacuation, and calling for supplies. He established a temporary supply depot at Sharpsburg on the 19th, much closer to the battlefield than Frederick. "Not only were our wounded supplied, but the wounded of the enemy, who fell into our hands, was furnished with all the medical and surgical appliances required for their use," wrote Letterman.[22]

On September 20, McClellan moved his headquarters to the west side of Antietam Creek. Letterman put surgeon John Howard Taylor in charge of the Pry farm's barn that now served as a field hospital for enlisted men, as well as in charge of hospitals on the R. F. Kennedy and Henry Neikirk farms a few miles away. At least 1,500 wounded men, initially short of adequate clothing and bedding, at the Hoffman farm and Pry Mill hospital among other locations, were the responsibility of Taylor.

By that point, Letterman faced a new challenge and with it came an opportunity. Repairs to the railroad bridge over Monocacy River at Frederick neared completion. Soon the flow of supplies toward the battlefield would accelerate. Letterman could then utilize the empty boxcars as patient transports back to recently expanded convalescent hospitals in Baltimore, Washington, and elsewhere. Wounded men who could withstand the journey in the back of a wagon were taken from hospitals near Sharpsburg to the rail head and nearby hospitals in Frederick. More than 10,000 men were admitted to Frederick's thirty-four hospitals, most on their way to larger cities.

The timing of their departure had to be meticulously planned so that their arrival in Frederick more than fifteen miles away coincided with the evacuation trains' schedule and capacity. "It was imperative that the trains [convoys of ambulance wagons] should leave at the proper hours, no one interfering with another; that they should halt at Middletown, where food and rest, with such surgical aid as might be required, could be given to the wounded; that food should be prepared at this village at the proper time, for the proper number; that the hospitals at Frederick should not be overcrowded, and the ambulances should arrive at the railroad depot in Frederick at the required time to meet the Baltimore trains," wrote Letterman.[23] His medical officers sent wounded men to the nearest hospital that still had capacity. They transferred Lieutenant Spurr by ambulance to Hagerstown, Maryland, for treatment of the gunshot wound in his thigh.

Thousands of wounded men, unable to travel to general hospitals in cities, remained at large hospitals at Keedysville, Smoketown, and in other nearby rural towns. These "hospitals," to which the majority of wounded men were taken, comprised a collection of tents. If the men were lucky, the tents were located in stands of trees that provided shade. A rural church, barn, or courthouse served as the hospital headquarters, operating room, recovery, and intensive care unit.

Letterman's Keedysville hospital was typical. "The principal hospital was established in the brick church near the upper end of town. Boards were laid on top of the seats, then straw and blankets, and most of the worse cases of wounded were taken to this, the headquarters. Comrades with wounds of all conceivable shapes were brought in and placed side by side as thick as they could lay, and the bloody work of amputation commenced. The Surgeons, myself and a corps of nurses with sleeves rolled up, worked with tender care and anxiety to relieve the pain and save the lives of all we could. A pit was dug under the window at the back of the church and as soon as a limb was amputated I would take it to the window and drop it outside into the pit. The arms, legs, feet and hands that were dropped into that hole would amount to several hundred pounds. On occasion I had to fish out a hand for its former owner, as he insisted that it was all cramped up and hurt him. As soon as the hand was straightened out he complained no more of the pain in the stump," wrote hospital orderly George Allen of the 76th New York Infantry.[24]

In other instances, in contemporary accounts, the term *hospital* in the singular represented a summary description of several impromptu medical facilities. "Smoketown hospital" represented field hospitals at several farms near the small settlement of Smoketown. The main hospital in a stand of oaks contained eighty tents, a post office, kitchen, chapel, dispensary and storerooms.

"The hospital is arranged nearly in the form of a square; the wards in which the patients are placed form one side of the square. There are now eight of these, each ward consisting of six or seven large tents, each ten being fourteen feet square. . . . There are streets running between them, which are swept every morning, if the weather permits. . . . The beds are all made of iron, with good ticks well filled with straw, and plenty of blankets. . . . Each tent has a good stove with an oven in it. There are five patients in each tent," wrote a newspaper reporter.[25]

As battlefield reports detailed the wasteland of death and injury in western Maryland, Letterman faced a new invasion: relatives and friends of the wounded. "Immediately after the battle, many persons came within our lines to remove their relatives or friends who had been injured—whose lives, in many instances, depended upon their remaining at rest. It was impossible to convince them that the removal of a dangerously wounded man would be made at the risk of his life—that risk they were perfectly willing to take, if he could only (at the end perhaps of a long and painful journey) be placed in a house. No greater mistake could be made. . . . A marked contrast could been seen, within a few yards, between the wounded in houses and barns, and those in the open air. Those in houses progressed less favorably than those in barns, those in the latter buildings less favorably than those in the open air; though all were treated alike in other respects," wrote Letterman.[26]

For all the authority granted Letterman, decisions by others in command had to become a source of frustration at times. It must have saddened him to see families take wounded sons, brothers, and fathers out of the field hospitals Letterman had worked hard to establish and take them to less healthy environments. Probably just as frustrating, McClellan allowed some state relief society representatives to take wounded soldiers back to their home states. Thousands of men were lost to the Army of the Potomac in this way, with their return to duty uncertain at best.

Families also scoured the battlefield in search of a relative or friend. Letterman could not ignore the sanitation hazards posed by the dead and dismembered body parts. Nearly a week after the battle, "the dead were almost wholly unburied, and the stench arising from it was such as to breed a pestilence in the regiment. We were ordered to bury the dead, collect arms, and accoutrements left upon the field. . . . I have seen, stretched along, in one straight line, ready for interment, at least a thousand blackened, bloated corpses with blood and gas protruding from every orifice, and maggots holding high carnival over the heads," wrote surgeon Holt.[27]

In the weeks following battle, the flow of wounded to the east matched waves of supplies finally reaching Maryland. "There was probably no campaign throughout the war which was conducted under greater disadvantages in respect to supplies of all kinds . . . the immense losses and terrible exhaustion of a week of battles, the consequent confusion and disorganization, and the impossibility of providing adequate means of transportation for the most necessary supplies, the Army which fought at Antietam was placed in the worst possible condition so far as its ability to care properly for its wounded was concerned," wrote Sanitary Commissioner Charles Stille.[28] Letterman may have disagreed with that statement, as his inspections convinced him they were reasonably supplied, with the exception of food in the days immediately following the battle. He could hardly deny the initial shortage of food as the Sanitary Commission, independent of the military-controlled railroad line, delivered 28,763 pieces of dry goods, 2,620 pounds of condensed milk, 3,188 pounds of farina, 5,000 pounds of beef stock and meat, 3,000 bottles of wine, and tea, sugar, spices, and crackers to area hospitals following the battle.[29]

Antietam demonstrated that both the military and civilian medical communities were needed to treat thousands of men who fell wounded within a few hours' fighting. Although some Sanitary Commission agents had found Letterman to be aloof, Antietam galvanized a relationship of mutual respect that overcame the army's reluctance to accept assistance from civilians. "I am pleased to state that the true relation of the Sanitary Commission to the Medical Department was fully recognized and appreciated as a body designed to supplement and not supplant the regular operations of the army," wrote a Sanitary Commission doctor.[30] After a year of war, the civilian-led Sanitary Commission, army medical professionals led by Surgeon General Hammond, and army medical directors such as Letterman began to tolerate and accept their respective roles in caring for tens of thousands of casualties. Those numbers became more overwhelming in the battles still to come.

Although the Confederates had been driven back into Virginia at Antietam, critics condemned McClellan's failure to decisively destroy Lee's army in the battle. Letterman's medical department came in for criticism as well. While his ambulance system had evacuated the entire battlefield in twenty-four hours, a respected publication of the day, the *American Medical Times*, characterized his efforts as "gross mismanagement and inefficiency . . . lack of system control," and reported allegations of theft by some ambulance drivers.[31]

Some Sanitary Commission agents also were critical. One focused on Letterman's department, complaining that some of the wounded were given only water the first day and then coffee and crackers the second day as they waited for a doctor. Yet according to Letterman, the Deputy Medical Inspector General of the British Army, in a visit to Antietam, "expressed the pleasure it afforded him to see the manner in which the wounded were attended, and remarked that although he had been on many battle-fields, he had never found them more carefully provided for, or attentively treated."[32]

Praise from a fellow medical officer meant more to Letterman than the opinions of civilians. He held a dim view of their ability to judge the unique challenges of military medicine and valued the professionalism and order he found in the military. His self-awareness and confidence left no need for accolades from those he felt unqualified to judge his emerging system.

Letterman was pleased with the first test of his ambulance philosophy, writing: "It is well to remember than no system devised by man can be perfect, and that no such system, even if it existed, could be carried out perfectly by human agency. Calling to mind the fact that the ambulance system, imperfect as it may be found, could not be fully put into service—remembering the magnitude of the engagement, the length of time the battle lasted, and the obstinacy with which it was contested—it affords me much gratification to state that so few instances of apparently unnecessary suffering were found to exist after that action and that the wounded were removed from that sanguinary field in so careful and expeditious a manner."

Some criticized the thousands of post-battle surgeries that left men disfigured or minus a limb. Some characterized it as butchery by incompetent doctors who had rushed to the battlefield as volunteers. Letterman saw it differently. While he acknowledged the care by a few contract civilian and state regiment volunteer doctors was poor, he felt that probably more amputations should have been conducted in what he viewed as "conservative surgery." He believed that given the likelihood of deadly infection following a severe leg or arm wound littered with dirt and debris, the conservative approach was prompt amputation to give the patient the best possible chance at survival.

Lieutenant Spurr's upper thigh wound made amputation impossible. A few days after the battle, an infection took hold and spread. Ten days after he had been wounded, at 9:00 a.m. on September 27, Spurr faded quickly as his eyes grew glassy. "Mother!" he cried, moments before he died. He became one of 20,950 Union and Confederate soldiers who were killed or wounded at Antietam, a battle that produced nearly five wounded men for every soldier killed outright on the battlefield.

Coping with families searching his hospitals, hoping to find that their loved one had survived the fighting, was one of Letterman's post-battle priorities. He also turned his attention to maximizing a rebuilt supply line that fed Frederick and dozens of hospitals in the region. He established procedures to transfer thousands of wounded men from rural barns to metropolitan hospitals, sometimes one hundred miles away. He also focused on post-battle analysis.

In the aftermath of General Lee's retreat to the South, Letterman knew that the Army of the Potomac's pursuit would produce massive battles, perhaps as large as the one that had been fought at Antietam. His battlefield evacuation system had been proven, despite inadequate time for training. However, the skyrocketing numbers of wounded from a single battle revealed the army's vulnerability to a poorly organized and fragmented supply system. The destruction of a single railroad bridge could put thousands of lives in jeopardy. Too many doctors at Antietam had been inadequately equipped for the initial wave of patients delivered to their operating table.

It also became clear that Letterman's encouragement of hospital organization by division was insufficient. The chain of care at the edge of the battlefield from aid station to field hospital to evacuation hospital to convalescent hospital had to be as comprehensively overhauled as he had reorganized the battlefield ambulance system. Battlefield care could not be a two way street. He had to reverse the tide of battlefield care from bringing surgeons to the wounded to efficiently transporting the wounded to an organized and tiered hospital structure that could move with the army and become established on as little as a few days' notice. To accomplish that, reliance on civilian transports instead of assigned military personnel could not continue.

Long before the last of the major Antietam hospitals at Keedysville and Smoketown were closed, Jonathan Letterman knew he had to turn his attention to supply and hospital structure. Reorganization of both might have to take place while the army marched. Having resisted a prompt pursuit of Lee after allowing him to escape into the South, McClellan faced mounting pressure from President Lincoln to take the initiative.

His reluctance to pursue began to cost him the confidence of some of his medical officers under Letterman. "I am loosing (sic) all confidence and respect for McClellan—a man who a year ago I verily believed to be an agent of God to put down the rebellion in the shortest, cheapest, and most approved manner. . . . Three times we have moved expecting to follow up their retreat; and three times we have not done it," surgeon Holt wrote in a letter to his wife.[33]

In approximately three months, the survival of thousands of men charging another sunken road would depend on how well McClellan, Letterman, and other officers could plan and coordinate the missions of combat, care, and if necessary, pursuit of the enemy.

6

FREDERICKSBURG

"A huge serpent of blue and steel"

J. H. Woodbury of Massachusetts, George Simons of New Hampshire, and Henry Dyke of New York were typical of those who volunteered to serve in their state's regiments as part of the Army of the Potomac. They joined an army still struggling to adapt to a new type of warfare that required far more mobility than any American army had faced in 1776, 1812, or 1846.

The army's medical department had been crippled by an outdated command structure that left it vulnerable to the quartermaster corps, which controlled a supply chain that sometimes overwhelmed and sometimes starved those who depended upon it. On more than one occasion, soldiers had to carry more rations than they could manage on the march. While they tossed food, coats, and knapsacks aside, medical officers went begging for missing wagons filled with medicines, tents, and other supplies that frequently were marooned at supply depots, abandoned in the rush to find the enemy, or commandeered by other officers for their personal use. Tens of thousands of wounded and dying young men had suffered as a result of unpreparedness and inefficiency.

Jonathan Letterman had now experienced firsthand the unique medical needs of an army equivalent to the combined populations of Pittsburgh, Memphis, Peoria, and Sacramento when it was on the march.[1] Standing atop a barren hilltop, he had watched massive armies collide on the battlefield at Antietam and had seen how Civil War battles could produce more casualties in a few hours than America had experienced throughout the Revolutionary War.

For the first time, Letterman had to look backward as well as forward in managing the Army of the Potomac's medical department. Thousands of the most-seriously wounded men facing extended and uncertain recovery as they lay in Antietam-area hospitals remained his responsibility. At the same time, Letterman had to prepare for the next clash between McClellan and Lee without knowing where it would take place.

Although Antietam generally had been judged as a victory both for Letterman and McClellan, both had faced public criticism in its aftermath. While that represented a new experience for Letterman, McClellan had long been the target of military critics. McClellan's commander in chief, President Lincoln, now was foremost among those who questioned McClellan's appetite for battle. After meeting with McClellan, Letterman, and others in early October, President Lincoln remained far from mollified, later calling the Army of Potomac "McClellan's bodyguard."[2] Letterman reported to a general who no longer enjoyed the confidence of his boss. McClellan defenders, however, argued that political meddling had kept the general from carrying the fight to Lee.

On the other hand, Letterman's organization of the ambulance corps three months earlier and his ability to plan for the unprecedented casualties at Antietam, had justified McClellan's original judgment of him. As an exhausted Army of the Potomac spent October in the Sharpsburg area following Antietam, the opportunity to complete his medical department's reorganization was at hand. Letterman turned his attention to overhauling the medical supply system and then the hospital structure as dozens of regiments arrived to create a 135,000-man army by October 20.[3]

As he had done with his ambulance reorganization, Letterman made a frank assessment of the waste of war and then, based on that assessment, took a logical approach to ensuring the optimal disbursement of medical supplies. After Antietam, he knew he had to calibrate the availability of medical supplies with the reality of war. "Hitherto medical supplies for three months had been furnished directly to regiments, and no wagons allowed expressly for their transportation. From these causes large quantities were lost, and in various ways wasted; and not unfrequently [sic] all the supplies of a regiment were thrown away by commanding officers, almost in sight of the enemy, that the wagons might be used for other purposes. I desired to reduce the waste which took place when a three months' supply was issued to regiments, to have a small quantity given them at one time, and to have it at all times replenished without difficulty; to avoid a multiplicity of accounts, and yet preserve a proper degree of responsibility; to have a fixed amount of transportation set apart for carrying these supplies, and used for no other purpose," wrote Letterman.[4]

Letterman conceived a tiered supply chain beginning at the brigade level and ending on the battlefield, perhaps on the backside of a hill that offered a fragile refuge for the wounded. With McClellan's consent, on October 4, 1862, he issued a set of standing orders that reflected the new medical supply protocols. Each brigade was assigned one hospital wagon filled with medical supplies in bulk; one filled medicine chest and one wagon of hospital supplies for each regiment in the brigade; and one medical knapsack for each medical officer in the regiment. Each brigade was issued one month of medical supplies, which could be replenished from a nearby supply depot, ideally near rail or water transport.

Regimental medical officers could requisition supplies for their knapsacks from the brigade without a receipt, but Letterman held brigade officers accountable for the consumption of their supplies and prompt resupply from the regional depot. Ambulances accompanying regiments also carried supplies. In this way, Letterman decentralized medical supplies from brigade headquarters in the rear to the regiments on the battlefield.

He also mandated what must be available in the brigade's supplies and aboard ambulances and hospital wagons. Required supplies for individual ambulances included beef stock; leather bucket; camp kettle; lantern and candle; tin spoons and tumblers; and ten pounds of hard bread. When regimental ambulances could not approach the battlefield with the troops, his order required an orderly to carry a knapsack filled with medical supplies instead. A hospital wagon had to be equipped with twelve pints of alcohol, eight dozen opium pills, one pound of opium tincture, twenty-four bottles of whiskey, ten pounds of arrowroot, one pound of zinc chloride, four quarts of castor oil, and twenty-four ounces of quinine as well as a variety of other chemicals, instruments, foodstuffs, bedding, and equipment.

With this single order, Letterman restructured the concept of military medical supply so that supplies could more reliably be delivered where needed on the battlefield. His fluid system reflected the increased mobility of armies. As the tide of battle flowed from invasions to flanking counterattacks to massive frontal collisions, the supply chain needed to expand and contract to match the exigencies of war and the movement of regiments, brigades, and divisions, and now it could. The wagons transporting the supplies were now the property of the medical department and no longer subject to misappropriation or abandonment by others. This meant less potential waste of precious materiel and a greater ability to reliably plan on their availability.

This restructuring of medical supply built on recent efforts to ensure the good health of the troops through proper nutrition. The average soldier's diet continued to be a concern of the army, particularly given the incidence of disease that had ravaged the weakened troops early in the war, and, two months before Letterman's medical-supply mandate, Congress had formally established the basic army ration:

> A ration is the established daily allowance of food for one person. For the United States Army it is composed as follows: twelve ounces of pork or bacon, or one pound and four ounces of salt or fresh beef; one pound and six ounces of soft bread or flour, or one pound of hard bread, or one pound and four ounces of corn-meal; and to every one hundred rations, fifteen pounds of beans or peas, and ten pounds of rice or hominy; ten pounds of green coffee or eight pounds of roasted (or roasted and ground) coffee, or one pound eight ounces of tea; fifteen pounds of sugar; four quarts of vinegar; one pound and four ounces of adamantine or star candies; four pounds of soap; three pounds and twelve ounces of salt; four ounces of pepper; thirty pounds of potatoes, when practicable, and one quart of molasses.[5]

Now, for the first time in the war, soldiers could with some reliability count on a structured and more nutritious diet as well as the availability of necessary medical supplies if they were wounded on the battlefield. These two improvements, guaranteeing adequate food and giving them confidence of good care for their wounds, addressed two of the fundamental needs crucial to ensuring the troops' morale.

The Army of the Potomac had less than three weeks to assimilate Letterman's medical supply system before it crossed the Potomac River at Harpers Ferry and Berlin, Maryland, in a cold rain, finally on the trail of General Lee. Its late-October pursuit into Virginia became a muddy one. It took six days to move the entire army across the river before it marched through a valley between the Blue Ridge and Bull Run Mountains toward Warrenton on a line almost due south toward Richmond.

As the Army of the Potomac marched through the Virginia countryside, Letterman's mission of reorganization was not yet complete. Although he had imposed a structure both for battlefield evacuation and medical supply, the flawed organization of military hospitals desperately needed a similar overhaul. When individual battles produced so many casualties that more than one hundred temporary hospitals could be required, fundamental changes had to be made in how triage and treatment were managed.

Letterman's experience at Antietam demonstrated that he needed to forge a more comprehensive and efficient organization: it would need to integrate battlefield first-aid stations that might lie behind rocks and in creek beds with field hospitals that were sometimes within range of enemy artillery and with general hospitals in major cities perhaps one hundred miles distant from the fighting. Having the benefit of experience, he now understood what was needed to treat thousands of men wounded in a single day's fighting. With respect to staffing, surgeons who refused to treat men who were not members of their regiment could not be tolerated. In addition, those selected to make critical treatment decisions and perform surgery had to be the best surgeons available, not simply those assigned to their posts on the basis of seniority or politics. Finally, there had to be a coordinated command-and-control structure that reflected the battlefield realities of more than 100,000 warring soldiers producing thousands of casualties in a single battle.

Letterman recognized that having hospitals dedicated to specific regiments was military medicine's weak link. At Antietam, regimental surgeons had sometimes turned away the wounded from other regiments, denying them timely treatment. Field hospitals that made no distinction about a soldier's regimental affiliation were critical to quick access to care. "As far as I knew, no system of field hospital existed in any of our armies, and, convinced on the necessity of devising some measures by which the wounded would receive the best surgical aid which the Army afforded with the least delay, my thoughts naturally turned to this most important subject," wrote Letterman.[6] Battlefield chaos, he understood, had to be channeled into coordinated care. "On the field of battle, where confusion in the Medical Department is most disastrous, it is most apt to occur, and unless some arrangement be adopted by which every Medical officer has his station pointed out and his duties defined beforehand, and his accountability strictly enforced, the wounded must suffer."[7]

Again with McClellan's endorsement, on October 30, 1862, Letterman issued a directive that recast the military hospital system as completely as his ambulance and medical supply orders had done in the preceding months. Letterman began by requiring a hospital for each division and setting standards for the number of surgeons and assistant surgeons in each. Some assistant surgeons were assigned record keeping duties, while others became specifically responsible for pitching hospital tents or organizing kitchens or burial details and ensuring adequate supplies for each. Surgeons chosen to perform operations were to be selected "solely on account of their known prudence, judgment, and skill."[8]

Letterman's order also converted what had been regimental hospitals close to the fighting into aid stations, designed to provide immediate lifesaving care before the wounded were transported to the newly designated field hospitals at the division level. Surgeons at the aid stations decided who among the seriously wounded had a chance at survival. The lucky ones might get a tourniquet to stop their bleeding, see some morphine sprinkled into their gaping wound, and be given some water or a swallow of whiskey before being carried to a collection point. Horse-drawn ambulances positioned at a nearby collection point could transport them to a division field hospital, often located in a church, courthouse, or barn. In the span of a few pages, Letterman's order created a "critical link—missing for most of military medical history—between the frontline aid stations and the rear-area general hospitals," according to one historian.[9] Just as his innovative approach organized regimental hospitals into aid stations, it established the division field hospital as the critical provider of intermediate care before the wounded were transferred to general hospitals.

This new system enabled medical officers at regimental aid stations to keep the slightly wounded closer to the battle and more readily available to return, while sending more seriously wounded soldiers to the mobile division field hospital. In addition, Letterman's order required hospital guards at both the regimental and division field hospitals to "be particularly careful that no stragglers be allowed about the hospitals, using the food and comforts prepared for the wounded."[10] Hospitals were no longer havens for thousands of soldiers looking to avoid battle.

Letterman's new system emphasized the role of division field hospitals in providing urgent care but also relied on the ability of those hospitals to evacuate the seriously wounded to general hospitals in major cities. Washington and other cities were already deluged with wounded. However, Letterman's order came at a time when efforts were under way to create new hospital space. With Surgeon General William Hammond overseeing a massive urban hospital construction initiative, government buildings that had been converted into makeshift hospitals—with no security, minimal ventilation, unacceptable hygiene, and minimal capacity—were giving way to newly built general hospitals. Earlier efforts by army medical directors had been plagued by private contractor profiteering. One hospital project, anticipated to cost $75 a bed, produced contractor bids of up to $400 per bed.[11]

In many ways Hammond was a visionary. A few months after Letterman's field hospital order, Hammond published a detailed treatise on the history and contemporary requirements of military hospitals. Early war experience had revealed proper ventilation as a vital control agent of contagious infections in frequently overcrowded general hospitals. Hammond recommended single-story hospital wards radiating from the center like spokes of a wheel, each 120 feet long under a tall roof with closeable openings at both ends to facilitate ventilation. Nearby buildings housed a kitchen, warehouse, operating rooms, ice house, pharmacy and offices. Both efficiency and hygiene were critical to caring for tens of thousands of wounded arriving from Letterman's field hospitals.

But the most contemporary military hospitals of the day sometimes strained the compassion of those who worked in them. "If our men were brave on the field, they were still braver in the hospital," wrote Union nurse Mary Livermore. "I can conceive that it may be easy to face death on the battlefield. . . . But to lie suffering in a hospital bed for months, cared for as a matter of routine and form, one's name dropped, and one only known as 'Number 10,' 'Number 20,' or 'Number 50'; with no companionship, no affection, none of the tender assiduities of home nursing, hearing from home irregularly and at rare intervals, utterly alone in the midst of hundreds; sick, in pain, sore-hearted and depressed, I declare this requires more courage to endure, than to face the most tragic death."[12]

Ingenuity led to modest and temporary advances in comfort. Poet Walt Whitman noted that in some hospitals soldiers dug a long trench under a row of hospital beds and then partially backfilled it with railroad iron and dirt. Fires built at either end of the trench where the railroad iron was exposed heated the metal, which conducted the warmth lengthwise to warm the surrounding soil under the hospital beds.

Letterman viewed one of his major priorities as maximizing McClellan's fighting force. He believed he could do that by keeping the sick and wounded out of Hammond's hospitals and as close to the army as possible, so they could return to duty more promptly. Too many Army of the Potomac soldiers disappeared when they traveled north into large cities to recover from wounds that could be treated nearby. Letterman also had to provide critical care for the seriously wounded as a prelude to evacuating them to the rear, and then ensure their efficient transportation to general hospitals in cities. His October 30 order reorganizing military hospitals in the field became the last step necessary to accomplishing those goals. Reorganized battlefield care, evacuation to a coordinated hospital structure, adequate supplies, and medical staff accountability were Letterman's military medicine cornerstones. All was in place by October 31, 1862.

By early November, McClellan and his army had reached Warrenton. McClellan couldn't conceal his unhappiness with the president's mounting pressure to attack Lee. "[T]he advance was made against his will, against his protestations, and on the imperative order of the President," wrote a reporter in the *New York Times*, a newspaper that supported McClellan in the partisan reporting of the war.[13] McClellan also regularly shared his dissatisfaction with the president in letters to his wife.

Late on November 7, he sat in his tent writing a letter when General Ambrose Burnside and Brigadier General Catharinus Buckingham interrupted him. Buckingham carried orders from the president removing McClellan from his command. For the second time, Lincoln had decided to fire the man who proved adept at developing the Army of the Potomac and at imposing structure among demoralized troops, but who resisted attacking the enemy.

McClellan and Letterman had shared a passion for the welfare of the men in their charge. In McClellan's case, it led to an aversion to aggressively engage the enemy. That cautiousness cost him his command. But McClellan's ouster had been much of his own doing. His imperial nature and overt disdain of politicians had alienated potential allies in Washington. He appeared more fearful of defeat than eager to defeat the enemy. While that trait generated widespread and passionate loyalty among most of the troops, who felt he had their best interest at heart, Lincoln, Secretary of War Edwin Stanton, and others no longer could tolerate a defensive general who was thought by some to be intellectually overmatched by General Lee.

Letterman had lost a friend. Early in his relationship with McClellan he had found common ground, their mutual passion for the welfare of the troops. Most of Letterman's few friendships similarly were based on professional relationships centered on a common cause. Those friendships ran deep. Now he would have to build a working relationship with McClellan's replacement, a man who might not share or appreciate Letterman's apolitical approach to battlefield medicine.

McClellan's ego and leadership style had unfortunately politicized the Army of the Potomac. McClellan had promoted some officers more on the basis of personal loyalty than seniority. That emboldened officers who agreed with him, and placed those who didn't in an impossible position. A key topic of disagreement was the purpose of the Civil War and what was required to end it. McClellan's subordinates served a general who believed the war necessary to preserve the union but not necessarily to emancipate slaves. The sole requirement for peace, in his view, was reunion and that emancipation could follow at some point in the future.

Minutes before McClellan was formally dismissed, Burnside reluctantly had accepted command of the army. His demeanor matched the early winter snowstorm that blanketed Warrenton that night. When congratulated on his appointment later, Burnside responded, "That, Sir, is the last thing on which I wish to be congratulated."[14] Yet command was his, and responsibility for an army that remained largely supportive of the outgoing McClellan despite eroded confidence among some officers.

Jonathan Letterman now reported to a general who considered himself wholly unfit to lead an army. Burnside had accepted the job so a rival, General Joseph Hooker, couldn't be offered the promotion. Jovial, fun-loving, quick to make friends, Burnside had a reputation among officers of an immensely likeable fellow devoid of leadership ability. It hardly inspired respect among fellow officers such as Letterman when the general resorted to his favorite expression, "trust to luck."

Burnside left McClellan's key senior officers, including Letterman, in place. He needed their experience and leadership, given his lackluster military career of modest accomplishment. He had graduated eighteenth in a class of thirty-eight at the U.S. Military Academy. He had left the army at one point, failed in business, and had turned to McClellan for help in 1858, when McClellan was an executive with the Illinois Central railroad.[15] Now Burnside had replaced his friend and relied heavily on his predecessor's military appointments. "He is a first-rate second-rate man," wrote one reporter assigned to Burnside's army.[16]

Mostly bald, he favored "side car" hair that extended down in front of his ears and spread into giant "mutton chops" that blanketed his checks before tapering and meeting as a moustache. He looked more barber than general, and his unique facial hair gave rise to the term "sideburns." His soft, puffy face sagged under the unwanted pressure of command. Three days after General Burnside replaced McClellan, according to one observer, "I saw him walking up and down the balcony of the hotel which he makes his headquarters, in an absorbed, distraught condition, seemingly overwhelmed by the weight of responsibility resting upon him."[17]

The snowstorm that had greeted Burnside's promotion signaled that the early winter window for a major offensive against Lee had grown short. Burnside reorganized his corps into three "grand divisions" and ordered his 115,000-man army to leave Warrenton for Fredericksburg, positioning it to both defend Washington and pose a serious threat to Richmond. Meanwhile, Lee's 78,000 soldiers were divided about equally between General James Longstreet in Culpeper to defend Richmond and General Stonewall Jackson in the Shenandoah Valley, who looked to attack Burnside's line of supply.

If Burnside could capture Fredericksburg, it would become an ideal staging area for an attack on Richmond along the route of the Potomac Railroad. It also had rail and water access back to Washington. The army marched from Warrenton on November 16, arriving at the bank of the Rappahannock River across from Fredericksburg three days later. Two months almost to the day after Antietam, the Army of the Potomac was ready to reengage the enemy.

Letterman had used the time to complete his overhaul of his medical department while an exhausted army rested, recovered, and prepared to mobilize. He had addressed what has since become the three cornerstones of battlefield medicine: evacuation, tiered care, and medical supply. Representatives of the Sanitary Commission assigned to the Army of the Potomac were impressed. "In no Department of the Army was the improvement more marked than in the medical service. Dr. Letterman, the Medical Director, with uncommon capacity for organizing his work, had a very high appreciation of the nature of the duties devolving upon him, and showed great energy in insisting that all the details of the service should be thoroughly and faithfully carried out by his subordinates."[18]

As civilians fled Fredericksburg, the Army of the Potomac massed on Stafford Heights, a bluff overlooking the Rappahannock's northern bank, for three days beginning on November 17. The Rappahannock flows northwest to southeast. The town, only five blocks wide, sat on the southern bank. About 900 yards southwest of the town's western boundary, Marye's Heights rose nearly 500 feet. It formed the southwestern border of the Rappahannock valley.

For the first time, Burnside experienced some of the logistical frustration that McClellan had endured, when he discovered that he had no way to cross the river. Pontoon bridges failed to arrive as expected, the result of bungled communication, poor leadership, torrential rain, and bridge barges running aground on sandbars. General Henry Halleck, responsible for logistical support as general in chief to the president, had failed to insure that the pontoons arrive on schedule for the Fredericksburg attack. McClellan had thought the brusque, impersonal, and alienating Halleck was the "most hopelessly stupid of all men in high position."[19]

While Burnside impatiently waited for the mobile bridges, Letterman prepared for battle. "Ample supplies of medicines, instruments, stimulants, and anesthetics were ordered from New York and Washington. . . . In addition to these supplies, large quantities, over and above what were required for issue, of beef stock, stimulants, dressings, milk, coffee, tea, blankets, and underclothing were ordered and kept on hand. . . . Horses, harness, stretchers, lanterns, and all that was necessary for putting the trains in serviceable order were procured, and officers were assigned, and men detailed to complete and render effective the organization," he wrote.[20]

Letterman had been given a few days' notice to prepare for Antietam. He had been forced to complete much of his planning while on the march. This time he had received several weeks' notice, which was prolonged further by the delay in the pontoons' arrival. He also had the benefit of reliable supply lines by rail and water so that large supply depots could be established. He scouted the area and established a division hospital site for each of the eighteen divisions in the army, and he could prepare the 550 medical officers in his command, who were responsible for 254 regiments.[21] This time Letterman had enough time to assemble approximately 1,000 ambulances, about one ambulance per hundred men.

But he could not anticipate how General Burnside's decisions during the battle might change medical needs on the battlefield or allow enemy fire to draw within range of field hospitals. He could not know when enemy fire might intensify in stagnated confrontations, producing unexpected casualties. Then, as counterattacks and breakthroughs unfolded, his medical supply depots could become vulnerable or too remote. There was no way Letterman could fully anticipate the course of a battle that would follow the largest cross-river landing in American military history to that time. Therefore, his pre-battle analysis and planning had to reflect the inevitable chaos of war.

For example, the pontoons' delay had allowed General Jackson's 40,000 men to complete a 175-mile march in twelve days to reinforce the 1,000 men defending Fredericksburg. By December 3, Union and Confederate armies were within sight of each other, while Jackson deployed his divisions in town and on ridges overlooking the river. The Army of the Potomac had lost another opportunity to overwhelm the enemy that now had deployed its forces along a seven-mile front.

When the fighting finally resumed, Letterman could be faced with massive casualties during an exposed river crossing. If the crossing proved successful, his medical officers could be confronted by one of the few instances of Civil War urban warfare if the Confederates chose to defend Fredericksburg, house by house. Or, he could face still more casualties if the Confederates defended the town and then fell back to the heavily fortified ridgeline and dared Union troops to cross an open plain.

For three weeks, the Confederates had built their defenses while Letterman planned for various casualty contingencies. The weather turned harsh and cold after five inches of snow fell on December 5. That night "[n]ot a fire could be started or a bed made for our men; but upon a bleak plain, destitute of every comfort . . . our poor men were compelled to remain all night standing in frozen pools, wet through the skin and famishing with hunger," wrote surgeon Daniel Holt of the 121st New York Regiment.[22]

On December 9, Burnside announced his battle plan. He assigned General Edwin Sumner 30,000 men in the Right Grand Division to assault Fredericksburg slightly upriver and attack General Longstreet's men in town and on Marye's Heights. General William Franklin's 50,000 troops in the Left Grand Division would cross the river south of town to face General Stonewall Jackson's men. It represented a wholly expected pincer assault in plain view of the Confederates. The Grand Center Division's General Joseph Hooker would hold his men in reserve on Stafford Heights. Several officers disagreed with what they considered a predictable strategy.

At 3:00 a.m. on December 11, the battle for Fredericksburg began when Union engineers began assembling the pontoon bridges that had finally arrived. Within minutes sand and shrapnel flew through the air as Confederate artillery blasted the assembly area. Burnside responded by ordering many of his 147 cannons on Stafford Heights to open fire on the town below. Dozens of homes, churches, stores, and stables shuddered and crumbled. Fires spread like an incoming tide. At mid-afternoon, pontoon boats filled with troops crossed the river, the lead elements firing on Confederates dug in along the river bank.

The first urban warfare in America's history began when Burnside blundered into a trap. As Confederates pulled back, their artillery on Marye's Heights pounded the Union soldiers as they entered the town a few feet from the river's edge. In less than twenty minutes, the 20th Massachusetts Regiment lost 97 of 307 men. But by nightfall, most of the pontoon bridges were completed, and the Army of the Potomac had established a small beachhead in Fredericksburg.

On December 12, thousands of Union soldiers crossed into Fredericksburg in a dense fog. They indiscriminately ransacked the town, littering the streets with clothing, broken china, family heirlooms, shattered glass, and furniture. Soldiers searched buildings still standing for caches of food and alcohol. They yanked curtains from their rods to serve as future bandages.

Letterman and General Lee had both concluded that the major battle would take place the next day across the open plain between town and the ridgeline of Marye's Heights. While Lee reinforced his position, Letterman searched the city "for the purpose of examining that part of it . . . to its adaptability for hospital purposes, I found desolation everywhere visible from the effects of the bombardment. . . . Some houses were shattered, others in ruins, and others burned. The courthouse, several churches, and other such buildings as were deemed suitable, were selected. . . . As many hospital wagons as were required were sent over, and the organization of each hospital commenced."[23]

A damp, cold fog had settled in the river valley by dawn on December 13. Thousands of men waited. Opposing skirmishers who had been within sight of each other on opposite sides of the river could only hear the movement of the enemy a few hundred yards away. Letterman's medical officers waited. Each had double-checked his supplies during the night. Letterman knew the battle for Fredericksburg would start near the southern edge of town. At 10:00 a.m., when the fog thinned, General Franklin attacked, committing approximately one-fourth of his troops after misinterpreting vague orders from Burnside.

When General George Meade's 3,800-soldier force assaulted Prospect Hill nearly three miles south of Fredericksburg, they were met by nearly 40,000 Confederates firing from an elevated and superior position. General Jackson had reinforced his line of defense, massing four men for every linear foot along his line of defense.[24] A thundering artillery exchange lasted almost three hours before Meade's men advanced across a half mile of open ground from the river toward Prospect Hill.

Meade finally drove through a weak spot in the Confederate line, reached a dense forest, and met the Confederates' second line of defense. There Union elements lost contact with each other, enabling Jackson to counterattack and drive the Union's advance force back into the open ground by early afternoon. The first phase of Burnside's battle plan had failed, and the wounded were being carried to hospitals that had been established on farms along the Rappahannock River. In less than four hours, nearly half of Meade's men were killed, wounded, or missing.[25]

Burnside turned to one of the oldest generals in the Union army, Edwin Sumner, to launch the second attack at 11:00 a.m., west out of Fredericksburg toward Marye's Heights. Sumner had served in the army since 1819 and commanded 30,000 men against 4,000 Confederates who had dug in behind a stone wall halfway up Marye's Heights. They were reinforced by artillery along the ridgeline.

Lee's men confidently looked down on the ground that Sumner's troops would have to cross. The Union attackers faced a plain 900 yards wide. Two bridges across a canal west of town forced them to concentrate their forces before advancing on the exposed ground. One Confederate wrote he could see "the bright lights of their bayonets glistening in the sunlight (which) made their lines look like a huge serpent of blue and steel."[26]

Waves of Union brigades, marching two hundred yards apart, became ideal targets for Confederate artillery. As they advanced, hundreds fell wounded under merciless hilltop Confederate artillery fire pointed almost straight down on their advance. Those who survived then faced a storm of small arms fire from hundreds of Confederates concealed behind the stone wall along a below-grade road halfway up the ridge. When a Confederate stood to fire, his level shot was almost directly into the belly of an advancing Union soldier, often less than one hundred yards away.

In three hours of battle, Letterman's medical officers confronted five thousand dead or wounded Union soldiers below Marye's Heights. Stretcher bearers who followed one regiment after another onto the battlefield carried wounded men to aid stations and hospitals in Fredericksburg. By the time the sun set, six assaults on Marye's Heights had failed. South of town, a second attack by General Franklin at mid-afternoon also had ended in a deadly defeat. Two distinct battlefields, now dark and bone-chilling cold, were covered with dead and wounded.

Hospitals in town and in Union-held territory across the river had already filled. Chatham House, a local landmark high atop the sloping eastern riverbank was typical. Letterman had established a hospital in the manor that also served as Sumner's headquarters. Rows of windows across the towering two-story building facing the river, 180 feet wide and 27 feet deep, could be seen from Fredericksburg.

Surgeons converted one room into an operating room and transformed nearby barns, a laundry shed, slave cabins, and a stable into patient wards. The operating room featured windows on three sides, providing excellent ventilation against the throat-grabbing stench of open belly wounds. After each

amputation, an assistant tossed the severed limb out a northern window onto a sickening pile of severed body parts under
a tree. Not far away, wounded men lay outside, waiting their
turn for attention. There were so many that "orderlies (placed)
patients outside on the cold, damp ground. . . . Think of it,
wounded and unable to help yourself, and lying on the ground
in the month of December with only a rubber blanket between
you and the cold earth; but it could not be helped," wrote Josiah
Murphey, who had been brought to Chatham after being shot
in the face.[27]

The fighting had been so intense and so close to Fredericksburg that Letterman's ambulance crews were of limited use. His
organized battlefield force of stretcher bearers stumbled through
the night across lumpy ground freshly plowed by the day's artillery explosions. "The night was very dark, and the difficulty
great in finding the objects of their search," wrote Letterman.
"The lanterns could not be used, as the glimmering of a candle
invariably drew the fire of the enemy. . . . [B]efore dawn, all the
wounded who were inside our lines had been taken to hospitals. . . . Here, throughout the night, the medical officers . . .
engaged in attendance upon them, as they were brought in,
blankets were fastened over the windows and every aperture
to conceal the lights, as every appearance of which drew a shot
from the enemy's guns planted on Marye's Heights."[28]

Letterman's surgeons faced a variety of wounds. "As wounded
soldiers arrived from the battle field, they are usually begrimed
with powder, smoke and dust, and often covered with mud. . . .
Their wounds, being mostly from gunshot or shell, seldom or
never bleed at first, unless some important artery is cut, and in
these cases they usually perish in the field. Their greatest danger
from hemorrhage comes with the sloughing process incident
to healing, some 15 or 20 days after. They usually utter no cries,
and a wounded hospital is, in the main, as still by night as the

house of death, save from the subdued tones of conversations of the wakeful or the movements of the attendants," wrote surgeon Franklin Hough.[29]

On many occasions, Letterman's surgeons could only provide comfort in the final moments of a man's life. "On the litter lies a man who has his leg nearly torn from his body, by a shell; he looks up into your face with a wishful expression and mildly asks 'Doctor as soon as can (be) convenient will you examine my leg?' He asks, 'Will it kill me?' Then comes the time to try the courage of the Surgeon: you have no time to beat around the bush; the answer must be plain. If 'Oh no,' he says 'Thank God!' If, as often is the case, 'I fear your wound is fatal,' he closes his eyes; you see his lips moving in prayer; you catch his accents as his eyes grow filmy, and hear him feebly imploring protection and care for his poor wife and children, 'Tell them I have done my duty faithfully as a good soldier and my last wish was for their welfare.'"[30]

The following day, as Letterman's casualty list grew to more than 9,000, the two shattered armies rested in place while Burnside's officers talked him out of a second attack. The Confederates remained in control of the high ground west of Fredericksburg, and the Union army huddled among the smoldering ruins of a town now littered with collapsed walls, household belongings, shredded trees, and abandoned equipment. That night they shivered as the temperature dropped into the thirties and an aurora borealis danced across the sky, turning from pale yellow to blood red. Surgeries had continued nonstop in the town's field hospitals but were interrupted when messengers arrived, telling the staff to evacuate all wounded east out of Fredericksburg and back across the pontoon bridges to the Army of the Potomac's original staging ground.

Sawdust, dirt, and pine branches were spread on the bridges to muffle the sound of Letterman's ambulances carrying the wounded across the river. Ambulances on the far side of the river entered town in unison and exited as a unit across a different bridge to the north. The one-way traffic made it clear to Confederate lookouts that an evacuation was under way. While surgeons in town prepared their wounded for transport, hundreds of ambulances rolled across the bridges through the night. Some of the most seriously wounded men were carried on stretchers by soldiers and orderlies to hospitals on the other side The daring retreat and entirely successful medical evacuation produced thousands of unexpected patients on the other bank that Letterman had expected would remain in the hospitals established in Fredericksburg.

The opposing armies were now back in their original positions after suffering nearly 2,000 dead, more than 13,000 wounded, and nearly 2,500 missing or taken prisoner. A temporary truce enabled Letterman's burial details to cross the river one last time to collect the dead and bury them. Some were "on their back with gaping jaws, some with eyes as large as walnuts, protruding with a glassy stare, some doubled up like a contortionist, here one without a head, there one without legs, yonder a head and legs without a trunk, everywhere horrible expressions, fear, rage, agony, madness, torture, lying in pools of blood, lying with heads half buried in mud, with fragments of shell sticking in oozing brain, with bullet holes all over the puffed limbs,"[31] wrote one man on burial detail.

When it became clear Burnside would not renew the attack, Letterman decided to keep as many wounded near Fredericksburg as possible to speed their recovery and return to duty. But Burnside overruled him ordering a mass evacuation by rail to Aquia Landing and then by steamers north to general hospitals in major cities. On December 18, 2,500 wounded men were evacuated, followed by 900 the next day. Within two weeks nearly all of the wounded who could travel

were evacuated. Hundreds of unscathed soldiers deserted the battlefield by hitching rides on the rail cars, raising Letterman's ire.

"These are cowardly stragglers who abandon their colors on
the field of battle for the slightest injury (often self-inflicted)
and raise a clamor which unhappily too many are fond to echo.
How different those, whether slightly or seriously wounded,
who have born the burden and the heat of the day!—rarely do
they complain of want or care; on the contrary, expressions of
thankfulness often escape their lips for the attention bestowed
upon them," he wrote.[32]

In one of the few documented disagreements between him
and his senior medical officers, Letterman edited surgeon John
Brinton's critique of the first stage of evacuation by railroad.
Brinton felt the conditions in the railroad cars were substandard
for the wounded, but amended Brinton's report to say there was
adequate bedding in the railcars for the wounded during the
thirty-minute ride to Aquia Landing.[33] In his postwar writing,
Letterman never explained why he edited Brinton's report.

Despite some criticism that Letterman wasn't adequately
prepared for Burnside's order to evacuate the wounded, Fredericksburg represented as large a victory for the medical department as it became a strategic loss for the Army of the Potomac.
Burnside was devastated by the losses he had suffered in his first
battle as commanding officer of the army. The pontoon bridges'
delay had cost him the element of surprise, but on the other
hand it had given Letterman invaluable time to prepare for a
battle whose location was certain for several weeks in advance.

As a result, Letterman had plenty of supplies, except for cold-
weather clothing necessitated by an early December snowstorm.
For that event, the Sanitary Commission had come to his rescue,
with 1,800 blankets, 900 quilts, more than 5,600 woolen shirts,
nearly 4,500 pair of woolen underwear, and more than 4,000

woolen socks.[34] Despite this assistance, the Sanitary Commission acknowledged that Letterman had prepared well for the battle, reporting "A minute inspection of these supplies was at once made, and it was found they (Letterman's hospitals) had nearly all been amply supplied by the Medical Purveyor with those means of succor first needed by wounded men."[35]

Fredericksburg became the first true test of Jonathan Letterman's reorganization and systematization of battlefield care. His ambulance crews were in place and trained. His surgeons had been reorganized according to a restructured hospital system that provided mobile field hospitals, the previously missing link between regimental hospitals that primarily served as aid stations and general hospitals. Medical supplies and transport had become the province and responsibility of medical officers, not the quartermaster corps. His entire system had been tested by approximately 100,000 soldiers in the Army of the Potomac. A new era in battlefield medicine had begun.

"The medical department has become so thoroughly systematized, that wounded and sick men were cared for better than they had ever been in any army before . . . (this) was perfected . . . by the efficient and earnest medical director of the army, Dr. Letterman; to whom belongs the honor of bringing about this most desirable change. By the new system, the surgeons were enabled to accomplish a far greater amount of work, and in much better order than under the old; and the wounded were better and more quickly cared for," wrote surgeon George Stevens of the Sixth Corps. Stevens appreciated Letterman's designation of operating surgeons, hospital organization personnel, and record keeping surgeons, and he noted that about one in fifteen medical officers performed surgeries.[36]

Stevens's commanding officer, Sixth Corps medical director Charles O'Leary, was equally impressed with Letterman's system: "During the engagements on the 13th, the ambulances being guided and governed with perfect control and with a precision rare even in military organizations, the wounded were brought without delay or confusion to the hospitals of their respective divisions. Not a single item provided for the organization of the Field Hospitals suffered the slightest derangement, and the celerity with which the wounded were treated, and the system pervading the whole Medical Department, from the stations in the field selected by the assistant-surgeons with the regiments, to the wards where the wounded were transferred from the hands of the surgeons to be attended by nurses, afforded the most pleasing contrast to what we had hitherto seen during the war."[37]

Despite glowing praise by military medical professionals, Letterman was roundly criticized by a single medical inspector, Thomas Perley. His was a lone voice almost a month following Fredericksburg when he wrote Secretary of War Edwin Stanton, saying "I do not believe I have ever seen greater misery from sickness than exists now in our Army of the Potomac. . . . In view of the condition of the Army of the Potomac, I am forced to the conclusion that the principal medical officer is not equal to his responsible station, and has failed in his duty, either from having too much to do or from neglect."[38]

At the time, Stanton was bitterly feuding with Surgeon General William Hammond. Whether Perley served as a lackey for Stanton, looking to find fault within Hammond's organization, is unclear. Perley wrote his report after his sole tour in the field, and there is no evidence that it merited serious consideration or action. He also wrote it after the Army of the Potomac had settled into its winter quarters near Aquia Landing.

By then, Letterman's anger may have subsided. He had made it clear that he disagreed with General Burnside's decision to evacuate so many wounded out of the region. His disgust at perhaps thousands more who deserted by commandeering rides of medical evacuation transports knew no bounds. And his sensitivity to the condition of those transports had led him to openly edit a surgeon's critical assessment of the supplies available during medical transportation. After his second major battle as medical director of the Army of the Potomac, Letterman was keenly aware that the effectiveness and perception of his department were vulnerable to differing combat philosophies as well as post-battle second guessing.

Cold, mud, and a lack of firewood defined the winter camp of the Army of the Potomac, a base of operations it had first established when it marched on Fredericksburg more than a month earlier. Following Letterman's battlefield success, he now faced increasing rates of typhoid, erysipelas, scurvy, and other maladies in a massive army camp whose sanitary conditions in thousands of unheated tents was substandard at best. An exhausted, demoralized army faced a long, cold winter at the start of 1863.

Meanwhile General Burnside sought redemption. On January 20, the Army of the Potomac marched in search of General Lee. Cold rain changed into snow as it blanketed Burnside's soldiers the first night of the march. It turned the Virginia countryside into fields of sticking, sucking mud that stripped men of shoes and stubbornly gripped wagon wheels. Cold, drained, and discouraged, the army lacked the strength to fight Lee and winter. Burnside turned the army around, retreating once against to the Aquia Landing region. The area had already been stripped of most of its natural resources by the massive army.

The Army of the Potomac now faced a long Virginia winter a few miles from its devastating defeat at Fredericksburg, where many soldiers had come to believe their comrades had died in vain. Battlefield deaths included J. H. Woodbury of Massachusetts, George Simons of New Hampshire, and Henry Dyke of New York. They were killed at Fredericksburg and had been buried side by side, less than one hundred yards from the Confederate artillery emplacements on Marye's Heights.

Although Jonathan Letterman had overhauled the military's battlefield care system in the latter half of 1862, in the first few weeks of 1863 the military camp health issues that he faced were the same ones that had plagued the army for years. He also soon would have to build a working relationship with his third commanding officer of the Army of the Potomac in less than four months.

Letterman had reported to one general who considered himself the Union's savior, and another who candidly acknowledged his lack of qualifications for command of an army. Tens of thousands of soldiers had been ordered to follow the commands of these men, engage the enemy in sometimes suicidal assaults, and place their health and potentially their survival in the hands of Jonathan Letterman.

Despite the instability of Army of the Potomac's command, Letterman had proven worthy of Surgeon General Hammond's confidence when Hammond appointed him medical director of the Army of the Potomac six months earlier. Hammond had made his respect for Letterman clear in his letter of appointment on June 19, 1862. "In making this assignment, I have been governed by what I conceive to be the best interests of the service. Your energy, determination, and faithful discharge of duty in all the different situations in which you have been placed during your service of thirteen years determined me to place you in the most arduous, responsible, and trying position you have yet occupied."[39]

Now, after six months of war experience, Letterman would stand between the army's wounded and sick and a new commanding officer, whose army's headquarters would become better known for bachelor pursuits than battle plans.

CHANCELLORSVILLE

"What will the country say?"

General Ambrose Burnside commanded a beaten and increasingly sick Army of the Potomac in the final few weeks of 1862. Some of his generals believed Ambrose wasn't the man for the job and planned a coup. It began on December 30, when two of Burnside's brigadier generals, John Newton and John Cochrane, took the extraordinary step of going over his head to meet directly with President Lincoln. They told the president Burnside already had lost the confidence of his generals, the army had fallen into disarray, and that Burnside planned to attack Lee at Fredericksburg again.

They met with the president at the behest of two of Burnside's major generals, William Franklin and William Smith. Other members of Burnside's most senior officers shared the sentiments of Franklin and Smith. Lincoln now faced open revolt in a critical army. He summoned Burnside to the White House where, on New Year's Eve, Burnside learned of the internal attack against him. Appalled and angered, he leveled accusations of his own, claiming that Secretary of War Stanton and General in Chief Halleck had lost the confidence of the nation. Burnside then offered his resignation.

On January 1, Lincoln refused to accept it, so Burnside returned to his army's headquarters to plan a midwinter assault against the Confederates that became known as the "Mud March." The short-lived January 20 advance came at a time when the Army of the Potomac was suffering from significant desertions, increasing illness, and dismal living conditions. On January 25, the president finally took action. He fired Burnside and appointed the Army of the Potomac's third commanding officer, Joseph Hooker.

Hooker had fought in the Mexican War and subsequently built an undistinguished record in California, where he became better known for a lifestyle that included varying degrees of drinking, fine food, prostitutes, and gambling. He had fought in the Peninsula Campaign and at Antietam and Fredericksburg, so Letterman was familiar with his new commanding officer. Hooker was cocky, likable, and immensely popular with the troops. He had lobbied for the job earlier and had been openly critical of Burnside, saying he had a brain the size of a hickory nut.[1] Lincoln reluctantly chose Hooker regardless. Politically, he could not return McClellan to command, and other senior generals in the Army of the Potomac had not distinguished themselves in battle. Hooker would have to suffice in the depth of the Virginia winter.

When Hooker took charge, Letterman was "engaged in the details of the organization which I had instituted the previous autumn, carrying out measures for improving the health of the Army— such as those regarding the location and police of the camps, the food, cooking, and police of the men; the reestablishment of regimental hospitals, etc."[2] For the time being, he could set aside the continuing refinement of battlefield care that he had organized. Fredericksburg validated the Letterman system. Though the system was Letterman's achievement, it had been built in part on the work of French surgeons more than sixty years before and of Union army surgeons under Ulysses S. Grant earlier in 1862.

Napoleon's chief surgeon, Dominique-Jean Larrey, developed the "flying ambulance" concept in which battlefield evacuation personnel followed advancing troops into battle. The tactical organization resembled the artillery supporting an army's lead infantry. In 1797, during a campaign in Italy, Larrey assembled more than 300 men that he divided into three medical divisions in support of frontline troops. About the same time, another French surgeon developed the concept of training stretcher bearers and moving them forward with troops to speed the evacuation of the wounded. Medical proximity and mobility were already becoming part of the battlefield. More than half a century later, in 1862, three Union physicians in General Grant's army, John Brinton, Henry Hewitt, and Bernard Irwin, began to redefine the roles of American battlefield hospitals.[3]

In February 1862, at the battle for Fort Donelson on the Cumberland River in Tennessee, Brinton (as acting director of the Department of Cairo) and General Grant's acting medical director, Hewitt, directed regimental medical officers to set up aid stations at the edge of the battlefield, and they established ambulance depots about one hundred yards away (but still within the enemy's artillery range). The two men had recognized the need to create more organizational structure in the medical department during battle. Their approach became an embryonic version of tiered battlefield medical care.

Two months later, at the Battle of Shiloh near Savannah, Tennessee, the resourceful Bernard Irwin served as medical director of General William Nelson's division in the Army of Ohio. At thirty-one years of age, Irwin had already garnered national notoriety. A year earlier he had received the Medal of Honor for his part in leading reinforcements to rescue outnumbered Union troops that were surrounded by Indians in a remote mountain pass in the Southwest.

The Confederates attacked Grant in early April and pushed his army two miles back to the Tennessee River. He left wounded soldiers and regiment tents in his wake. After reinforcements from the Army of the Ohio arrived during the night, Grant counterattacked the following day and drove the enemy back from ground and tents it had captured the day before.

Irwin recognized Grant's advance as a medical opportunity for treating more than 8,000 wounded men. He seized abandoned tents and organized them into a fledgling field hospital. Irwin commandeered enough tents to house 2,500 wounded soldiers. Creating the first field hospital entirely comprised of tents, he organized it in sections of 125 beds, with each section divided into four wards. Although it lacked substantial postoperative care, Irwin's plan provided more comprehensive treatment for Grant's wounded closer to the battlefield than had been seen before. In many ways, it became a precursor to Letterman's field hospital organization at Antietam six months later.[4]

While Irwin stayed in the field, in May 1862 Surgeon General William Hammond had summoned Brinton and Letterman to his office in Washington to become part of his new team of medical inspectors, examiners, and bureaucratic administrators. Hammond had read the Shiloh medical reports written by Irwin. In addition, Brinton likely had discussed his aid station concept with both Letterman and Hammond in the month that he and Letterman spent together in Washington before the latter received orders for the Army of the Potomac in early July.

Brinton remained in Washington to begin a massive research and documentation project that would become the *Medical & Surgical History of the War of the Rebellion*. He also served on a medical examining board that reviewed the qualifications of volunteer surgeons. When the examiners rejected too many at first, Secretary of War Stanton threatened Brinton and his colleagues

with elimination of the board unless they lowered their standards and accepted more volunteer doctors. More medical volunteers were soon entering the service.[5]

So, when Letterman had forged a battlefield evacuation and
hospitalization system in his first six months as medical director
of the Army of the Potomac, it was partly based on the work of
Irwin and Brinton. Letterman's system had been tested by more
than 24,000 casualties in two of the most brutal battles of the
Civil War, which took place less than ninety days apart. Now,
once those wounded in battle were treated and transferred to
hospitals in the North, midwinter disease, diet, and sanitation
became Letterman's enemies.

As Hooker disbanded Burnside's "grand division" organization of the Army of the Potomac and returned to a corps-
based structure, Letterman also focused on organization as well
as communication and accountability. In October, he had created a medical examination board of three doctors that investi-
gated allegations of physician incompetence, and he reactivated
it now. The board quickly confirmed a number of instances of
bad medical care.

Also in January, assistant surgeon Warren Webster became
medical inspector of the army at Letterman's request. Webster had
graduated from Harvard's medical school two years earlier. Only
twenty-seven years old, Webster had been ordered to build hospitals in Washington shortly after the outbreak of the Civil War. He
probably had gotten to know Letterman when Letterman served
briefly on Surgeon General Hammond's Washington staff.

Webster supervised the corps medical directors who in turn
appointed medical inspectors. In this way, Letterman established
a chain of enforcement and accountability that extended from
his office at the Army of the Potomac's headquarters through
the entire army as it expanded to nearly 120,000 men with the
addition of fifty-six new regiments.

Every wave of new regiments posed health problems for Letterman, particularly in the middle of winter. Venereal disease was particularly prevalent among new arrivals. Letterman established a venereal disease hospital in Washington and "hoped the result of treatment would be valuable to science, and more easily obtained than from scattered records of the various hospitals through the country."[6]

Both Letterman and Hooker shared the belief that good food led to improved troop health and morale. The common soldier diet of salt pork boiled in bacon grease and beans weakened the men and allowed scurvy to take hold. If not strictly supervised and held accountable, commissary officers might not promptly distribute perishable supplies such as potatoes while soldiers might continue unhealthy food preparation habits such as rolling rice, beans, and flour into a ball before boiling the concoction in grease.

Letterman wasted no time in asking his new commanding officer to issue new diet regulations. Within days of his promotion to command in late January, Hooker endorsed Letterman's two-pronged attack against malnourishment by holding commissary officers and soldiers accountable for food distribution and preparation. On February 3, Letterman told his medical directors that potatoes should be issued three times a week, onions twice a week, and bread as often as possible. He ordered them to assess the availability of fresh vegetables in their weekly reports. Although the medical directors could not require the improved diet, a reporting mechanism now was in place. Four days later, Hooker ordered his chief commissary officer, Colonel Henry Clarke, to report when and why fresh vegetables were not being issued. With monitoring and accountability established by Hooker and Letterman, vegetable distribution improved and pilferage along the route of distribution declined. The health and morale of the troops improved. In the month following Letterman's dietary improvements, he noted that cases of diarrhea declined by 32 percent in February and typhoid fevers decreased by 28 percent.[7]

Meanwhile, Letterman began to focus on the sanitary conditions of an army encamped across twenty miles along the Rappahannock River. As dozens of new regiments arrived, the Army of the Potomac remained officially classified as on active duty. As a result, permanent winter living quarters were not built. The army maintained a state of readiness in the snowbound Virginia countryside with too few tents and too many makeshift huts. For sleeping quarters, soldiers often dug a wide, shallow pit in the near-frozen mud, erected primitive side walls of scavenged pine logs, and covered the top with canvas or mud mixed with brush.

A massive supply depot at Aquia Creek furnished the more than 100,000 men with approximately 700 tons of food daily as well as 800 tons of forage daily for horses.[8] Regardless, the soldiers' living conditions in thousands of these crude huts with dangerous fireplaces, the scarcity of firewood, and the dearth of basic supplies worried Letterman.

The apparent indifference of many regimental officers' to squalid conditions also dismayed Letterman. On March 9, he issued housing orders, requiring soldiers to move out of temporary tents into better-built structures and transferring the soldiers who were living in muddy dugouts to more permanent huts. He also required that new huts' roofs be removed twice a week and that bedding be hung outdoors daily, weather permitting. Letterman knew that ventilation had been proven critical to the troops' health. The overall illness rate following his orders declined to about 8 percent.[9]

Corps medical inspectors submitted weekly reports of their inspections to their corps commanders, who in turn submitted monthly summaries to the corps medical directors. That single reorganization placed senior line officers in the middle of the medical department's preventive health and sanitation com-munication chain. No one could claim ignorance. Letterman tolerated no deviation from the reporting forms he devised. Uniformity was integral to accountability.

He subscribed to the "you get what you inspect" school of military command when he wrote, "It cannot be too strongly impressed upon your attention that the object of these inspec-tions is to secure reliable information as to the actual condition of the Medical Department of this Army, and to bring to notice all errors, neglects, deficiencies, and wants of every kind; to bring to notice also the cases of prompt and intelligent attention to duty, and of earnest endeavor to promote the best interests of the service; to bring to light the good as well as the bad."[10]

His new standards did encounter resistance. Many line offi-cers did not hold medical officers in high regard, regardless of the medical officers' rank. Many perceived the medical department as secondary to the fighting units. Some line officers apparently resented a more regimented preventive health program. Though the new medical department regulations written by Letterman carried the signature of General Hooker, in some cases line offi-cers simply ignored them.

In one of the rare instances where Letterman revealed his anger, he wrote, "It is a popular delusion that the highest duties of Medical officers are performed in prescribing a drug or amputating a limb . . . it is a matter of surprise that such preju-dice should exist in this enlightened age . . . and were it well if commanding officers would disabuse their minds of it, and per-mit our armies to profit more fully by the beneficial advice of those who, for years, have made the laws of life a study."[11]

By April the health of Hooker's army had improved consid-erably. In a written report to Hooker, Letterman's outlined the reasons for the improvement. "This favorable state of the health of the army, and the decrease in the severity of the cases of disease, is in great measure to be attributed to the improvement in the diet of the men, commenced about the first of February by the issue of fresh bread and fresh vegetables, which has caused the disappearance of the symptoms of scurvy that in January began to assume a serious aspect throughout the army; to the increased attention to sanitary regulations; to the more general practice of cooking by companies; and to the zeal and energy displayed by the medical officers of the corps."[12]

Improved morale fueled Hooker's confidence in an army that had increased to twice the size of General Lee's force a few miles away on the other side of the Rappahannock, near Fredericksburg. Letterman was proud of what had been accomplished. "I have necessarily impressed upon all officers of this department, the primary importance of carrying into effect sanitary measures to prevent sickness, and my directions and suggestions have been carried out with an intelligence and zeal which it affords me great satisfaction to bring to the notice of the Commanding general," he wrote.[13]

As Hooker prepared his battle plan for the coming combat season, Letterman inadvertently found himself at the center of a national controversy. An officer in Surgeon General Hammond's office mistakenly allowed a reporter from the *Washington Morning Chronicle* to read one of Letterman's reports. From Letterman's detailed sickness rates, General Lee calculated the size and organization of Hooker's army, less than a month before what would become the Battle of Chancellorsville. Lee estimated Hooker's total strength at 159,000 men. Hooker later said his intelligence officer would have paid $1,000 for similar information about Lee's troop strength.

By mid-April, Letterman knew that the fighting would begin within a few weeks. Hooker planned to march a major force west-northwest along the Rappahannock, flanking Lee's left. His men would then turn south and cross the Rappahannock and

Rapidan Rivers, work their way through the rugged area called the "Wilderness," and take control of key transportation routes near Chancellorsville to cut Lee's army off from Richmond.

A smaller force would again attack at Fredericksburg, but only as a diversionary tactic. Unlike Burnside, who had concentrated his men around Fredericksburg, Hooker planned to attack on two fronts, ten miles apart, posing new challenges for Letterman and his medical department. In Letterman's battlefield experience, both Antietam and especially Fredericksburg had been relatively concentrated battles.

However, experience and advance notice enabled Letterman to be far better prepared for the huge numbers of wounded such a battle likely would produce. He established hospitals along the railroad route from Fredericksburg to the Aquia Landing depot. He organized them by division and corps, reflecting Letterman's belief that wounded men fared better when hospitalized with men from the same unit. He concentrated the hospitals so that a single supply officer could be assigned to all of them. Efficiency, too, was a priority for him.

The imminent battle would be the first time Letterman had the time to prepare adequately for the specific location and expected course of fighting. Perhaps because of this, he appeared confident in his department's ability to handle the coming casualties. He telegraphed Hammond and requested that civilian surgeons be barred from the battlefield. He also required Sanitary Commission agents with supplies to travel with the medical department and not act independently of his staff.

Now a combat veteran, on April 27, Letterman issued a number of orders to his medical department in anticipation of the renewed fighting. Among them, he required detailed information on available troop strength. He also notified his officers that he expected action reports during battle. Previously he had designated medical record keepers, made it clear what he expected of them, and noted he didn't care if the reporting system was cumbersome or intrusive. "The knowledge which the officers of this department have had, and may yet have opportunities of gathering, is of such a character and of such an extent as will, when made known, go far toward filling the hiatus which now exists in that branch of the science in which we are now engaged—that of military surgery," he wrote.[14]

Also on April 27, many of Hooker's officers learned the march toward the enemy would begin the following day. As rain pelted orchards of blooming peach and cherry trees and then slackened on April 28, the Army of the Potomac began skirting the enemy. Confederate lookouts in Fredericksburg rang church bells when they spotted tens of thousands of men on the far side of the river heading toward the west. Although General Sedgwick remained across the river from Fredericksburg with two corps, Hooker had no intention of suicidal front assaults against Lee. Hooker's rested men prepared to engage Lee at a time and place of Hooker's choosing. It would be up to Letterman's medical department to keep up.

The following day, the bulk of Hooker's force completed a ten-mile march, crossed the Rappahannock and Rapidan Rivers, and arrived in the area appropriately called the Wilderness. It was a seventy-square-mile region of dense, second-growth timber, tangled underbrush, creeks, bogs, and few roads, and here Hooker's army was poised to attack the western flank of Lee's forces. Letterman, however, had already been restricted by Hooker's battle plan.

It had been Union army doctrine since 1861 that pre-battle priorities were ammunition, commissary, medical supplies, and general baggage in that order. Over Letterman's objections, Hooker allowed no more than two ambulances to accompany each division when it crossed the Rappahannock and entered the Wilderness to the south. Letterman could establish hospitals only north of the river, several miles from where he expected the battle to take place. He also had to establish his medical supply depot on the far side of the river, about six miles from the expected battlefield. Alarmed, Letterman appealed to the general and convinced him to allow a few medicine wagons to cross the river (he also filled the limited empty ambulances with medical supplies), but nearly all stretcher bearers were kept on the far side of the river. While Letterman never directly criticized Hooker for this, his subsequent description of the battle almost always included a reference to how Hooker limited his options by sometimes delaying the arrival of medical supplies to allow troops and ammunition to be brought forward first.[15]

As the rain resumed on April 29, Hooker felt almost ready to attack a badly outnumbered Lee. However, he turned cautious like McClellan. He halted his force of three corps near the Chancellor family's two-story brick home and tavern, grandly called Chancellorsville, to await reinforcements despite his significant numerical advantage. That single decision perhaps dictated the course of the battle and determined the number of casualties Letterman would face.

For Lee used the delay to his advantage. He split his troops, leaving some at Fredericksburg and positioning approximately 36,000 men to blunt Hooker's position at Chancellorsville. Lee took a huge chance, dividing his already outnumbered force and sending most of it to confront Hooker's 50,000 men (with more on the way), who were supported by approximately one hundred artillery pieces. As Hooker dallied on April 29 and again on April 30, Lee's men dug fortifications in the forest. For their part, Letterman's medical officers utilized the lull to establish aid stations. Letterman focused on the evacuation routes back to the Rappahannock and Rapidan Rivers and constructing hospitals on the far side.

April 30 ended with Hooker arriving at the Chancellor house at 6:00 p.m. As was his custom, Letterman had established a hospital at Hooker's headquarters and planned to stay there as long as battle conditions permitted. That would enable him to receive field reports as quickly as possible so he could make necessary and timely medical decisions. It also allowed him to take advantage of Hooker's couriers and telegraph operators, who sent and received battlefield reports. Hooker rejoiced that night. He believed Lee had been caught in a trap.

On May 1, early morning ground fog delayed Hooker's attack. When it cleared, 30,000 men attacked the Confederates at 11:00 a.m. Stiff resistance produced more casualties than expected. As they began arriving at Chancellorsville, Hooker again took a cautious route. He confounded many of his officers when he ordered lead units to fall back. As his men withdrew into a more consolidated position and as Confederate reinforcements reached the battlefield, Letterman began transferring as many patients as possible north and across the rivers. The battle had hardly begun, yet limited resources near the battlefield and Hooker's cautious tactical decisions already were influencing Letterman's medical decisions. Although Hooker claimed to be pleased with the day's battle, he had lost momentum, which forced Letterman to react from a position of poorly equipped weakness.

Then it got worse. On the night of May 1, Lee took another gamble by splitting his force a second time. He assigned 28,000 men to General Stonewall Jackson and ordered him to march double-quick to the west in an attempt to flank Hooker's army, just as Hooker had done to Lee. That left about 12,000 men, commanded by Lee, to face Hooker in the woods surrounding Chancellorsville.

At about the same time that night, Letterman also made a strategic decision. He had planned to evacuate the wounded over a good road to Fredericksburg, about ten miles away. But enemy positions now threatened that route, so Letterman decided to evacuate patients the next day to hospitals established north of the river and beyond, over twenty-five miles of bad roads, to Potomac Creek. Heartbreaking gasps of pain marked each wagon's progress toward the patient depot. Men wrapped in bandages that oozed red dreaded every roadbed rut, ridge, and rock in wagons that jolted over every obstacle. While Letterman felt he had managed to get enough supplies onto the battlefield, evacuation to remote hospitals became a major concern.

Late on the afternoon of May 2, Jackson attacked. In less than an hour, General Hooker's original grand plan of flanking and attacking unraveled. The Confederates had seized the initiative. Hooker's right flank, commanded by General Otis Howard, crumbled under Jackson's assault as the sun set. The enemy overran Union positions and casualties began streaming into Letterman's Chancellorsville hospital. Thousands of Union troops fled toward the army's headquarters. As forward aid stations were abandoned, the enemy captured Union surgeons, patients, and medical supplies. The battle turned into a rout. Within an hour, the Confederates advanced one-and-a-half miles to within four miles of Letterman and Hooker. For the second consecutive day, Hooker's position had become more concentrated around Chancellorsville. Heightened protection of retreat routes north to the Rappahannock became a priority.

By late afternoon, enemy artillery fire pounded Hooker and Letterman at Chancellorsville. Letterman's wry sense of humor, or perhaps frustration, surfaced when he later wrote, "[T]his building came within range of the enemy's guns, planted on his left, centre (sic), and right, being the centre of a converging fire—a location for which Commanding Generals of the Army of the Potomac seemed to have a peculiar partiality."[16] As night settled on the forest, Letterman's medical corps struggled to carry wounded men off the battlefield while its ambulances sat idle miles away on the far side of the Rappahannock and Rapidan.

Horror struck on May 3. The Confederates attacked a thin section of the Union line at 5:30 that morning. Within two hours they broke through. More casualties arrived at Chancellorsville. When Hooker inexplicably ceded an open area called Hazel Grove to the Confederates, enemy artillery fire from that region soon landed at Chancellorsville. The Union army's headquarters came under direct attack.

As Hooker stood on the Chancellor house's expansive veranda, which held a broad view of the battlefield, an aide handed him a field report. Letterman stood nearby. At that instant an artillery shell hit the base of the pillar next to Hooker. The wood pillar hit him squarely, knocking him to the floor and unconscious. Letterman ordered him taken to his room inside the house. Hooker likely had suffered a severe concussion when he fell to the ground. He was unconscious for nearly an hour. After he revived, he tried to mount his horse to reassure nearby troops but promptly collapsed and vomited. For the rest of the day, he appeared stunned and was at times incoherent. Just as the Battle of Chancellorsville reached its climax, Hooker had been knocked senseless.

What could Letterman do? Hooker's respected chief of staff, Major General Daniel Butterfield, was in the field and could not be reached. Other officers at headquarters at the time lacked seniority and experience. With Hooker obviously incapacitated, Letterman did not have the authority to require transfer of command. In his postwar writings, he never indicated whether he thought Hooker so incapacitated that command could or should have been transferred, He left it to others to speculate on whether the battle's outcome might have been different if a less-cautious general had taken over.

As the eastern side of the Union's line at Chancellorsville disintegrated and Hooker lay senseless at midmorning, Sedgwick attacked Lee's remaining men at Fredericksburg. Once again, Union soldiers stormed Marye's Heights east of the town.

Jonathan Letterman had only thirteen years' medical experience in military outposts when he became medical director of the 100,000-soldier Army of the Potomac. *U.S. Army Medical Museum*

Letterman grew up in this building, where his father also practiced medicine beginning in the 1820s. *James Herron Collection*

Letterman founded Beta Theta Pi at Jefferson College. Fraternity brothers included a future congressman, governors, college professors, and a state supreme court justice. *James Herron Collection*

Fort Union in New Mexico was typical of Letterman's pre-war experience: remote locations, inadequate nutrition, vermin infestation, extreme weather conditions, and poorly built buildings. *National Archives*

This church at the Battle of Bull Run became a field hospital where Union surgeons volunteered to remain with five hundred wounded men until all were captured and became Confederate prisoners of war. *Library of Congress*

Charles Tripler failed to earn the respect of General George McClellan or Surgeon General William Hammond. He resigned after the Peninsula Campaign, creating the opportunity for Letterman to reform battlefield care. *National Library of Medicine*

Until Letterman improved army nutrition, many soldiers had to buy much of their food from merchants (called sutlers) who followed the armies. *National Archives*

Secretary of War
Edwin Stanton's
bitter feud with
Surgeon General
William Hammond
became so intense
that Letterman's
career was briefly
stalled at one point.
Library of Congress

A renowned medical
researcher before
he became surgeon
general, Hammond
enabled Letterman
to implement wide-
ranging reforms
in battlefield care.
Library of Congress

Letterman routinely commandeered farms, barns, public buildings, and homes such as the Pry House (above) overlooking the Antietam battlefield. *National Park Service*

Hundreds of hospitals following a battle were little more than clearings in stands of timber or a collection of haphazard tents in farm fields. *National Park Service*

The Army of the Potomac typically fought within a day's ride of the nation's capital, making it possible for President Lincoln (seated, left) to visit the battlefield and meet directly with the army's generals. Here he meets with General McClellan. *National Park Service*

As the new medical director of the Army of the Potomac, Letterman (fifth from the left) and his staff had only a few weeks to prepare for what would become the bloodiest day in American history: Antietam. *Library of Congress*

General George McClellan often criticized what he saw as inappropriate interference by President Lincoln in statements to reporters and in letters to his wife, Mary. *Library of Congress*

From his vantage point about two miles away, Letterman could watch the fighting in the center of the Antietam battle, near Dunker Church, but relied on couriers for reports on casualties and medical needs from his surgeons. *Library of Congress*

The Army of the Potomac was perhaps the Union's highest-profile army. President Lincoln (center right) visited the army several times. His coat nearly unbuttoned, Letterman stands to the left of Lincoln. *Library of Congress*

Fredericksburg was the first major Civil War battle where wounded soldiers benefited from Letterman's overhaul of battlefield evacuation, hospital organization, camp hygiene, and diet standards. *Library of Congress*

Letterman established strict hygiene and nutrition standards, including recipes and company kitchen construction requirements that elevated kitchens out of the dirt. *National Archives*

Letterman's system of battlefield evacuation and tiered hospital care greatly improved his surgeons' ability to treat thousands of men wounded in a single day's fighting. *Library of Congress*

Major General Joseph
Hooker shared
Letterman's belief that
good food and proper
nutrition were critical
to his troops' morale
and fighting strength.
Library of Congress

Letterman established professional ambulance crews with specific training requirements.
Derelict soldiers and army band members no longer were entrusted with the evacuation
of the wounded. *Library of Congress*

Efficient battlefield evacuation became possible only when Letterman gained control of ambulances, which no longer could be taken for other purposes. *Library of Congress*

At Chancellorsville, Letterman had to negotiate with General Robert E. Lee's medical director, LaFayette Guild, a former classmate at Jefferson Medical College, for the return of twelve hundred wounded prisoners of war. *National Archives*

Major General Gouverneur Warren believed he knew more about his troop's medical needs than any trained doctor, including Letterman. Warren became one of the few outspoken critics of Letterman. *Library of Congress*

General George Meade drew the ire of Letterman when he delayed the advance of badly needed medical supplies at Gettysburg early in the fighting. Meade said troop supplies, including ammunition, took priority. *Library of Congress*

This farmhouse became the headquarters for Letterman and Meade on the eve of Gettysburg. *Library of Congress*

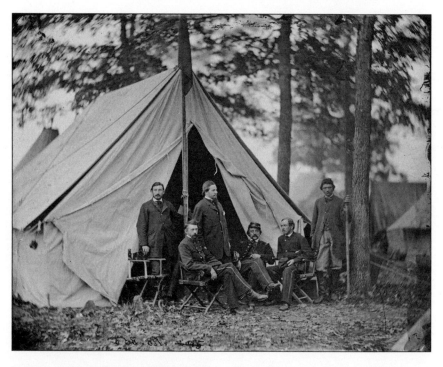

Letterman (seated) relied on about 100 medical officers to treat more than 20,000 Union and Confederate wounded soldiers scattered among twenty-four Gettysburg-area hospitals. *National Archives*

General in Chief Henry Halleck opposed army-wide adoption of the "Letterman system" but later became a powerful political ally following the war. *Library of Congress*

This wooden derrick in the rugged and isolated foothills north of Los Angeles was typical of the oil wells drilled by Letterman in a failed wildcatter career. *California Oil Museum, Santa Paula*

A SKELETON IN HIS CLOSET.

Despite political risk in an era of intense anti-Chinese sentiment, coroner Letterman decried the living conditions of the Chinese in his report to San Francisco officials. *Elizabeth Thomas Collection*

Within one hour, Letterman's medical department delivered more than 1,000 wounded men to the same hospitals in town that his officers had established the previous December. "Such sites are too much for the human eyes to behold. Dying, screaming and groaning in every quarter and the blood almost running on the floor," wrote hospital steward John Hieber.[17]

Sedgwick's men were too far away to reinforce Hooker, and vague orders had left Sedgwick unclear on whether he had authorization to proceed to Chancellorsville after clearing the enemy off Marye's Heights. At Chancellorsville, chaos reigned. Hooker abandoned the Chancellor house and ordered the Army of the Potomac to pull back toward the river crossings. As the army retreated, the enemy overran some of Letterman's field hospitals. Union doctors and wounded soldiers were taken prisoner. Meanwhile, those who had been wounded and evacuated the day before were transferred to hospitals at Aquia Creek and Potomac Creek to make room for fresh casualties.

By nightfall on May 3, most of Hooker's troops had dug in along the retreat route back to the Rappahannock River. More than 1,000 wounded men and medical officers had been taken prisoner. Letterman faced more than 9,600 wounded soldiers. Nearly 1,700 had been killed. The much smaller Confederate army had suffered nearly the same number of casualties. Taken together, only the Antietam casualty total exceeded the 21,000 casualties at Chancellorsville.[18] In the course of eight months, Letterman had been the senior medical officer in two of the Civil War's ten bloodiest battles.

After months of preparation, after accumulating an overwhelming manpower and firepower edge and seizing the initial advantage, General Hooker and the Army of the Potomac had been beaten in less than a week. On the night of May 4, Hooker ordered a retreat back across the Rapidan and Rappahannock Rivers. Again the orders crippled Letterman's ability to take care of the wounded. Letterman learned on the morning of the 5th that all wounded were to be taken across the rivers. But he could use only the ambulances already south of the river. Worse, when an ambulance took wounded men across to the northern bank, it would not be allowed to return.

Once more, Letterman appealed to Hooker, arguing the impracticality of using only those ambulances already south of the rivers and using each ambulance just once. "[A]fter much solicitation I was permitted, late in the day, to manage the matter in my own way. I then ordered a sufficient number of ambulances from the north side of the river, and all the wounded were taken across before the troops began to pass the stream," he later wrote.[19] The wounded were ferried in a steady rain, much like the rain that had soaked the army when it marched around Fredericksburg to outflank Lee nine days earlier.

They were deposited at temporary field hospitals in the wet forest, little more than patient depots comprised of crude huts, pine boughs, and sometimes canvas. They waited, many in pain, for comprehensive care that came later, when they reached larger hospitals in the north and east. "I found many of their wounds had had no attention whatever since the first dressing on the battlefield, the limbs in many instances had become so swollen that the stopping of the circulation by the bandages resulted in the most intense pain. I worked until my materials were exhausted," wrote William Stewart, who had graduated from medical school two months earlier.[20]

Although Lee had not been able to prevent the Army of the Potomac from escaping, once again he had outwitted its commanding officer with guile and daring. He had inflicted massive casualties on an army that routinely had held a significant manpower and firepower advantage. When President Lincoln received word of Hooker's defeat, he was stunned at the news, asking, "Oh God! What will the country say?"[21]

Letterman turned his attention to the nearly 1,200 men and nineteen surgeons who remained prisoners of war. Fiercely loyal to his captured men and their patients, he grew more and more frustrated in the days following the battle as negotiations for their return dragged on. Finally, on May 8 and 9, Letterman received authorization to send twenty-six medical officers, five army wagons filled with supplies, and 2,500 rations of bread, beef, coffee, sugar, salt and candles to the wounded men held captive. That brought only temporary relief to the captured Union wounded.

Lee's agreement on May 11 to allow the return of some of the Union's wounded soldiers to Letterman's field hospitals across the river proved to be a hollow victory. The men, wounded more than a week earlier, desperately needed medical care. Letterman asked that a pontoon bridge be erected across the Rappahannock to enable enough ambulances to cross and collect the wounded in one trip. Hooker's chief of staff, Butterfield, denied the request. Instead, he directed Letterman to use pontoon rafts, which carried only two ambulances at a time. Letterman needed hundreds of ambulances to cross the river for the more than 1,000 wounded soldiers who were waiting. The ambulances could not cross the river without bridge or raft, due to its depth, steep bank, and rocky bottom. So the bloodied and maimed soldiers remained out of his reach.

Letterman sought and finally received permission to negotiate directly with Lee's medical director, LaFayette Guild, for the return of remaining surgeons and wounded prisoners. The Alabama native had graduated one year ahead of Letterman at Jefferson Medical College in 1848. Given the relatively small size of the student body, it's entirely possible they had known each other as medical students. Guild was among the Union surgeons who had been dismissed from the service in 1861 for refusing to take an oath of allegiance at the outbreak of the Civil War.

He went to Richmond to join the Confederacy and within a
year became medical director of the Army of Northern Virginia
during the Peninsula campaign in 1862.

It must have been an awkward meeting between former
classmates dedicated to saving lives, who now found themselves
in opposing armies sworn to destroy each other. Within one
day the two surgeons reached an agreement. Letterman prepared 450 ambulances for the trip to the Chancellorsville area.
He then went over Butterfield's head, asking Hooker (who had
traveled to Washington to face the president's disappointment)
to authorize a pontoon bridge. Hooker agreed. The bridge was
completed on May 13. The following day Letterman's medical
corps collected and returned 1,160 patients and their captive
surgeons to Union-held territory.

Intrigue gripped a defeated Army of the Potomac. Some generals
under Hooker's command sought another coup, aiming to position
General George Meade as their preferred replacement. But when
Meade declined to cooperate, the plot dissipated.[22] Hooker, for his
part, did little to strengthen his questionable standing. Worse, he
ordered Letterman and others not to reveal the number of casualties the Army of the Potomac had suffered, a decision that weakened his position in the eyes of some in Washington. It also placed
Letterman in an impossible position. How could he order adequate medical supplies for wounded who did not officially exist?

Secretary of War Stanton ordered Surgeon General Hammond to determine how many men the Army of the Potomac
had lost. Hammond ordered a surgeon who knew Letterman
and who held Hammond's respect and trust to find out. His
written order to John Brinton ostensibly was to "collect patho-
logical specimens" at Chancellorsville, but on the back was the
real mission: "Order in reality to ascertain the number of casualties at Chancellorsville which had been concealed."[23]

Brinton thought that might be an easy task when he learned that Letterman was in Washington having dinner with Hammond one night shortly after the battle. He went to Hammond's house and asked if he could talk to Letterman directly. But Hammond said no, and added that Brinton would have to travel to Chancellorsville because Letterman was not authorized to discuss "specimens." Letterman obeyed Hooker's gag order, and Brinton set forth.[24]

Letterman's position was untenable. After having been hampered in his duties by Hooker when the general kept most ambulances on the north side of Rapidan River, away from the battlefield, he was now ordered to conceal the Army of the Potomac's losses. However, in his post-battle reports and written recollection, he made clear that he thought Hooker's decision about ambulance deployment had caused additional suffering. He wrote: "Great difficulty was experienced in removing the wounded, for want of ambulances (plenty of which were parked on the north bank of the river). . . . That portion of the field under our control was searched and all the wounded were brought in and every wounded man was safely removed across the river before the Army commenced its march for camp. . . . I have seen no battle in which the wounded were so well cared for; and had not military necessity deprived us of the use of our ambulance train on the south side of the river, nearly every man could have been comfortably placed in our corps hospitals (near Potomac Creek) within twenty-four hours of receipt of his wounds."[25]

Meanwhile, Lee sought to parlay his victory at Chancellorsville into another advance into Maryland. He withdrew two corps of the Army of Northern Virginia from Chancellorsville beginning on June 3. The following day, Hooker admitted in writing that he had no idea where they were headed. A week later, intelligence reports confirmed that another advance into

Northern territory by the Confederates appeared likely. The following day, Letterman began preparing for the second major campaign of the year, probably in Maryland, in two months.

Once again, Letterman supervised the post-battle flow of wounded from the battlefield to general hospitals in Washington while the Army of the Potomac chased General Lee. His army's march, covering up to twenty-five miles a day, was exhausting. It had not rained in nearly a month. Giant clouds of dust hung in the sultry summer air as tens of thousands of Union soldiers tramped through the Maryland countryside. Many collapsed from a shortage of water as the army crossed the state line into Pennsylvania.

In his haste to counter Lee's advance, Hooker once more made Letterman's supplies a second priority. As rain finally brought relief and then turned roads into mud, Hooker reduced the number of medical supply wagons allowed to accompany the army, once more over Letterman's objections. "On June 19 while the army was on the march, as it were, from before Fredericksburg to some unknown point north of the Potomac River, the headquarters being near the Fairfax Court-House, Va., the transportation of the (medical) department was cut down by Major-General Hooker, on an average of two wagons in a brigade, in opposition to my opinion, expressed verbally and in writing."[26]

Supplies now became a major concern. On June 25, Letterman ordered Surgeon Jeremiah Brinton to Washington to collect more, although there were still some supply wagons from the Sanitary Commission accompanying the Army of the Potomac. Letterman told Brinton to take the supplies he obtained to Frederick, Maryland, for experience had taught him that Frederick would be a good location for a depot should the next battle take place in western Maryland or central Pennsylvania. As Letterman focused on medical logistics for a battle whose location was yet uncertain, he didn't know he also would have to forge a working relationship with still another commanding officer of the Army of the Potomac.

As Hooker continued to blame some of his generals for his army's defeat at Chancellorsville, his pleas for reinforcements from Harpers Ferry were denied. President Lincoln knew that Hooker had lost the confidence of some of his generals. Once again, he was confronted with a badly fractured command structure in the Army of the Potomac, and he wrote Hooker, "I must tell you that I have some painful intimations that some of your corps and division commanders are not giving you their entire confidence."[27]

Like Burnside before him, Hooker also suffered from a poor relationship with crotchety general in chief Henry Halleck. When Halleck refused Hooker's reinforcement request, Hooker committed the tactical blunder of threatening in a telegram to resign. "I have now imposed upon me, in addition, an enemy in my front of more than my number, I beg to be understood, respectfully but firmly, that I am unable to comply with this condition with the means at my disposal, and earnestly request that I may at once be relieved from the position I occupy," Hooker wrote.[28] Five hours later on the night of June 27, Halleck made it clear who would decide Hooker's fate when he replied by telegram: "As you were appointed to this command by the President, I have no power to relieve you. Your dispatch has been duly referred for Executive action."[29]

When Halleck showed Hooker's message to Lincoln, Hooker's fate was sealed. Lincoln decided to make another change at the top of the Army of the Potomac, practically on the eve of battle. Secretary of War Stanton's chief of staff, Colonel James Hardie, delivered the news in the middle of the night to Hooker a few miles outside Frederick, where Hooker learned command had been transferred to George Meade. Many considered it a

surprise appointment. Lincoln once again had appointed a commander whose leadership style was in stark contrast to his predecessor's, which the president had found lacking.

Lincoln replaced the outgoing Hooker with a tall, gaunt,
bespectacled man whose glasses sat on a large Roman nose
and framed sad eyes weighted down by dark bags. The bachelor Hooker had been replaced by a thoughtful man who wrote
long, pensive letters to his wife. Fluent in French and valuing
modestly and a reserved decorum, Meade had a leadership style
that was nearly bereft of charisma and that sparked little inspira-
tion among the troops.

Meade had graduated in the middle of his 1831 West Point
class and had served in Florida and Massachusetts before resigning from the army in 1836 to become a civil engineer. This son
of a wealthy businessman found civilian life unfulfilling, and he
returned to the army six years later. He surveyed coastlines, built
lighthouses, and had little command experience before joining
the Army of the Potomac. Lincoln had placed the leadership of
the Army of the Potomac in the hands of a logical man who
relied on common sense, was generally cautious, and who was
called a "snapping turtle" by subordinates who bore the brunt of
his hair-trigger temper.[30]

Three days after taking command, Meade followed in the
footsteps of his predecessor by limiting Letterman's ability to
treat wounded in the coming battle. Not knowing precisely
where Lee's army was located, he issued an order concentrating
much of Letterman's medical supplies to an area between Union
Mills and Westminster, Maryland. Only the bulk of ammunition and ambulances proceeded with the Army of the Potomac
in search of Lee.

It had to appear like déjà vu to Letterman, who wrote, "The
expediency of the order I, of course, do not pretend to question,
but its effect was to deprive the (medical) department of the

appliances necessary for the proper care of the wounded, without which it is impossible to have them properly attended to as it is to fight a battle without ammunition."[31]

On June 29, Meade's Army of the Potomac marched toward Gettysburg, Pennsylvania, still unsure of Lee's tactical plan. After three major battles in nine months that produced more than 38,000 casualties, the army and Letterman's medical corps proceeded on a collision course with an enemy army for the fourth time in less than a year. He and his medical officers would be confronted by a deluge of human destruction and death in what remains the most deadly battle fought on American soil.

8

GETTYSBURG

"I turned away and cried."

Grit and sweat coated many of Jonathan Letterman's sur-geons as they marched with approximately 95,000 men northwest across Maryland in late June 1863. Billowing clouds of dust marked the Army of the Potomac's path toward battle. General George Meade, pushing his men up to thirty miles a day and sometimes through the night, had to find General Lee first before he could stop his advance into the North. Exhaustion became Letterman's enemy days before Lee's 70,000 men opened fire.

Frederick, Maryland, would play a key role in the coming confrontation regardless of the battlefield's precise location. Antietam, Fredericksburg, and Chancellorsville had demonstrated the need for reliable rail lines for pre-battle supply as well as post-battle evacuation. The quartermaster corps remained dependent on rail, while relief organizations such as the Sanitary Commission and United States Christian Commission stood ready to provide tons of needed supplies if reliable rail routes could be protected. Otherwise, delivery by wagons on rutted roads would be agonizingly slow. After two years of battle, the Army of the

Potomac remained dependent on the supplies provided by these private organizations.

On June 28, on orders from Letterman, Brinton arrived in Frederick with twenty-five wagonloads of supplies. Accompanying the army's headquarters group, Letterman had left the day before, headed for Taneytown, Maryland, approximately twenty-five miles northwest of Frederick and near the Pennsylvania border. Meanwhile, the army itself, grouped into three massive wings, moved northward toward the state border. Brinton and his wagons stayed in Frederick as the primary supply depot in support of the army's northerly advance.

Although General Hooker had briefed Meade shortly after Meade replaced him, Meade urgently needed field intelligence in order to reposition his army to protect both Baltimore and Washington while tracking Lee in search of an opportunity to attack. The pressure became evident in a man inexperienced at commanding an army. Meade began to lose sleep, miss meals, and frequently change his mind.[1] In drawing him farther and farther away from Baltimore and Washington, Lee hoped to neutralize the Army of the Potomac's manpower and firepower superiority with an aggressive offensive strategy on a battlefield of his choosing.

On June 29, Meade sent a dispatch to General in Chief Halleck, informing him that as Meade's army advanced toward Gettysburg, Pennsylvania, he remained mindful of protecting routes to Washington, Baltimore, and Harrisburg. His infantry and cavalry corps were at various locations in Pennsylvania and Maryland and had not yet consolidated. As he searched for Lee, he considered Big Pipe Creek, about fifteen miles south of Gettysburg, a possible point of engagement or a fallback position.

On June 30, as more of Meade's units crossed into Pennsylvania, an army circular ordered soldiers to draw three days' rations.

This represented the first real evidence that Meade's chase of Lee was about to end, and possibly the first concrete indication received by the medical department of where the battle might erupt. That same day, a cavalry division led by General John Buford encountered Confederate troops near the crossroads town of Gettysburg. Buford established defensive blocking positions west and north of Gettysburg. That night he informed General John Reynolds, commander of the First Corps located eight miles south of Gettysburg, of the actions he had taken. Reynolds approved Buford's troop deployment and made plans to advance toward Buford. Meade, and Letterman, knew battle was near.

Generals Lee and Meade had positioned their military firepower on a battlefield chessboard with Gettysburg at the center. While Meade anticipated the battle would take place probably south of Gettysburg, the precise location was impossible to predict, and Letterman had to factor in that uncertainty during the few days he had to prepare. He commanded approximately 650 doctors, deployed among more than 225 regiments, and controlled approximately 1,000 ambulances, one per hundred men.

By now, Letterman's ambulance system had become battle tested, highly organized, and likely was the least of Letterman's concerns. A corps chief of ambulances summarized the state of Letterman's ambulance organization, noting each division possessed a train of forty two-horse ambulances, several supply wagons, and a forge wagon for repairs. The total medical force for the corps included thirteen officers, 350 men, more than 300 horses, approximately 100 ambulances, and about a dozen supply and forge wagons. The ambulances had seats for the lightly wounded that could be adjusted to allow three men to lie horizontally. A water keg was fastened to the back of the ambulance; beef stock, bandages, and other supplies were stored under the front seat; and a canvas stretcher was hung on each side.[2]

However, as Meade had moved his troops toward Gettysburg, he restricted the advancement of medical supplies, following Union army doctrine that gave precedence to ammunition and commissary over medical supplies and general baggage. Ammunition and food supplies had to be at the front of the line as Meade searched for Lee and positioned his corps for imminent battle. Letterman would have to wait until the battlefield was known and established before completing his preparation.

Meanwhile, Letterman shifted the army's supply depot from Frederick to the railhead at Westminster, about twenty-five miles from Gettysburg. That brought Letterman's supplies closer, but still miles away from potential battle. A single railroad line to Baltimore, nearly fifty miles away with no sidings or telegraph, served the supply depot. An army that required 700 tons of supplies daily became dependent on a single railroad and wagon trains that faced a long trip from Baltimore through Philadelphia to the Gettysburg area.

The crack of a carbine cut through the thick, humid air and reached Gettysburg at about 7:30 a.m. on July 1. Confederate General Henry Heth's lead elements collided with Buford's defensive line west of Gettysburg. A three-hour battle ensued. Wagons carried Union casualties to field hospitals established by Letterman's surgeons in Gettysburg churches and public buildings but soon spilled over into Pennsylvania College, the Lutheran Theological Seminary, High Street School, the courthouse, and several homes. The battle of Gettysburg had begun, sooner than Meade or Lee had anticipated.

A second wave of Confederates attacked Union defenders at 2:00 p.m., this time from the north under the command of General Richard Ewell. As the battle raged, Confederate general Jubal Early launched an attack on the Union's Eleventh Corps from the northeast. The Union's infantry line began to collapse.

By late afternoon it became clear Union reinforcements could not reach the fighting north of Gettysburg in time to avoid a rout by Lee. Union general Oliver Howard ordered a Union retreat to Cemetery Hill south of town.

The enemy fire dissolved an orderly retreat by Union defenders into a chaotic flight back through Gettysburg and south a short distance to Cemetery Hill. Letterman's ambulances, which had efficiently brought the wounded into Gettysburg, now faced a frantic evacuation of the same casualties out of Gettysburg to hospitals established on dozens of farms south of town. Hundreds of wounded soldiers had to be left behind.

As the first day's battle drifted south of Gettysburg, some late-arriving Union army units marched "double quick" toward Cemetery Ridge. The exhausting advance took a heavy toll on men who had yet to see the enemy. "Soon men began to stagger from the ranks, and fall by the wayside. Every piece of woods through which we passed was filled with prostrate men from previous columns; and others all along the roadside, with no one to care for them, lay dying, and not a few dead," wrote one officer.[3]

When Confederate general Ewell declined to press the Rebel advantage with an attack on Cemetery Hill, the first day's battle ended. As Meade's commanders consolidated the Union position on the nearby Cemetery Ridge with reinforcements late in the day, Letterman's medical corps had already been faced with 4,550 wounded men. Some had been abandoned in the frantic retreat out of Gettysburg. Many had made it to Cemetery Hill before being taken to field hospitals at White Church and the George Spangler farm. Others remained at makeshift aid stations.

Meade, and presumably Letterman, had not learned of the fighting until 11:30 a.m., when the first messenger from the battlefield reached the general. Reports came in during the afternoon as the fighting slowly moved south, reaching Gettysburg about 4:00 p.m., and farther south as the lead Union units retreated toward Cemetery Ridge. A few hours' fighting had proven that a great battle would take place on the outskirts of the small market town of 2,400 residents that sat at the intersection of twelve major roads.

Both armies concentrated their forces under a full moon the night of July 1. At approximately midnight, Meade arrived at a small, white farmhouse on Taneytown Road, about a mile south of Gettysburg. Letterman typically established his headquarters at or adjacent to his commanding officer's base. Meade's diminutive farmhouse was divided into two ground-floor rooms and a small loft. A barn, about thirty yards away, towered over a peach and apple orchard. Regiments of exhausted soldiers marched through adjacent rolling fields of corn, wheat, barley, and rye nearly ready for harvest. They tethered their horses to split-rail fences in anticipation of battle.[4]

After midnight, Letterman rode down the Taneytown Road, canvassing the location of various hospitals. Now a battle-tested veteran, he knew how an unexpected enemy advance could threaten hospitals once thought to be outside the enemy's reach. Were any of his hospitals potentially vulnerable? What if Lee broke through the Union line after daybreak? And where might that breach occur? Who would be threatened? Letterman advised at least one hospital to relocate immediately because he expected the enemy to begin shelling the area at dawn.[5]

That night, Lee's and Meade's troops established their lines along two parallel arcs south of Gettysburg. Confederate troops were closest to Gettysburg, having pushed Meade farther south. Lee deployed his men along Seminary Ridge southwest of town. Their line ran generally north along the ridge up to the southwestern edge of Gettysburg, then east along the southern edge of town, and then bent south to the Culp's Hill area. Inside that arc, Meade's smaller arc, shaped like a fish hook, began in the southwest in the vicinity of two hills, Little Round Top and

Round Top, extended generally north toward Gettysburg along Cemetery Ridge, turned east at Cemetery Hill, and extended to the east before turning south at Culp's Hill. The two massive armies had squared off against one another in parallel arcs, about a mile apart, each hugging a ridge line and daring the other to attack.

At approximately 1:00 p.m. on July 2, Lee committed his army. He ordered General James Longstreet to march his two divisions southward from Herr Ridge to roll up the Union left flank. Then on his own initiative, Union general Daniel Sickles pushed his men forward at the southwestern end of the Union arc in search of more defensible ground. After stopping about two-thirds of a mile in front of the Union line, Sickels's men had become vulnerable on two sides.

Longstreet engaged Sickles's men about 3:30 p.m. with artillery, after taking several hours to get into position. Waves of Confederates attacked the thin Union line arrayed from a rocky outcropping known as Devil's Den, through a nineteen–acre wheat field, to the peach orchard where the Union line bent northward on the Emmitsburg Road. The Second Corps' General Winfield Hancock had thinned his Union forces in order to reinforce Sickles to the southwest. Hancock then rebuilt his line by sending exhausted troops that had just reached Gettysburg directly into battle. Some of the most intense fighting of the Civil War ensued. One regiment from Minnesota suffered a casualty rate of 80 percent.

Confederates also raced up the slopes of Little Round Top where Union defenders stubbornly held their ground. Aid stations were established on the back sides of hills and then abandoned when the enemy gained ground. Sickles shifted several units of his Third Corps to blunt the assault. Brutal fighting ensued around Little Round Top and a nearby wheat field as thousands fell dead and wounded.

The battlefield soon thickened with smoke in the still air as Letterman's ambulance corps sought makeshift aid stations, sometimes established in pockets of rocks fifty yards from the fighting. When the smoke thinned or volleys of fire paused, ambulance drivers spotted the stations' plain red or yellow flags and could hear the cries of injured men, bleeding and desperate for evacuation to a field hospital.

Longstreet's attack became the opening foray of what developed into a three-pronged Confederate assault on July 2. While Longstreet pressed the Union left flank, General Ewell attacked the Union right on Culp's Hill to keep Meade from shifting units westward toward Longstreet. Darkness halted the assault before the troops could become fully engaged. About 8 p.m. the Confederates attacked the center of Meade's forces near Cemetery Hill. The casualty toll mounted as the Union line held.

July 2, 1863, became one of the bloodiest days of the Civil War by the time the fighting ended. The Confederate flanking attack on the Union left had gained some ground; its assault on the Union right had gained partial control of Culp's Hill; and the attack in the center of the Union line had nearly been successful but failed to generate a strategic advantage. Meade had positioned reinforcements quickly, while Lee's commanders faced longer realignment distances and suffered from faulty coordination and communication.

After two days of fighting, 12,000 wounded men had become the responsibility of Letterman's medical corps.[6] More than five thousand had been wounded in the wheat field and peach orchard.[7] That night, flickering ambulance lanterns cast a dancing, ghostly glow across the battlefield as crews collected the wounded and took them to more than 100 temporary hospitals that had been established in farmhouses and barns and along creeks. Within six hours after the fighting had stopped, nearly all of the wounded not in enemy territory had been collected by the ambulance corps and regiment volunteers, who braved enemy fire while searching for the injured soldiers.

With one exception, a lack of supplies had plagued Letterman's surgeons throughout two days of fighting. Only the Twelfth Corps remained in good shape, because its medical director, John McNulty, had disregarded the army's standing order of leaving medical supplies in the rear prior to battle and had retained his full complement. As a result, McNulty gathered and treated all his wounded within six hours after the fighting stopped and performed all necessary operations within twenty-four hours.

Although Letterman's supplies remained largely confined to Westminster, supply wagons from the Sanitary Commission and Christian Commission originating in Frederick had skirted the worst of the fighting throughout the day in search of Letterman's hospitals. The First, Second, Third, Fifth, Eleventh, and Twelfth Corps all benefitted from Sanitary Commission wagons delivering brandy, beef soup, sponges, chloroform, lint, and bandages. "U.S. SAN. COM." became a welcome sign on the side of a wagon rolling to a stop in front of a barn filled with wounded, dehydrated, and hungry men.[8]

Letterman's corps and division medical officers had established hospitals while on the move throughout the day. As battle lines shifted, seemingly safe locations became vulnerable to enemy artillery fire. As the Army of the Potomac's position gradually became more concentrated, Letterman's relocated hospitals were squeezed into a more confined area, inside a triangle formed by Emmitsburg Road approaching Gettysburg from the southwest and the Baltimore Pike approaching Gettysburg from the southeast. Six corps hospitals were located within the triangle, four of them alongside the winding Rock Creek. Fresh water was a requisite for any field hospital. Although, close together like this, the hospitals were easier to supply, they also became vulnerable en masse if the Confederates broke through the Union line defending them.

Nearly every major farm inside the triangle was turned into a hospital. Commandeered by Eleventh Corps medical officers, George Spangler's farm was typical. The massive, "Pennsylvania Bank Barn" was cut into a hillside, creating a ground-level entrance on the low side and a second-story entrance on the uphill side. The smells of manure, straw, and dust soon mixed with those of open wounds and lacerated bellies. About 150 men lay side by side inside the barn, with more than 1,000 a few yards away in tents and unprotected in farm fields.

Despite suffering nearly 12,000 casualties over two days, Lee decided to launch one final assault against Meade on July 3. This time Lee would amass more than 12,000 men opposite the center of Meade's army, pummel Meade's men with approximately 150 pieces of artillery, and then stampede the Union line, shoulder to shoulder and on foot. A desperate tactic by a frequently aggressive general, it was certain to produce prodigious numbers of casualties on both sides. Lee turned to General Longstreet to lead the all-or-nothing charge.

The temperature reached eighty-seven degrees with 70 percent humidity early in the afternoon of July 3. Pale gray clouds massed to the west as Union units waited along sunken roads, in creek beds, and behind stone walls. Most of the stands of timber between farm fields groaned with wounded men, most of them lying on the shaded ground where they had been placed after evacuation from the open battlefield. Those attendants not assisting surgeons during marathon operating sessions walked among the wounded, reassuring them that medical supplies surely would be arriving soon.

At approximately 1:00 p.m., the Confederate artillery opened fire in volleys so thunderous they could be heard miles away. After nearly two hours, the responding Union artillery slowed to conserve dwindling supplies of ordnance. A smoldering and quieted battlefield separated thousands of men prepared to charge across 1,400 yards of open ground toward each other, their rifles primed and ready. The Confederates then attacked across the open ground, reaching a broken fence along the Emmitsburg Road, where the Union infantry concentrated its fire in a flood of lead that pulverized faces, chests, and torsos. Hundreds fell dead and wounded in what became known as Pickett's Charge. Confederate losses amounted to approximately 50 percent in one of the deadliest assaults of the war.

Again, Meade reinforced at the point of attack, at the same time as he and his staff abandoned his headquarters when it came within range of enemy artillery. Once more, Letterman asked Meade that wagons filled with medical supplies and tents be brought forward as the casualties mounted. Again, Meade demurred, but this time he allowed half of Letterman's wagons to be driven onto the battlefield.[9]

As Pickett's Charge bogged down in pools of fresh blood, the Army of Northern Virginia's defeat at Gettysburg became certain. The cost to both armies exceeded the catastrophic. The Army of the Potomac had suffered nearly 15,000 wounded casualties and more than 3,000 deaths. Including those listed as missing, Meade had lost about one in four men, and Lee had suffered a cumulative loss of approximately one in three.[10] Some units in the heaviest areas of battle on July 1 and 2 had suffered unbearable losses: Letterman's medical officers managed casualty rates in makeshift aid stations and primitive, barnyard hospitals that approached 52 percent in the 19th Indiana Regiment; 56 percent in the 24th Michigan; 60 percent in the 2nd Wisconsin; and 68 percent in the 1st Minnesota.[11] Overall, the two armies lost more than 50,000 men in about twenty-four hours of fighting over three days.

July 4, 1863, was the first anniversary of Letterman's promotion to medical director of the Army of the Potomac. In the year that had elapsed, he had forged the army's most forward-thinking and best-organized medical department, despite the turnover in his commanding officer after almost every major battle. He spent part of the day pleading for supplies and making sure those still on the battlefield were found and ferried to a field hospital. "I have it from the most reliable authority and my own observation that not one wounded man . . . was left on the field within our lines on the morning of July 4. A few were found after daylight beyond our farthest pickets, and these were brought in, although the ambulance men were fired upon when engaged in this duty by the enemy," wrote Letterman.[12]

Lee expected a counterattack by Meade on July 4. But neither bloodied army had the strength to attack the other in established positions. Like several of his predecessors, Meade opted not to press the Army of the Potomac's numerical advantage without a more precise assessment of the enemy. Instead, he planned a reconnaissance mission for July 5. By the time a torrential overnight downpour eased on the morning of the fifth, General Lee's army had disappeared.[13] His invasion of the North had ended in failure, and now his exhausted and demoralized men faced a long march back to Virginia in the mud. The Confederate wounded who had not been left behind for Letterman's surgeons faced a ghastly wagon ride back to Virginia over gutted and rutted countryside roads.

The sight of Lee's men retreating away from Gettysburg shocked Reverend J. C. Smith. "A more crestfallen, woebegone mob may never have been seen. Hurry was the order of the day. . . . No one counted the wounded. They could not be counted because hundreds of wagons loaded with them were part of this train. . . . When passing over any part of the street where the wagons would jolt, they would yell and groan in pain. Many had received their hurt on Wednesday or Thursday with no attention paid to them by surgeons, the doctors having been kept busy with graver injuries. All who were wounded in the head, the arms, the shoulders, the nonvital parts of the body, were compelled to walk through the mud ankle-deep, with no food save a little flour mixed with water and baked on a few coals."[14]

The slow, agonizing march did not include approximately 6,000 wounded Confederate soldiers and nearly 100 surgeons left behind in twenty-four hospitals within twelve miles of Gettysburg. The wounded Confederates added to the 15,000 wounded men already the responsibility of Letterman's surgeons.

Letterman's ambulance corps cleared the battlefield of wounded so completely that the torrent of injured men arriving at dozens of temporary field hospitals resulted in chaotic overcrowding in the days following the battle. Some surgeons could not adequately prepare for so many wounded because they had had to move their hospitals during the fighting. Others remained critically short of medical supplies due to the temporary embargo that had been placed on delivery prior to and during the battle.

After every day of battle and in the immediate aftermath, mangled bodies littered the ground. Some squirmed and others twitched among the countless dead lying in ditches, on logs, and across fences. Shell-shocked whimpering mixed with gasps and groans from bodies that yet held life. More than 4,500 men were wounded the first day. Twenty-four hours later, Letterman's surgeons faced an additional 7,250 wounded men. Then, on the third day, more than 2,700 wounded soldiers arrived at aid stations and hospitals.

"There were some (wounded) in churches, some in barns, some in tents among the fruit trees, some in tents in the fields, some under such shelter as a farmer would be ashamed to show for his cows. Some were under blankets hung over cross-sticks, and some without even so much shelter as that. There were some scattered groups of men outside the hospitals. It some-times appeared as if an experiment had been made to see how many wounded could be crowded in a given space in a house," wrote medical inspector G. K. Johnston.[15]

Many surgeons, attendants, and volunteer nurses became haunted by the sounds of care and complaint. "Shrieks, cries and groans resounded on all sides, not only from those in the tents but on the amputating tables, which were almost constantly occupied; and who could pass them without a dreadful shudder at those ghastly bleeding limbs heaped without, which the eye, however cautious, could not always avoid," wrote nurse Jane Moore.[16]

Civilians, with no training in medical care, gagged at the smell of war. Gettysburg resident Sarah Broadhead agonized over the condition of the wounded her family tended in their home. "It is heart-sickening to think of these noble fellows sac-rificing everything for us, and saving us, and it is out of our power to render any assistance of consequence. I turned away and cried."[17] Volunteer nurse Cornelia Hancock, twenty-three years old, felt equally overwhelmed, writing: "So appalling was the number of wounded as yet unsuccored, so helpless seemed the few who were battling against tremendous odds to save life, and so overwhelming was the demand for any kind of aid that could be given quickly, that one's senses were benumbed by the awful responsibility that fell to the living." Hancock also wrote her cousin that "[i]t is a very beautiful rolling country here; under favorable circumstances I should think healthy, but now for five miles around, there is an awful smell of putrefaction."[18]

After most of the wounded had been carried off the battle-field, the sight and stench sucked the breath out of most observers who struggled to find context or comparison. The following account is typical of attempts by observers to convey the cluttered lunar landscape abandoned by the two armies: "The appearance of the field was as if an army of men, with every kind of material, had started up in the night, leaving everything but what was fastened to their bodies. Knapsacks, blankets, coats, hats, shoes, stockings, testaments, letters, cards, plates, knives, bread, crackers, meat, candles, cartridge boxes, percussion caps and bullets without count, ramrods drawn to load, and in the fury of battle thrown away to use their bayonet or butt of the guns, broken guns, broken wagons of ammunition and of cannons, wheels that had been driven a hundred yards from the wagon by a cannon ball or shell, shells by the wagon load which had not yet exploded, solid shot, and fragments of shells in every direction."[19]

As the eggs laid on dead bodies by millions of green bottle flies hatched into maggots, survivors searched for wells that had not been sucked dry by tens of thousands of soldiers. Supplies of chloride of lime used to staunch the smell of putrid flesh of man and animal proved woefully inadequate.

Even as Letterman began to organize his post-battle hospitals, Meade was anticipating an attack by Lee on the following day, July 5. He believed that if the Confederates attacked it would ". . . probably determine the fate of the country."[20] No attack came, and Letterman ultimately had three days to assess the total carnage, determine the precise location of dozens of temporary field hospitals, and find ways to move medical supplies forward onto the battlefield. On July 6, the bulk of the Army of the Potomac, including Letterman and the majority of his medical department, left Gettysburg in pursuit of General Lee and his retreating Army of Northern Virginia.

Before leaving Gettysburg, Letterman assigned the overall treatment of the wounded to Dr. Henry Janes, a young and inexperienced surgeon who had demonstrated the knack for organization that Letterman so highly valued. Letterman departed knowing that tents for patients had become more widely available as medical supplies had begun arriving the day before. On July 5 to 6, 30,000 rations arrived in the Gettysburg area.

The day Letterman left with the army, it is unclear whether he and his superiors had a complete understanding of the unprecedented number of wounded in light of available surgeons, ambulances, and supplies. On July 6, Surgeon General Hammond remained convinced that there were adequate numbers of surgeons and accommodations at Gettysburg. The same day, a notice appeared in the *Pittsburgh Gazette* asking that civilian doctors not be sent to Gettysburg in the absence of a working railroad. Letterman also told General Robert Schenck in Baltimore not to send civilian surgeons, possibly because he didn't think they were needed or perhaps because Letterman viewed civilian doctors on the battlefield as counterproductive.[21]

The Confederates had burned key bridges on the main rail line leading to the Union army's main supply depot at Westminster, so distribution of supplies to more than one hundred hospitals took time. Reports from across the battlefield made it clear a critical shortage of supplies, tents, and experienced surgeons persisted. On July 8, a nurse reported: "The men lie on the ground their clothes having been cut off them to dress their wounds; they are half naked, having nothing to eat only as Sanitary Commissions, Christian Commissions, and so forth have to give them."[22]

Starving and dehydrated soldiers suffered in the brutal heat that gripped the Pennsylvania countryside. It became so stifling hot that officers suspended noncritical work by troops on July 8.

However, relief remained elusive for the thousands of wounded men lying in barns, tents, and fields. The battle at Gettysburg was far from over for the medical corps that Letterman had left behind.

What few supplies might be found among Gettysburg farmers came at a steep price. Some of Letterman's surgeons became furious with Gettysburg farmers once the fighting stopped. Farmers shocked Surgeon William Watson when they offered bread that had cost ten cents a loaf before the war to the surgeons and their patients for seventy-five cents each. He lamented: "The brave army that has protected this State deserved better treatment."[23] A newspaper reporter shared his indignation when he wrote: "Here is a farmer who has twelve stray cows, all of which he had milked daily, in addition to his own, whose farm and crops have been protected from the hands of the despoiler, by the blood of the slain, and whose barn is filled with two hundred bleeding, dying patriots. Does he give them milk when they ask and plead for it? Yes. At five cents a pint! Does he give them one loaf of bread when they have saved him ten thousand? Yes. At forty cents a loaf. . . . They [the farmers] seem to be proud of the opportunity, and laugh at their cunning in counting their gains—it is not cunning, it is something less than duplicity."[24]

Several field hospitals benefitted from supplies provided by the Sanitary Commission. Its deliveries amounted to more than 11,000 pounds of poultry and mutton, 10,000 loaves of bread, 8,500 dozen eggs, 7,100 shirts, and more than 6,000 pounds of butter.[25] Sometimes donated parcels included handwritten notes. "This is a poor gift, but it is all I had; I have given my husband and my boy, and only wish I have some more to give, but I haven't," was written on a package of bandages. Another: "This pillow belonged to my little boy, who died resting on it; it was a precious treasure to me, but I give it to the soldiers."[26]

Some army surgeons chafed at the credit given to the relief organizations. "A mistaken idea prevailed at home, that the agents of the Sanitary Commission resorted to the battle-field, ministering to the wants of the wounded, dressing the wounds, bringing the crippled from the field, and feeding the hungry. . . . Nothing of the sort was done," wrote surgeon George Stevens of the 77th New York Regiment.[27] He noted the commission's agents were confined to "large hospitals after the roar of the battles had passed away; but they had nothing to do with the care of the wounded on the battle-field."

It took nearly a week following the end of the fighting to repair secondary rail lines in the Gettysburg area so that reasonably adequate supplies could be distributed from the regional supply depot at Westminster. The Union army's railroad engineer, Herman Haupt repaired the York & Cumberland Railroad from Gettysburg to York by July 7. Work on the line leading from Hanover to Gettysburg progressed. On July 9, the army quartermaster reported he had amassed 300,000 rations at the regional supply depot.[28]

The surgeon Letterman had placed in charge of Gettysburg area hospitals, thirty-one-year-old Henry Janes, turned his attention to building a central field hospital and consolidating the region's wounded. Janes had worked closely with Letterman during the fighting as the medical director for the First Corps, which had lost more men than any comparable unit in the battle. More than 3,200 had been wounded, and some of Janes's doctors had been taken prisoner.

Despite Letterman's lack of respect for civilian doctors and confidence in Janes, he asked Surgeon General Hammond in mid-July to send twenty volunteer civilian surgeons to Gettysburg to support the 106 surgeons Letterman had left behind. In his official Gettysburg report, Letterman noted, "No reliance can be placed on surgeons from the civil life during or after a battle. They cannot or will not submit to the privations and discomforts which are necessary, and the great majority think more of their own personal comfort than they do the wounded. Little more can be said of those officers who have for a long period been in the hospitals."[29] Regardless, nearly two weeks after the fight Letterman knew his medical officers needed help at Gettysburg.

They also needed more ambulances. Letterman had left six ambulances and four wagons per corps at Gettysburg when his medical department left with the rest of the army on July 6. That quantity proved to be horribly inadequate, as thousands of wounded had to be transported to consolidated hospitals and then to the railroad depot for evacuation to larger cities.

Evacuation of patients who could stand the trip to Philadelphia, Baltimore, and other cities on the railroad network that had been repaired in the week following battle became a top priority. Soon 800 men a day were being loaded into railroad cars for the trip from various field hospitals to Philadelphia-area hospitals and others in the region. The trip could be as long as 150 miles, depending upon a wounded man's final destination. Each train had a medical officer in charge, along with a bevy of relief agency representatives who distributed bed pans, urinals, and water to the wounded, who typically sat or lay on straw. Janes's problem became finding enough ambulances to get the wounded to the railroad.

Not everyone could be evacuated, however, as the fighting at Gettysburg had produced a higher-than-average number of casualties with serious wounds. Thousands could not be left for an extended period of time in muddy barns that reeked of manure and torn flesh. Those requiring intensive care needed to be consolidated in a central general hospital that didn't yet exist. On July 4, Letterman had ordered that a general hospital be built among the ruins of the battlefield.

Janes authorized an elevated eighty-acre knoll with a nearby timber lot for the new hospital. Located about a mile-and-a-half east of Gettysburg on the George Wolf farm along the York Pike, sat about 500 feet from a railroad line. The site was an ideal location, regularly swept by a gentle, prevailing breeze, supplied by a reliable spring, and protected by natural drainage with an adequate supply of nearby firewood.

Janes organized the hospital as logically as a military outpost. Six rows totaling approximately 100 patient tents were laid out on a precise imaginary grid, separated by paths of wagon width. The cookhouse and bakery were built off to one side, near the spring. On the downwind side, there was a long latrine ditch, graveyard, and dead house for embalmers.[30] Living quarters for officers and the enlisted completed the layout. Construction began on July 10, four days after Letterman had departed. In honor of the Army of the Potomac's medical director, the largest military general hospital built on the battlefield to date was named Camp Letterman.

Shortly after Camp Letterman opened on July 22, more than 16,000 men had been evacuated from the region. That left about 5,000 seriously wounded patients, most of them suffering from penetration wounds to the head, chest, abdomen, and pelvis, as well as serious fractures. The central purpose of Camp Letterman was to get patients "train ready" as quickly as possible for convalescence in permanent hospitals elsewhere. By the end of the month, Janes's staff closed the remaining Gettysburg hospitals located in the seminary, high school, and railroad office and transferred those patients to Camp Letterman.

In the three weeks following the fighting at Gettysburg, critics of Letterman's post-battle medical plan emerged. Despite Letterman's need to take most of his medical department with Meade in pursuit of Lee, some felt Letterman's ambulance-and-wagon allocation per corps and the approximately 100 surgeons he left behind at Gettysburg were woefully inadequate for more than 14,000 wounded Union soldiers, plus thousands of wounded Confederates. Gettysburg produced more wounded than had Antietam, Fredericksburg, or Chancellorsville.

In response to some of the critics, Secretary of War Stanton sent Surgeon General Hammond on an inspection trip to Gettysburg. Hammond blamed the shortage of medical supplies on General Meade, noting that General Hooker also had reduced Letterman's medical transportation at Chancellorsville as well. "I cannot but attribute a considerable amount of the suffering at Gettysburg to this cause," wrote Hammond.[31]

At about the same time as his Gettysburg visit, Hammond transferred the responsibility for Gettysburg hospitals from Letterman to the Department of the Susquehanna's medical director, W. S. King, and directed King to close all Gettysburg hospitals as soon as practical. King had geographic responsibility for the Gettysburg area. With the majority of those moderately wounded at Gettysburg having been sent to cities elsewhere by late July, Letterman no longer determined how the most seriously wounded would be treated in his namesake hospital. Camp Letterman would operate until November 1863.[32]

Although Letterman remained unapologetic for the numbers of surgeons and ambulances he had left at Gettysburg, on July 29 he sent one of his surgeons back to Gettysburg to assess the situation in the face of continuing criticism. Some army hospital inspectors had sided with Letterman's post-battle allocation of surgeons and wagons because another confrontation with Lee was expected. Others decried the suffering for lack of adequate shelter, prompt medical attention, and supplies. Letterman's inspector generally gave the situation passing marks, but reported that the need for tents remained.[33]

For several weeks, Meade's march across western Maryland almost parallel to Lee's retreat toward Virginia had resulted in a few skirmishes and modest casualties. That had given Letterman time to reorganize and resupply his medical department, and he believed he had prepared it for another battle of comparable intensity to the Battle of Gettysburg. He had received an additional fifty surgeons after leaving one-sixth of his surgeons behind to treat the wounded at Gettysburg. He had also taken receipt of 500 tents as rumors swirled that Meade was about to catch Lee and force another confrontation.

By the end of July, Lee's army had encamped near the Rapidan River. A few miles away Meade's Army of the Potomac had reached the Rappahannock River, a little more than a mile north of the Rapidan. Meade had pushed his army hard, sometimes through heavy rains that turned gear and clothing moldy. By July 28, some men had marched more than 400 miles in the previous forty-two days, and now suffered from a lack of shoes and stockings.[34] The sultry Virginia summer heat sapped both energy and spirit. As some regiments' enlistment obligations were met and soldiers sent home, dozens more arrived to replace them. Meanwhile, part of Lee's Army of Northern Virginia was transferred to the fighting in the western theater. Neither Lee nor Meade had the means or strategic advantage to reengage.

August became an opportunity for Letterman to complete his vision of how a wounded soldier should be treated when he fell on the battlefield. In less than two years he had organized an ambulances corps on the battlefield. He had instituted a more comprehensive, tiered hospital system. He had elevated preventive medicine to a priority that became the responsibility of line officers. Systemization and accountability had been the cornerstones of each milestone. It became time to instill greater accountability and a true sense of military organization within the fledgling ambulance corps. Military discipline had to be as fully inculcated into the medical department as it was in the army's cavalry or artillery.

The logic of Letterman's next phase of reorganization in battlefield medicine appealed to Meade, the former civil engineer. On August 24, 1863, General Meade issued General Orders, No. 85, written by Letterman. The mandate overlaid military organization onto the Army of the Potomac's ambulance system. A captain became responsible for the entire ambulance corps; a first lieutenant in charge of each division's ambulance allotment; a second lieutenant responsible in each brigade; and a sergeant became responsible in each regiment.

The new regulations delineated the duties of each to avoid any miscommunication and assign responsibility. The captain became responsible for the condition of the entire corps' ambulances. He was required to conduct training drills that included the proper way to pick up a wounded man and place him in the standard two-wheel ambulance. The captain ensured ambulances were not used for any other purpose, including those dictated by the whims of line officers. Letterman also required weekly and monthly inspection reports, as well as reports following every battle.

The first lieutenant at the division level became an acting quartermaster. He issued his ambulances by receipt, and commanded a staff that included a blacksmith with a cavalry forge and saddler. In one stroke, Letterman had eliminated much of his medical department's dependence on the army's quartermaster. He also had taken the logistical management of ambulances out of the hands of his medical officers and placed it in the hands of officers solely responsible for those ambulances.

The order also required two medical officers and two assistants to accompany each division's ambulances when on the march. Their job was to make sure only the sick and wounded rode in ambulances and that line officers did not appropriate the ambulances for other purposes. When in camp, the order also established stable standards for the ambulance horses and set specific requirements for ambulance maintenance.

Letterman considered recognition of newly elevated corps vital. This, in part, required an ambulance corps insignia, and Meade's order also established a specific insignia for ambulance corps sergeants and privates. "This corps will be designated for sergeants, by a green band, one and a quarter inches broad, around the cap, and chevrons of the same material, with the point toward the shoulder, on each arm above the elbow. For privates, by a band, the same as for sergeants, around the cap, and a half chevron of the same material on each arm above the elbow."[35]

Letterman went one step further. He purchased red, white, and blue flags consistent with each division's flag to be displayed at the front of each division's ambulance train. Division medical officers received unique flags as well. His ambulance corps now had clearly designated and largely independent authority, standards of accountability, and a unified organization. But as Letterman's ongoing reorganization of the medical corps neared completion, Letterman's longtime mentor, William Hammond, was losing his grip on the surgeon general's post. Hammond's fate could greatly influence whether key appointees such as Letterman, who also often were his friends, would keep their jobs.

William Hammond had been the maverick at the top of the army's medical department who had been necessary for Jonathan Letterman to implement his organizational initiatives. Hammond's path to the surgeon general's post had been marked by scientific inquiry, robust self confidence, a proclivity to question military authority and medical tradition, and the strong support of the medical officers he trusted.

In 1854, when Hammond was stationed in Kansas, he and other military outpost officers became involved in a real estate development scheme in anticipation of the territory becoming a state and the capital being established nearby. When irregularities surfaced and an investigation ensued, Hammond's testimony in part led to a senior officer being discharged from the army. Hammond also testified against the territorial governor, Andrew Reeder. Although Reeder was proslavery and Hammond owned slaves when stationed in Kansas, Reeder never forgave Hammond for his testimony.

Following Hammond's appointment as surgeon general in April 1862, largely due to the political strength of the Sanitary Commission, he and Secretary of War Edwin Stanton quickly grew to dislike each other. Stanton felt the Sanitary Commission unnecessarily meddled in medical department affairs, including its campaign to get Hammond appointed surgeon general over a number of more senior medical officers. Stanton resented Hammond's ego and grand self-image. Many Washington politicos considered Stanton opinionated, stubborn, intent, focused, and vengeful. He often felt he was superior to others in the room. He could be openly disrespectful of the president when he disagreed with Lincoln's position or a member of his administration. Given Stanton's combative personality, a confrontation with Hammond became inevitable.

The feud between the two had been developing for more than a year when Stanton launched a campaign in July 1863 to discredit and fire Hammond. He appointed a committee to look into Hammond's medical department affairs, and stacked it with Hammond critics. He found his opening for the campaign after decisions by the surgeon general had generated critics on the battlefield as well as in Washington.

On May 4, 1863, Hammond had banned the routine use of two cathartics, calomel and tartar emetic, by army surgeons.

Hammond and many educated physicians were concerned with the dangers of calomel, which contained mercurous chloride, as well as tartar emetic, which contained antimony and potassium. Concentrations of mercury could cause extreme salivation and facial ulcers that could leave patients horrifically and permanently disfigured. The heavy use of these drugs produced massive diarrhea and vomiting as part of "heroic treatment" used by many doctors who believed it necessary to balance a patient's system. Hammond did not believe in the heroic treatment philosophy, considering it ill-advised and potentially dangerous. Many military surgeons, however, vehemently disagreed with the surgeon general, and some sought non-military sources for the cathartics so they could continue treating sick soldiers the way they saw fit. Hammond's order cost him allies within the medical department, and the American Medical Association criticized Hammond's order.[36]

Stanton named Andrew Reeder from Kansas to head the three-man investigative committee, the same Reeder who had been damaged politically by Hammond's real estate trial testimony more than eighteen years earlier. Reeder's goal became clear, according to a close friend, Samuel Gross, who wrote in his autobiography: "Andrew Reeder was employed to collect testimony in this city by the examination of witnesses against the late Surgeon-General (Hammond) and I have never saw a man who entered more eagerly upon the discharge of his duties of his office. His object was to revenge himself upon his Kansas enemy."[37]

One of the investigators assigned to the committee was Silas Swetland who earlier had lobbied Hammond for an appointment as a liquor inspector. Despite Swetland's endorsement by several Congressmen, Hammond declined, noting he saw no need for a liquor inspector in his medical department. Now Swetland's job was to find misconduct, negligence, or incompetence by Hammond. Toward that end, Stanton also asked for

every medical report from every medical director, dating back
to the start of the Civil War.

Stanton wanted Hammond out of Washington and out of
reach of his political allies in the early months of his committee's
investigation. So, in August, he sent Hammond on an inspection tour of military posts in the West and as far south as New
Orleans, a tour that Stanton had declined to authorize earlier.

That same month, Stanton promoted army surgeon Joseph
K. Barnes to inspector general, replacing a beleaguered Thomas
Perley, who had criticized Letterman after Fredericksburg but
ultimately had proven to be poorly suited as inspector general.
Barnes and Stanton were particularly close. Barnes had served
as Stanton's personal physician for more than a year, as Stanton suffered from a variety of maladies, including congestive
heart failure, asthma, and liver problems. Their wives vacationed
together.[38] With Stanton as his political patron, Barnes became
a potential candidate to replace Hammond as surgeon general.
As Stanton positioned his political allies, Hammond remained
confident that nothing substantial would come out of the
investigation.

By his actions and in his reports to superiors, Letterman had
demonstrated an analytical mind and a keen awareness of what
transpired around him. He had seized the initiative when the
opportunity for reform presented itself. A self-reliant man,
he had been quick to praise professional medical officers who
were reliable, required minimal oversight, and had the confidence to make critical decisions under fire. An inner resolve
had surfaced in his style of leadership that bore little regard for
ego or hurt feelings. Yet he remained a privately emotional man,
and the human carnage of war placed an exhausting burden on
the man responsible for an army's survival. While the bulk of
Letterman's personal correspondence from the war no longer

exists, the handful of photographs of him taken in the war reveal a man who aged markedly in less than three years, as heavy dark rings developed under his eyes, casting a somber pall across his face.

In four battles, he and his medical corps had been confronted by more than 60,000 casualties, likely the most faced by any single army medical director to that time.[39] Thirty-eight years old and never married, he had served in the military for more than a third of his life. He had been stationed in the swamps of Florida, among the red mesas of Arizona, and in Pennsylvania farm country where a man fell wounded every six seconds over twenty-four hours' total fighting. Now, with characteristic personal reserve, Jonathan Letterman made private plans far from the battlefield.

9

VALIDATION

"Little more remained to be done."

Between some of the Civil War's bloodiest and most horrific battles, Jonathan Letterman had fallen in love. He had met Mary Digges Lee when her brother, Dr. Charles Carroll Lee, took Letterman to the Lees' Maryland home near Burkittsville on October 8, 1862, following the Battle of Antietam. Lee had entered the Civil War an assistant surgeon with the 1st Maryland Cavalry, which had been attached to the Army of the Potomac.

Letterman, Lee, and the commanding officer of the Army of the Potomac at the time, George McClellan, spent two hours at the Lee estate, called Old Needwood. Petite, with a long face and soulful countenance, Mary served her houseguests in the first-floor parlor. They made an impression during their brief stay. In an October 26 letter to her brother Thomas Sim Lee, who was studying in Rome to become a priest, Mary called McClellan "my hero."[1]

Old Needwood was part of Needwood Forest, a tract that had been in Mary's family since the late 1770s, when her grandfather, also Thomas Sim Lee, purchased the parcel. Rolling farmland, stands of timber, and mountains to the west marked it as an estate worthy of the Lee family's standing in Maryland.

Lee had been a leader in the Revolutionary War and served as Maryland's second governor. Mary's father, John Lee, had served in Congress in the 1820s. Her mother's great grandfather, Charles Carroll, had signed the Declaration of Independence.

The family remodeled a former schoolhouse into a towering, two-story Georgian-style manor, featuring expansive, two-story porches on the east and west sides. It was one of four family homes that formed a square. Nearby were agricultural outbuildings and quarters for slaves. When Letterman visited, Mary's mother owned the 144-acre Old Needwood. Her father's frequent financial troubles had forced the purchase of the property by Mary's grandmother, who deeded it back only to Mary's mother, Harriett Chew Carroll.

Unfortunately, no correspondence between Letterman and Mary survives, but the next documented Letterman visit to Old Needwood followed Gettysburg nine months later, this time with General George Meade, who knew Mary's mother. By that time Letterman had become an important part of the Lee household and the subject of family correspondence. On August 11, 1863, Thomas Sim Lee wrote Mary from Rome. "I know how anxious you must have been during the invasion of Maryland and Penna, nor is the war yet over. However the safety with which Dr. L (Letterman) has passed through so many bloody battles, is an earnest of his future preservation from harm. . . . I am very glad that Dr. L. has not offended the political foresight of the blind president (Lincoln). His is not to tear down but to build up, and therefore cannot injure the opposite party."[2]

Jonathan Letterman married Mary Digges Lee on October 15, 1863, in a small ceremony at Old Needwood, two days short of her thirtieth birthday. Since Letterman was not a Catholic, Mary's brother in Rome had obtained special dispensation for the marriage to take place. Letterman was nine years older than his bride. Michael Tuffer of the Society of Jesus and Thomas

Foley from the Baltimore Cathedral officiated in the family chapel. A few family members served as witnesses, including Outerbridge Horsey who owned a nearby distillery.

According to one newspaper report, Letterman's medical officers presented the couple with a $2,000 silver set. A note accompanied it, saying "The Medical Officers of the Army of the Potomac request you accept the accompanying present as a mark of their great regard for you as an officer and a gentleman, with best wishes for the happiness of yourself and lady." A thank-you note written by Letterman two days later while on his honeymoon in Washington revealed his deep affection for his colleagues: "It is well known to you how deep an interest I have felt in being an officer of (the Army of the Potomac), and while I have felt this interest in its officers, in their reputation and usefulness, it is a source of deepest pleasure to be assured of the feelings of kindness which this present so handsomely makes known and entertained towards me by the Medical Officers of the Army of the Potomac."[3]

A few weeks later Letterman returned to the Army of the Potomac and a battlefield he knew well. By late November, Meade and Lee's armies had drifted south through the Virginia countryside, east of the Blue Ridge Mountains, in a series of battles that amounted to little more than skirmishes compared to what both sides had endured at Gettysburg four months earlier.

On October 13, the Confederates' Major General J. E. B. Stuart cavalry had discovered the Army of the Potomac's rear guard near Warrenton, about thirty miles south of the Maryland border. Both armies had been depleted the previous month when Lee sent part of one corps to the western theater and Meade sent two corps to reinforce Union armies in Tennessee.

A series of small battles had ensued over the next three weeks, at Auburn, Buckland Mills, and then south near the Rappahannock River. By the second week in November, Lee had withdrawn to a position south of the Rapidan River, destroying the Orange & Alexandria Railroad as he retreated. Lee's army sat only a few miles west of Chancellorsville, while the Army of the Potomac encamped north of the Rapidan, near Culpeper. The series of five engagements had produced about 2,300 wounded and killed on both sides, less than the losses suffered in a single hour's fighting at Gettysburg.

As winter approached, Meade commanded a superior force of approximately 80,000 men, far more than Lee's 50,000 troops. The Union general still held out hope for a decisive victory before both armies settled into winter quarters. But just as bad weather had hampered earlier Army of the Potomac advances, heavy rains again stalled a Union attack that had been planned to begin on November 24.

On November 26, the Army of the Potomac celebrated America's first Thanksgiving by crossing the Rapidan.[4] The delayed crossing, nearly impassable roads, and scouting reports gave Lee time to reposition some of his forces to blunt what Meade had hoped would be an unexpected and lightning-fast attack on the Confederates' position. Counterattacks followed enemy advances over the course of several days. Flanking strategies were thwarted by shifts in the enemy's troop deployment and by overnight temperatures that plunged below freezing, sapping troop energy.

By November 30, it became evident to Meade that a final thrust into the heart of Lee's army near Mine Run on the eve of winter had failed. There would be no decisive victory to blunt criticism of him for not aggressively pursuing Lee after Gettysburg. Low on supplies, Meade retreated back across the Rapidan under the cover of darkness, cold, and rain on December 1. Letterman agreed with Meade's decision when he later wrote: "it required high moral courage in the Commanding General to order a retreat; in Major-General Meade that courage was fortunately found, and the Army retired, during the night of December 1st, to its former camp on the north side of the Rapidan."[5]

Following Jonathan Letterman's fifth campaign in a year and a half, the Army of the Potomac settled into winter quarters, not far from where it had waged major battles at Fredericksburg and Chancellorsville. After he had taken medical command of a badly depleted army following the Peninsula Campaign, his medical department had seen and contributed to strategic victories at Antietam and Gettysburg. His medical officers had coped with crushing Union defeats at Chancellorsville and Fredericksburg. In what would prove to be Jonathan Letterman's final battlefield campaign, Mine Run had ended in a draw of modest strategic consequence.

He now faced a long and cold winter apart from his wife, who often rented a room at Tudor Place, a grand mansion in the Georgetown Heights area of Washington that had been designed by William Thornton, the architect of the U.S. Capitol. The owners regularly entertained political and business leaders.

In December, he returned his attention to troop health as the army dug in for the Virginia winter. He continued to establish more structured and comprehensive standards of medical care and expected his medical officers to adopt them. That month he restricted the dispensing of alcohol, which doctors administered or prescribed as a stimulant. Prevalent prescription of alcohol "led to hasty and therefore incomplete examination of cases of disease. It is easy, in the case of a weak pulse, to prescribe stimulates, and this practice accords with ideas of unprofessional persons, and the cause of the disease is apt to be overlooked," he wrote.[6]

Yet, after eighteen months of war, he concluded he had completed his mission on the battlefield. Through the course of battles that left tens of thousands of wounded men in their wake, Letterman had remained focused on reorganizing nearly every aspect of the battlefield medical department. The realities of war that he had confronted and the resulting requirements for battlefield medicine that he had addressed had dwarfed the medical needs of soldiers assigned to remote military outposts before the war. A single artillery shell at Gettysburg produced more casualties in an instant than a weeks-long patrol into Indian territory. Serving with the Army of the Potomac, Letterman had faced an unimagined scale of human suffering that demanded critical and analytical retooling of battlefield care. In responding, he implemented a fundamental shift from outpost medicine to effective mass-casualty combat care.

In December 1863, Letterman asked to be relieved of medical command of the Army of the Potomac. "It is evident no military movements can be made by either army. . . .The medical department has been fully reorganized in its branches," he wrote.[7] He made it clear his decision had been a difficult one, that weighed intense personal loyalty to the men he served and treated against the intellectual conclusion that he had done all he could to prepare an army's medical department for the new realities of war.

"For eighteen months of arduous and eventful service, I had shared the varying fortunes of that gallant Army (of the Potomac), and formed many warm friendships with the best and bravest, some of whom were not fated to accompany their comrades, on many a bloody field, to the final triumph that purchased our peace, and restored our Union. But whether the grass grows over them, or they are wanderers, far from the scene of their perils and victories, those who labored together with but one heart, in their country's hour of agony, will live among the many memories that cluster around the dear old Army of the Potomac," he wrote after the end of the war.[8] He also left his post with pride, noting the army sick call rate had dropped from an unacceptable 20 percent when he had joined the Army of the Potomac in 1862 to 3 percent when he left.[9]

Letterman offered no detail in his military reports and post-war writing on what led to his decision to ask for a transfer. His mentor, Surgeon General William Hammond, was under increasing political fire from Stanton and his allies in Washington, and that may have played a role. If Hammond were to lose his job, Letterman may not retain his unfettered authority to enact sweeping changes. Having very recently married at the relatively advanced age of thirty-eight, perhaps he desired to be near his wife and start a family.

While Letterman may have seen his job as complete, his philosophy of battlefield care had yet to become Union army doctrine, even as public support for an army-wide ambulance system had grown throughout 1863. Much of that support had stemmed from a campaign by a vehement abolitionist, Henry Bowditch, who also was a physician and professor of clinical medicine at Harvard.

Bowditch's son had died from an abdomen wound earlier in the war. He had lain unattended on the battlefield next to his dead horse, and Bowditch claimed that army doctors at nearby field hospitals were powerless to help for want of available ambulances. The scarcity of ambulances enraged him in particular because his son had lain in the rear area of the army, easily retrievable, and not in enemy-held territory. Bowditch wrote a widely distributed pamphlet decrying the lack of an ambulance corps in all Union armies. He contended that: "[A] corps of detailed soldiers, or, what may be deemed better, a corps of honest, brave, and humane men, enlisted for this special (ambulance) duty is needed. Such a corps exists in every army in Europe . . . by having such a corps, the number of combatants would not be so rapidly lessened, as it is now, by several men taking one wounded from the field."[10] He cited Letterman's system as the desired forerunner of what all Union armies needed and offered a written endorsement by General McClellan of an army-wide ambulance system.

On December 23, 1863, Senator Henry Wilson of Massachusetts introduced ambulance corps legislation. As chairman of the Military Affairs Committee, he wielded significant influence. Massachusetts governor John Andrew was among those who endorsed the systemization of the Letterman approach.

Not everyone shared that belief. Major General Gouverneur K. Warren, a corps commander of the Army of the Potomac, became an outspoken critic of institutionalizing an ambulance corps. Trained as an engineer, Warren had been teaching at West Point at the start of the war. He had risen to prominence as General Meade's chief engineer at Fredericksburg and Chancellorsville. Warren believed that he had a better understanding of the medical needs of his men than his medical officers. "Responsible as I am for the safety and success of the command which I am entrusted, I claim to know better with my experience what is better in any subordinate part of my command even than the officer who devotes himself to that part especially," wrote Warren.[11]

Letterman had known for several months that Warren opposed his system. During the Bristoe Campaign in October, Warren assumed that he could prorate Letterman's required number of ambulances per regiment in regiments that were not at full strength. Letterman believed it impractical to know precise troop levels in all regiments at all times, so it made more sense to allocate a set number of ambulances to each regiment. When

Warren's medical director, Justin Dwinelle, sent Letterman an
October 31 report detailing Warren's reduction of ambulances,
Letterman became so angry that he filed a complaint against
the corps commander. Warren staunchly defended his actions,
disagreeing with nearly all of the premises on which Letterman
had forged his ambulance corps plan.

Warren had been told by his medical director that more than
1,000 able-bodied men had fled to Second Corps field hospitals
one night during the battle of Gettysburg. That came at a time
when Letterman's ambulance system was in place throughout
the Army of the Potomac. Although Letterman believed that
a designated ambulance corps would reduce the likelihood of
healthy or frightened soldiers leaving the battlefield to help the
wounded to the rear, Warren felt vindicated. "I think, then, the
ambulance detail as a means of increasing effective strength of
this army on the battle-field is a failure, even if the officers do
their duty," Warren wrote in one report.[12]

He also contended that the number of ambulances in a corps,
that was prescribed by Letterman's ratio of ambulances per regiment occupied as much road space as a division of frontline
troops, which was too much; and that ambulance trains, division
trains, and ammunition trains became confused in the heat of
battle. Large trains produced vulnerable targets for the enemy, he
maintained. "To put (ambulance) wagons in large groups would
leave places in the column without any defense, and an attack
of the enemy at such point would cut the column in two and
destroy entirely the control of the commander over one part
or the other of his army, and probably prove disastrous." He
acknowledged the same held true for ammunition and artillery
trains but noted those were necessary for battle.[13]

While public debate of the Ambulance Act continued in
January 1864, Letterman reported to the Department of the

Susquehanna, under the command of Major General Darius Couch. Couch had been given command of the Pennsylvania's militia, which had been established in June 1863 to repel General Lee's invasion of the state. Couch previously had commanded the Second Corps at Fredericksburg and Chancellorsville, making it likely that he and Letterman at least were acquainted.

The 1846 graduate of West Point had proven himself a solid and aggressive tactician and despite generally poor health, was well known for his poise in battle. He had served in the Army of the Potomac since Letterman's arrival. He had served under Generals Burnside and Hooker, both of whom had rebuffed his proposals to attack Lee. Frustrated, Couch had taken the extraordinary step of going over Hooker's head and complaining directly to President Lincoln. He then refused Lincoln's offer of command of the Army of the Potomac. When Hooker retained command, Couch resigned from that army and was given command of the Department of the Susquehanna.[14]

Letterman made a lateral transfer not to become Couch's medical director but rather a medical inspector of hospitals. Although there is no written record documenting it, it seems plausible that Letterman may have specifically requested a posting in the Department of the Susquehanna, since its area of operations was within a few days' ride of his in-laws' Needwood estate in Maryland. It was also close to Washington, the epicenter of the Union army's medical department. As a hospital inspector, he would remain involved with the thousands of casualties at Gettysburg, many of whom were still recovering in the region's hospitals. It was also a relatively pleasant posting. Army hospital inspectors often traveled between cities by rail and stayed in hotels with their wives. Gone were the days of pitching a tent in the cold or choking on the dust of a massive army on the move. It wasn't uncommon to see a well-regarded battlefield medical officer be rewarded with a hospital inspection post off

the battlefield. Best of all, Jonathan could spend more time with
Mary, his bride.

Now his inspections enforced many of the military medicine standards he had pioneered with the Army of the Potomac.
His oversight responsibilities included officers' quarters, enlisted
men's barracks, hospitals, medical supplies, camps, field hospitals
and transportation. Treatment of disease, wound care, preventive
medicine, nutrition, hygiene, and recordkeeping by hundreds
of medical personnel for tens of thousands of men became his
responsibility.

The Department of the Susquehanna sat on the fringe of
the Civil War in early 1864. A rumored Confederate incursion into Pennsylvania had failed to materialize. As President
Lincoln issued calls for tens of thousands of additional volunteers, Couch spent much of his time arguing with Secretary
of War Stanton about how best to recruit local volunteers and
whether they should become part of the state militia or part
of the United States service. Once again, Letterman's commanding officer was waging a personal war with the Union's
Secretary of War.

Letterman's legacy on the battlefield persisted nonetheless.
His fellow medical officers presented a memorial to the Senate's
Military Committee, proposing that Letterman be promoted
and receive attendant raises in pay.[15] They wrote:

> We express not the sentiments of Medical Officers only;
> we give the opinion of Military Commanders, when we
> affirm that not only the remarkable state of health, but
> in great measure the tone, the vigor, and in part the dis-
> cipline of this Army, is due to the efficient officer at the
> head of its Medical Department. When we contrast this
> Army at present, with what it was when Surgeon Let-
> terman assumed the charge of its medical department,

when the tide of men flowing to the rear depleted its ranks, owing to a lax system of discharges, or no system at all, and owing to an unchecked license of granting passes to hospitals; when we compare the provisions now made for the wounded with what they were before his time, we cannot help congratulating the Army and the country upon the change, and cannot forbear bringing to your notice the merit of the officer to whom that change is due.

We may search history in vain for campaigns of equal severity, for battles of equal magnitude, with those of this Army for the past eighteen months, and we challenge history to produce a battle wherein the hundreds of wounded have been so well and so rapidly cared for, as the thousands in the great battles of this Army.[16]

Letterman's supporters sought more senior ranks for medical directors, beyond that of major and on a par with other department heads. It wasn't until 1865 that Congress acquiesced.

Letterman's work had greatly improved the public perception of the army's medical department. Blistering early-war criticism of the wounded lying abandoned at Bull Run for days had been replaced by increasing recognition and respect of medical department reforms. Letterman had overhauled battlefield care, hundreds of military hospitals had been built, and the medical department had evolved to a level of military organization that had not existed at the outset of the war. In early 1864, a Philadelphia newspaper reporter wrote: "We have alluded to this subject in order that the friends and relatives of those who are now imperiling their lives in defence (sic) of their country may have some idea of what is done by a humane and bountiful government for the relief of those who fall in its battles; and that they may rest easy in the confident assurance that there is a department of the government which looks after the wounded and the sick with the utmost care, and provides for all their wants."[17]

Despite growing recognition for these accomplishments, a key ally who had made Letterman's reforms possible, Surgeon General William Hammond, had seen his political stock plummet. After Stanton had sent Hammond on his extensive tour of western medical facilities in September 1863, Stanton's investigative committee did its appointed work. Hammond's allies feared the worst, based on emerging rumors of what the investigation might reveal.

A few weeks before Letterman asked for his transfer, on December 6, 1863, *The New York Times* previewed the committee's not-yet-published investigative report: ". . . is said to be terrible in the management of that Bureau while under Surgeon-Gen. Hammond. It is proved that he instructed the Medical Purveyor in Philadelphia to cease purchasing drugs in open market at quotation prices, and contracted with other parties in that city for the same articles at from twenty-five to thirty percent higher rates than the testifying parties offered to furnish them for. A New-York blanket contract; the hospital bedstead contract, made with a secesh firm in this city, and whisky and other minor contracts of this bureau are said to be soaked with fraud."[18]

Hammond was arrested when he returned to Washington, on January 17, 1864, while Letterman was settling into his new post as hospital inspector in Pennsylvania. Charges of malfeasance and fraud—personally authorizing medical supply purchases without going through the medical purveyor and allowing the purchase of substandard supplies—mirrored the claims of the investigative committee. His trial began two days later and dragged on for several months.

Three days earlier, January 14, Letterman's post in the Army of the Potomac had been filled by surgeon Thomas McParlin. He had joined the Union army the same year that Letterman had enlisted. McParlin became assistant surgeon at Fort Union, New Mexico, in 1851, a post Letterman held five years later. McParlin assumed medical command for the Army of the Potomac in midwinter, finding an army in far better condition than when Letterman had assumed medical command less than two years earlier. Camp hygiene, military diet, a more reliable supply of provisions, and accountability, all hallmarks of Letterman's regime, were evident in McParlin's early assessments as his successor.

The army's winter camp was comprised "for the most part of log huts about eight feet square, with walls four feet high, and roofed with shelter tents, each hut accommodating from three to five men. Much skill and taste was evinced in the arrangement of many of the camps. . . . The rations furnished . . . were abundant in quantity, and of good quality and variety, the average weekly issue (included) three days' rations of fresh beef, three-and-a-half of fresh bread, four-and-a-half of potatoes and two-and-a-third of other vegetables," he wrote on January 26.[19] Two weeks later he had expressed equal satisfaction with the Army of the Potomac's hospitals. "These hospitals are floored with boards, and heated by means of open fireplaces, and their condition . . . was in every way good. Jellies and canned fruits are kept on hand and issued by the medical purveyor and from the fund created by the tax on newspaper vendors and sutlers, which has been put at the disposal of the medical director of the army."[20]

Meanwhile, Letterman inspected the Department of the Susquehanna's eighteen hospitals that housed more than 4,000 patients. He had become responsible for about 10 percent of all Union army hospitals as the spring campaign season approached. Only the Department of Washington and

Department of the Ohio operated more hospitals and patients. However, Susquehanna hospitals had a 37 percent occupancy rate, compared with an overall 54 percent occupancy rate in the Union army's 190 total hospitals.[21]

Letterman also became involved in the ongoing Congressional deliberation over the proposal to create an army-wide ambulance corps. Submitting his comments through General Meade, Letterman argued for a federal ambulance corps instead of one based on regiments. Several Army of the Potomac corps commanders, including Generals French, Pleasanton, and Howard, supported the legislation, based largely on their experience with the Letterman system. An unnamed Army of the Potomac surgeon wrote *The New York Times* that "From more than a year's experience in the hard-fought engagements of this army, I can affirm that I have not known wounded to lie on the battle-field two hours after their injuries were received . . . except . . . where the field remained in possession of the enemy.[22] General Gouverneur Warren remained one of the few senior line officers critical of Letterman's approach and wrote letters to the Senate military committee opposing army-wide adoption.

On March 11, 1864, Letterman's system became federal law. Other than a provision that assigned ambulances based on regiment size, the legislation matched nearly all of the provisions contained in General Orders No. 147 issued by General McClellan on August 2, 1862, at Letterman's behest. Less than eighteen months after Letterman had conceived of this overhaul of battlefield care, forged partially on the work of others, it became the required standard for the entire Union army. More than 86,000 casualties in Civil War battles yet to come would benefit from the medical department's transformation from outpost medicine to combat care.

Soldiers in the Army of the Potomac, however, saw little difference after the law's adoption. "As the provision of the ambulance law corresponded in all essential particulars to the system already instituted in the Army by Surg. Letterman, no difficulty or delay occurred in its adoption. All of the ambulances were thoroughly repaired, painted, and marked with the distinctive badge of their several corps, details of medical officers and men for the ambulance service were made, and the persons so selected carefully examined. As was to be expected, a large portion of those first detailed were rejected, regimental commanders having attempted to rid themselves of their weak and worthless men. The men attached to the ambulances were carefully and regularly drilled, minute inspections of everything connected with the ambulances and horses were made, and guidons and hospital flags were procured and distributed," wrote McParlin.[23]

By that point, the medical department in the Army of the Potomac had evolved to become a major component of near-equal standing with other units. On May 1, its ambulance corps included 592 ambulances, forty medicine wagons, 209 army wagons, fifteen forges, nearly 1,900 horses, almost 1,200 mules and a like number of stretchers, six officers, and more than 2,200 enlisted men.[24]

Four weeks later, Letterman became more removed from the war. On May 30, he traveled to West Point, New York, to conduct physical examinations of the latest graduating class of the U.S. Military Academy. Fifty-two graduates passed muster on July 1, all of them between sixteen and twenty years of age. In preparation to become military officers they had studied mathematics, literature, French and Spanish, military tactics, drawing, chemistry, philosophy, and engineering.[25]

The office of Letterman's medical director was located in Philadelphia, and the Lettermans were "living for the summer in a very pretty village outside Germantown," according to Letterman's wife. In June, Mary's mother wrote her son in Rome that she planned to rent a room near Philadelphia's Logan Square to be closer to her daughter and son-in-law. However, it appeared Jonathan and Mary's future was in New York. In mid-July, Mary asked a family friend to watch for homes that were for sale "not over $5,000 at Yonkers or nearer New York."[26]

Meanwhile, Letterman's inspector duties required him to travel frequently, living out of his luggage in hotels. He was miserable, away from his wife and far from the battlefield where his authority and decisions directly affected the lives of tens of thousands of men. His letters to Mary provided a rare glimpse into man who had found a purpose in life outside the military. After fighting against an unending torrent of human slaughter, of stained and dirty faces looking up from blood-soaked straw desperate for a glimmer of hope in the surgeon's face, his salvation from a life of disease, death, and disability had become Mary.

"To tell you that I am disgusted with this business would be to express myself in the mildest manner. It is a kind of business that I have no fancy for under the most favorable circumstances. . . . I am not by any means in good humor," he wrote his wife. "I felt it would be hard to be separated from you . . . (but) I am deeper in love than I thought, your goodness, your exquisitely fine sense of all that is good and beautiful and true . . . (is) exemplified in all your thoughts and feelings and actions. How often you are in my thoughts and how pleasant it is to linger upon thoughts of you, you may never know, for I can tell you but little how dearly you are cherished."[27]

While Letterman had turned his attention to West Point's future officers, his mentor became the subject of national debate and sometimes ridicule. On May 4, Surgeon General William Hammond was found guilty of the charges of sidestepping the medical purveyor and purchasing medical supplies found to be inferior and overly priced. He also was found guilty of conduct unbecoming an officer for telling a Philadelphia medical purveyor that he was obliged to fire him on orders from General in Chief Henry Halleck. Halleck claimed no recollection of such an order, and in his defense Hammond could only allege that documents proving the order came from his superior had been stolen from his office.

The four-month trial had featured extensive testimony by witnesses on both sides, sometimes disputing the quality of the goods sold. The prosecution relied heavily on civilian physicians who worked in military hospitals, while Hammond's attorneys called several career military physicians, including Letterman, who testified on Hammond's behalf. Despite early support of the Sanitary Commission, *The New York Times, American Medical Times,* and *Boston Medical and Surgical Journal,* Hammond was dismissed from the army and prohibited from holding another federal government post.

By August, many of Hammond's supporters had abandoned him. Although no allegations claimed that Hammond personally profited by his conduct, a reporter from *The New York Times* lambasted the former surgeon general, saying, "He not only directly violated the law in order to indulge favoritism in giving out contracts for supplies, but he stooped to the level of the lowest shoddy knave in knowingly taking supplies of medicines and of blankets of an inferior and unsuitable quality for an exorbitant price. . . . In an evil hour he listened to temptation, and the result is that he will be remembered only to be loathed, and to serve as an example of the infatuation of betraying the public trust for gold."[28]

With his political enemy out of the way, Secretary of War Edwin Stanton erased Hammond's influence in the surgeon general's office. Surgeon John Brinton, a supporter of Hammond and friend of Letterman, was transferred out of the office in late

September to a post in Kentucky. Although Brinton considered
Stanton honest and patriotic, he knew that anyone associated
with Hammond had a limited medical department future in the
army. "Believing himself to be right, he [Stanton] regarded all
those who differed in opinion from him to be wrong thinkers
and wrong-doers, criminal, in fact, and that it was his duty as
Secretary of War to punish them, when he conveniently could.
Now, I not only was a friend of Hammond's, but a relative, a
blood-relative of General McClellan who, in the esteem of the
Democratic Party, and a possible candidate for the presidency
of the United States, was in the eyes of Mr. Stanton little less
wicked than the Arch Fiend himself."[29]

Another Stanton foe and Letterman ally, General George
McClellan, prepared to make a comeback on the national stage.
As Hammond left his office, the Democratic Party nominated
McClellan as its candidate against President Lincoln, the man
who had relieved McClellan of his command.

A reluctant candidate, McClellan felt saddled by a plank
of the party platform that called the war a failure and sought
unconditional peace. McClellan rejected that position and
believed reunion was a necessary condition for ending the war.
His personal views didn't matter, though, as Republicans seized
on the Democrats' peace plank to level their attack on him.
When McClellan decided to make only two campaign appear-
ances over three months, the race dimmed to a war of words
waged by allies among the partisan newspapers.

On November 8, more than 4 million votes were cast, giving
the victory to Lincoln by a 10 percent margin. In the electoral
college, it was a landslide for the president, as McClellan only
carried New Jersey, Delaware, and Kentucky, losing 212–21.
McClellan had relied heavily on Union troops for support, yet
Lincoln carried the army vote by an overwhelming 78 to 22
percent margin. The results were nearly as bad for McClellan in

his former command. Seventy percent of the men in the Army of the Potomac voted for Lincoln.

McClellan resigned his army commission on election day, telling friends and family he had not looked forward to the burdens of the presidency. His lack of campaigning reflected that reticence. He remained optimistic, however, believing his political defeat was "part of the grand plan for the Almighty, who designed that the cup should be drained even to the bitter dregs, that the people might be made worthy of being saved."[30] But as the weeks passed, McClellan grew discouraged. On November 28, he had not found a job after being passed over for the president's post with the Morris & Essex Railroad. "Were it not for the house on 31st St. I should now be almost penniless," he wrote a friend.[31]

As McClellan adjusted to a life outside the army, on December 2, Letterman received orders for the Department of the Missouri, commanded by General William S. Rosecrans. It had been two years since Letterman had served under Rosecrans in the Department of West Virginia, within the overall command of McClellan. After Letterman had been summoned to the Army of the Potomac, Rosecrans had served in western Tennessee before a transfer to Missouri, a command of modest military significance.

Letterman faced another assignment on the outskirts of the Civil War. Just as the Department of the Susquehanna had guarded the Pennsylvania flank of the North, skirmishes and raids occupied the Department of the Missouri in the southwestern corner of the war.

Unbeknownst to his closest colleagues Letterman was thinking seriously about refusing an army order for the first time in his career. In fact, he was contemplating an even bigger decision, one that would set a new course for the Lettermans, who had been married a little over a year, and would allow them to build a life together. On December 22, 1864, Jonathan Letterman

declined the Missouri assignment. He shocked friends and colleagues by submitting his resignation from the Union army.

Letterman had decided to end a fifteen-year military career
with the outcome of the Civil War not yet certain. With characteristic reserve, he offered nothing personal that might have
revealed the reasons for his decision. Colleagues could only speculate that the decision may have been born out of exhaustion,
disenchantment over the fate of his mentor, William Hammond,
or perhaps due to increasingly chronic poor health.

Jonathan Letterman had turned forty years of age less than
two weeks prior to his resignation. Colleagues talked of a
chronic digestive ailment of vague origin that had plagued the
surgeon for some time. His face had grown gray as the war's toll
became evident in the darkened bags that developed under his
eyes. Letterman gave every appearance of exhaustion after three
years of war, after experiencing some of the war's most devastating battles.

His decision to resign from the army came at a point in the
war when a soldier's likelihood of surviving disease or a wound
on the battlefield had greatly improved. Over the course of three
years, army diet and hygiene had seen significant improvement.
His ambulance system had improved the speed with which a
wounded soldier received treatment. Transportation to hospitals
in the North had become far better organized. By mid-1864
there were 190 general hospitals in the north with 120,000
beds.[32] As a result, the 9 percent mortality rate that the Army
of the Potomac had suffered at Gettysburg was about one-third
of what it had suffered in the Peninsula Campaign of 1862 (26
percent) two years earlier.[33]

His final twelve months of service to his country had taken
Letterman off the battlefield and to a big-city military life in
the rear, where he lived and worked in the Philadelphia area.
He traveled to nearby cities such as New York City and, freed

from a life of army marches and commandeered barns and farmhouses, shared his military life with civilians for the first time. His wife's family, well-respected throughout the Maryland region, had high-profile business and social connections.

Jonathan Letterman thought about a life outside the military. About a new life whose path would return him to a remote stretch of Central California marked by expansive ranchos, Indian settlements, and rolling hills that might hold the promise of America's industrial future: oil.

10

WILDCATTER

"A good kind husband"

his son of a physician had known only the military medical life. He had never practiced medicine outside the confines of a camp or military hospital, or practiced any other profession. However, as a senior Union officer of some note, who had married into one of Maryland's prominent, landed families, Letterman had the opportunity during his job inspecting hospitals away from the battlefield to meet some of Philadelphia's civic and business leaders. One was a bold, charming, and persuasive man, Thomas A. Scott.

Scott was vice president of the Pennsylvania Railroad Corporation. Known as a workaholic with an ingratiating personality, Scott had played an indirect role in Letterman's chain of battlefield evacuation. In 1861, Secretary of War Simon Cameron asked Scott to build a railroad from Philadelphia to Washington to carry the wounded to a rapidly expanding cadre of hospitals under construction. Scott became Assistant Secretary of War, responsible for all railroads and telegraphs, and served as acting Secretary of War for a brief period before returning to Pennsylvania Railroad in 1862.

Scott and the company's president, J. Edgar Thomson, built railroads for the government in the war's western theater and explored for gold and silver along anticipated new railroad projects in the Far West. The war proved to be a boom period for aggressive railroad executives, who sought bright and accomplished army officers to their expanding corporate ranks to manage their growth plans. They envisioned a postwar expansionist era that would require thousands of miles of new railroads across land potentially rich in minerals and a natural resource quickly becoming an obsession: oil.

Pennsylvania and Ohio oil wells produced commercially viable oil that was superior for illumination and lubrication to whale- and lard-based oils. Expanding railroads in the West were making likely looking oil fields viable. Rail transport was critical for getting oil from wells to seaports and major cities for distribution. The first well in the Rocky Mountains was drilled in Canon City, Colorado in 1862, and tar seeps in California appeared promising. As Scott and others turned their attention to the West, speculators in California canvassed the western part of the state for tar seepages that could indicate the presence of substantial oil reserves.

Shortly after Letterman returned to the battlefield from his honeymoon in late 1863, three speculators acquired 100,000 acres in the Ojai Rancho area near Santa Barbara, California. Natural seepages of thick, tar-like oil that oozed out of the ground, dried, and formed large deposits that resembled asphalt proliferated in that part of the state. For generations, Native Americans had used the tar as a natural home-construction binding agent, as roof weatherproofing material, and to seal baskets and canoes. When the white man arrived, the natural resource became known as "Indian grease" and proved useful for lubricating wagon wheels.

The speculators hired one of the nation's foremost petroleum experts, Benjamin Silliman, Jr., to evaluate their holdings. They could not have selected a more widely respected expert at the time. In 1855, Silliman had demonstrated that Pennsylvania oil could be distilled into a kerosene of higher quality than whale oil. It was cheaper to produce at a time when the whaling industry was declining. Less than five years later, the nation's first oil boom happened, in Pennsylvania. In 1863, Silliman became one of the nation's fifty leading scientists to be included in the National Academy of Sciences established by Congress. Erudite and articulate, according to one contemporary, "[i]n society he was most genial, abounding with conversation based on a remarkable range of information on general topics and with an anecdote ready for the entertainment of the guests."[1]

As Letterman inspected hospitals in the spring of 1864, Silliman visited the Ojai property, guided by Santa Barbara County Surveyor, Thomas Sprague, who dreamed of becoming part of an oil boom in California. He collected handsome consulting fees from several oil speculators, and he could influence part of the tour by Silliman on their behalf. Silliman inspected the Ojai and nearby properties before writing his report in July. He concluded: "This property covers an area of eighteen thousand acres in one body, on which there are at present at least twenty natural oil-wells, some of them of the largest size. The oil is struggling to the surface at every available point, and is running away down the rivers for miles and miles."[2]

Apart from evoking rivers of oil, Silliman cited a report by Colonel James Williamson, who had surveyed the area twelve years earlier for a new railroad route. Williamson reported about one oil seep that it "is probably safe to estimate its contents on a mile square at one yard in depth, which would give over three million cubic yards of fuel."[3] Silliman in turn estimated that the mass would produce 144 million gallons of oil and, at a cost of $1,000 to $5,000 to drill a well, ten successful wells would produce annual profits of $1.365 million.[4]

Silliman left Ojai and traveled to Arizona, where he met an exploration team that Scott had commissioned on behalf of

Pennsylvania Railroad. When Silliman reported his California findings, the expedition abandoned its quest for gold and silver in Arizona and headed for the rivers of oil in California. Within six months after it was diverted from Arizona, Scott's expedition resulted in the acquisition of 187,000 acres in California, acreage that included the Ojai Rancho where Silliman had focused most of his attention as well as the Simi, San Francisco, and Las Posas Ranchos. The Pennsylvania Railroad Corporation placed a massive bet on more than 290 square miles of California land at a time when the price of oil was rising from $3 to $14 a barrel.[5]

The speculators needed to raise capital for each of two oil companies they were forming in California and began distributing glowing prospectuses to investors in search of 1 million shares at $40 each. According to them, "[t]here can be no reasonable doubt as to the fact of immense deposits of Petroleum, need only proper equipment." The prospectus painted a picture of a vast oil reserve that connected oil outcroppings that "are very numerous in a direct line for nearly fifteen miles . . . there appears to be no reason why the oil may not be conducted through pipes from the wells to reservoirs near the shore (about six miles from the property), from which shipments might be directly made."

The prospectus claimed that oil could be produced in the foothills, transported to ships on the coast, and shipped to New York at a cost not exceeding $5 per barrel. Their market assumptions were equally optimistic. "To supply the present, and increasing trade in this article to California, Australia and other points on the Pacific Coast, oil can be furnished most profitably, and can be shipped from California to China and all other parts of Europe; it is perhaps not exaggerations to say that it can compete in the New York market with the product of the Eastern States, and realize large profits to the producer. . . . This Property, when measured by the value of Oil lands in our Eastern States, appears fabulous in wealth."[6]

They may not have known that Silliman had spent less than a week on two of the three properties they had bought and that he had viewed most of it from a stagecoach.[7] But that had not stopped Silliman from describing nearly unbounded oil potential. "From what I have myself seen, and from all I can learn from the observation of others, I have reason to believe that, as an oil state, it is unsurpassed by any other in California. . . . Some of the natural wells of petroleum and tar are forty or more feet in diameter, troubled by the escape of gas, and surrounded sometimes by a quagmire of pitch in which wild and domestic animals become mired. . . . Hill-sides are covered often for hundreds of square acres, with hardened asphaltum, where in an earlier day oil springs, now no longer active, have found vent."[8] He also predicted that, based on his samples, the oil "proves itself to be of almost unequalled quality, and justifies the expectation that, when drawn fresh from the wells, it will rank among the very best samples of crude Petroleum produced in the world."[9]

Soon Thomson and Scott would need accomplished and well-regarded executives to run their two California ventures: the Philadelphia & California Petroleum Company to develop the Simi, San Francisco, and Las Posas Ranchos; and the California Petroleum Company to develop the Ojai Rancho. Armed with Silliman's report, they traveled in Philadelphia social circles that likely would have included senior officers of the Union army stationed in the city. Philadelphia newspapers had carried reports of how Letterman's organizational accomplishments had forged order out of battlefield chaos. His proven administrative acumen, his experience in living in rugged conditions, and as a bonus his familiarity with the region from his tour of duty at Fort Tejon and Camp Fitzgerald made him an ideal candidate to organize an oil-exploration operation in California. Letterman's lack of oil exploration experience wasn't a major factor in the embryonic oil industry. Newly trained petroleum chemists and experienced well-drilling teams from Pennsylvania would handle the technical and heavy field work.

Jonathan Letterman had coped with more than 100,000 wounded men during his Army of the Potomac command and while with the Department of the Susquehanna. At forty years of age, he had been married one year, and the prospect of family life finally had arrived. After living his entire adult life on an army officer's pay, he was offered a job by Scott that brought with it an opportunity to invest in a venture that could generate significant, if not astronomical, wealth.

Letterman's health concerns must have been a factor in his considerations. Along with hundreds of thousands of other soldiers, he suffered from gastrointestinal ailments. Diarrhea and dysentery had proven to be the scourges of the Civil War. Although the disease was poorly understood by doctors at its most basic bacterial level, Letterman instinctively had known that his pioneering camp hygiene standards were the first line of defense against it and similar diseases that sapped an army's fighting strength. Yet despite standing at the forefront of protecting troop health, he drank the same water and ate the same food as those for whose health he held responsibility.

Although incidence rates of nearly 1,400 per thousand men in 1861 had dropped to approximately 500 per thousand in 1865, armies generally remained malnourished, emaciated, and sometimes dehydrated. The Union army suffered more than 1.5 million cases of acute diarrhea and dysentery in the Civil War.[10] Chronic diarrhea led to ulcerated intestines. Amebic and bacillary dysentery, which included the involuntary discharge of blood, could rupture intestinal walls, and produce abscesses that reduced liver, lung, and brain function.[11] Many of those who survived the battlefield faced a lifetime of

chronic dysentery and potential premature death. Both plagued
military and civilian physicians.

Letterman bought 400 shares of Philadelphia & California
Petroleum stock and moved to California in February 1865,
accompanied by Mary and their infant daughter, Mary Catherine ("Cassie"), who had been born in Philadelphia the year
before. At a cost of $40 per share, the $16,000 investment represented nearly eight years of Letterman's salary as an officer in the
army.[12] It's likely the money came from his wife, Mary, whose
family was wealthy. For at least three generations, her relatives
had owned substantial property and successful business ventures
in Maryland and elsewhere.

Letterman reached San Francisco in the midst of a gold and
silver mining frenzy. The Comstock lode discovered in Nevada
more than five years earlier, just as California's gold ore reserves
showed signs of exhaustion, had fueled a transformation of the
city. Much of the Comstock ore was exported through San
Francisco, the closest city with seagoing access to the rest of the
world. In 1861, 1,453 commercial and residential buildings were
started or completed. That same year, the Pony Express reached
Sacramento, a day's ride to the east, linking San Francisco with
the rest of the nation.[13]

The Civil War had been good to San Francisco. Hostilities
in the East had created opportunities for expanded manufacturing, mining, agriculture, and exporting businesses on the
West Coast. Prosperity reigned in a city that had supported
pro-slavery politicians in the 1850s but had backed President
Lincoln throughout the war. San Franciscans enthusiastically
supported the humanitarian efforts of the Sanitary Commission in the war, contributing $300,000 in gold in the second
half of 1862 and accounting for one-fourth of all the cash
donated to the commission by Californians.[14]

Letterman bought drilling equipment in San Francisco, chartered a boat, and sailed to Port Hueneme near Santa Barbara. He and his family moved inland to the Camulos Rancho in the Santa Clara River Valley. The river, less than ninety miles long, drained California's western foothills to the coast, between present-day Oxnard and Ventura. Located between Los Angeles and Ventura, the rolling hills, arid grazing pastures, and stands of oak resembled the terrain surrounding Fort Tejon, about fifty miles away, where he had served four years earlier.

Letterman had been named the general superintendent of Philadelphia & California Petroleum. Not far away, Thomas Bard organized oil operations on the Ojai Rancho as general superintendent of California Petroleum. Only twenty-four years of age when he arrived in California, Bard had been a railroad businessman in Pennsylvania where he had met Scott. He had served as a volunteer militiaman at Antietam.

Within a few weeks, an experienced, six-man oil-drilling team arrived from Pennsylvania and joined Letterman. In April, Letterman staked his future on a stretch of level ground, not far from the Santa Clara River. The site lay on an imaginary line between two oil seeps on opposite sides of the river drainage. They were among dozens of seeps on the property, and Letterman began his venture in high spirits. He told a reporter for the *Daily Alta California* newspaper that samples from some of the seeps produced extremely high-quality oil and that Letterman expected to strike an underground river of oil that connected the outflows.[15]

As the days warmed, Letterman first built carpenter and blacksmith shops. Next his crew constructed a thick-timbered derrick fourteen feet square and more than forty feet tall. A boiler assembly followed, to feed a ten-horsepower engine that would drive the derrick's bit into the earth. Crude living conditions at the drilling site forced Letterman's family to reside several miles away in a ranch house. By May 18, Letterman had drilled sixty-five feet in search of California oil.

Letterman had not been forgotten by the army. In April, he had become a founding member of the Military Order of the Loyal Legion of the United States, an association of noted Union army officers established to help preserve the Union in the aftermath of President Lincoln's assassination on April 14. Others included Ulysses S. Grant, Philip Sheridan, and Letterman's friend, George McClellan. The month before, his philosophy of battlefield evacuation and care had been institutionalized by an act of Congress.

Letterman, though, remained intent of finding oil. On July 3, the *Daily Alta California* issued another glowing report as Letterman's well passed 150 feet and had produced "an extraordinary discharge of gas. When we consider that the place selected for this well is nearly two miles distant from any outflow or outcrop of oil, and near the middle of the valley, the fact of striking oil so far from direction indications is of very high importance . . . we may now expect daily to hear that oil has risen to the surface and the well become a flowing one."[16]

Although the public relations campaign in newspapers crafted glowing prospects for the sixty venture companies now exploring for oil in California, a groundswell of skepticism developed. Others who had visited Letterman's operation reported that at 117 feet he had hit a layer of maltha, material nearly as hard as asphalt that made drilling almost impossible.[17] Seismic activity over eons of California history had uplifted and twisted subsurface layers of varying density, which made drilling more difficult than in Pennsylvania and Ohio oil fields.

As Letterman's operation struggled after a few months, it appeared that skeptics of California's oil potential might prevail. For about a year, the California State geologist, Josiah Whitney, and a colleague, William Brewer, had openly disputed Silliman's claims of an untapped California oil bounty. Both had traveled the alleged oil fields and did not believe they held commercially viable oil. Just as Letterman had been getting started in March, Brewer had voiced his concerns publicly when he wrote, "I think that at the present state of our knowledge, good illuminating and lubricating oil cannot be profitably made in California."[18]

Then, in July, the refiner for California Petroleum, Stephen Peckham, joined the ranks of the skeptics after arriving at the Ojai Rancho following his discharge from the army on May 26, 1865. Peckham had studied to become a chemist before serving as a hospital steward in the Civil War. An oil venture in Rhode Island that promptly failed led him to sail for San Francisco to join the oil rush in early July. Neither he nor Letterman could find any oil that approached the quality of oil Silliman said he had collected in California the year before. Although Silliman steadfastly defended his samples and their analysis by citing the work of three independent laboratories, sales of stock in both companies plummeted.[19]

As Letterman's drilling slowly progressed, Mary fell ill. Living conditions in a remote ranch house in the California foothills were rugged at best. Conditions at Letterman's drilling site were worse. What could Letterman do? He had to stay at the site, knowing that his wife and young daughter, miles away, suffered from illness and his absence. Yet duty called. Newspaper reporters frequently rode to the drill site in quest of promising news. His bosses in Philadelphia were anxious for news on progress and prospect. So Letterman made what had to be an agonizing decision. At the end of August he sent Mary and their daughter several miles west to Santa Barbara on the coast. Once again Letterman would have to live apart from the only love of his life. He likely took some comfort knowing that the Santa Barbara climate was much milder than the inland summer heat. Summer temperatures typically climbed at least one degree for every mile inland from the ocean.

Mary said she planned to rejoin Letterman in October where he "is still hard at work boring for Petroleum. I shall be glad to get to my journey's end & to be with my husband, whom I have only been able to see once a fortnight, since I came to Cala. For by necessity (we live) five miles apart. The Ranch on which we are going to live was the first place from which gold was exported, & is still rich in metal, tho' there are not the necessary facilities for washing the ore. The oil is there in great quantities in surface springs, but the boring for a well, is very tedious. It is such a remote spot, they often have to wait a long time for the proper machinery, tools & pipes & the latter have caved in time so that there is full trial of one's faith and patience."[20]

Mary's letters to her brother in Rome revealed Mary had domestic help in her husband's absence, although at times it developed into a source of frustration. She complained of servants who left without notice, noting "one must have some troubles, & while I have a good kind husband, who does every thing on earth to try to make me happy, I am grateful for my blessings." In Letterman's absence, she also took great joy in her daughter. She wrote: "Your little god child grows & thrives, she is a blended likeness of both Parents, but most like her Father in her silent but warm temprament (sic)." She missed her brother, telling him: "I know if anything prevents this (seeing her brother again), you will always take an interest in my little child and pray for her Father's conversion. . . . Cassie sends much love to her Uncle; so would Dr. L if he were here."[21] Although Mary found the summers to be uncomfortably hot and had been disappointed in the roughshod aspects of San Francisco upon arrival in California, she had grown to admire "this wonderful interesting country" surrounding Santa Barbara.[22]

But when she rejoined Letterman inland in late 1865, the prospect of striking oil had dimmed substantially. Letterman's

eight-month career as a wildcatter had resulted in little more
than 700 feet of dry holes. Peckham's attempts on the Ojai
Rancho were similarly unproductive. The proximity of oil
seeps did not become a harbinger of riches within reach of
primitive drilling equipment. "If we strike it, I shall consider it
very much in the same light as I presume the ancient Hebrews
regarded the water which flowed at the touch of Moses' rod,"
he wrote a friend."[23] It appeared increasingly likely that Whitney and Brewer, far more familiar with California geology
than any group of speculators and their experts from the East,
were correct in their pessimistic assessment of California's oil
future.

Letterman was not yet ready to quit, however. With his family now living a few miles away, he decided to try new locations. He drilled a well in Tapo Canyon south of the Santa
Clara River, a flat expanse of barren ground along a seasonal
creek bed, surrounded by ridges. This time he found a very
modest flow of oil at twenty feet. He tried again at the mouth
of Eureka Canyon, less than five miles to the west. Letterman
drilled more than 400 feet. The well produced at most fifteen
gallons of poor-quality oil. Letterman distilled some of it and
sold the kerosene to a Los Angeles merchant. It burned a dim
reddish color, clogged lamp wicks, and produced a sulfur odor.
It, too, bore no resemblance to the oil samples Silliman said he
had collected in 1864.

By this point, Peckham had given up on finding oil on Ojai
Rancho after a number of dry holes. Just one well produced fifteen to twenty barrels a day and became California's first commercially productive well. He resigned and joined Whitney's
geological survey, collecting samples from a number of ranchos
in the area. When he met with Letterman in March 1866, Letterman confirmed he had found no oil that had approached
the Silliman sample quality. Peckham characterized Letterman's

attempts as futile, producing mostly gas and in some cases water high in salt content. He summarized Letterman's conclusion "that if a depth of one thousand feet failed to reach oil, it was of very little use to expect to obtain oil by boring."[24]

Criticism of Silliman's overly enthusiastic view of California petroleum reserves became more widespread. When state geologist Whitney published *Geology, Report of Progress and Synopsis of Field Work, 1860–1864*, he harshly criticized what he considered dishonest speculators who had duped naïve stockholders with false claims of oil quality and quantity. He stopped short of naming names but referred to companies in New York and Philadelphia.

As he concluded what had proved to be a disastrous oil venture, Letterman remained emotionally connected with his previous army life. In 1866, he published *Medical Recollections of the Army of the Potomac*. Like Letterman, the frank, concise, and analytical treatise offered little in terms of his personal feelings. It read more as a post-battle report than a personal diary or memoir that revealed the private man. His preface set the tone.

> The following account of the Medical Department of the Army of the Potomac, has been prepared amidst pressing engagements, in the hope that the labors of the Medical Officers of that Army may be known to an intelligent people, with whom to know is to appreciate; and as an affectionate tribute to the many—long my zealous and efficient colleagues—who, in the days of trial and danger, which have passed, let us hope never to return, evinced their devotion to their country and to the cause of humanity, without hope or promotion, or expectation of reward.
>
> Near San Buenaventura, Cal.
> February 1st, 1866[25]

A few passages, however, revealed insights into Letterman's character and values. His basis for praising the Army of Potomac's assistant medical director, Bennett Augustine Clements, was typical of what he often wrote when lauding other surgeons: "In all my duties I received most valuable assistance from Assistant-Medical Director Clements; his unwearied industry, and unfailing devotion to duty, and his ability, called forth my admiration, while his kindness of heart and refinement of feeling awakened a friendship that can never be broken."[26]

Letterman, in fact, formed some close relationships during his military career. One was with Colonel Benjamin Franklin Davis, who had served with him in California. As the post surgeon and a second lieutenant at the time, respectively, they had accompanied Major James Carleton on his search for restive Indians in the Mojave Desert in 1860. Letterman had treated two of Davis's men who had been shot with arrows. They spent several months together in the desert before returning to Camp Tejon. A year later, they were stationed at Camp Fitzgerald near Los Angeles. Friendships between soldiers stationed together in remote outposts for months at a time grew strong and deep. Their common experience became the foundation for mutual admiration and respect that lasted a lifetime.

In an unusual twist of assignments, the Mississippi-born Davis joined the 8th New York that fought at Antietam and had remained part of the Army of the Potomac. On June 9, 1863, now a colonel and brigade commander, Davis died in fighting at Brandy Station. Three years later, Letterman's recollection of Davis remained painful. "This officer, who so successfully extricated his regiment from Harper's Ferry when that post was surrendered by General Miles—who fought so gallantly on our march through Virginia in the autumn of 1862—had been my companion in more than one campaign among the Indians; my mess-mate at stations far beyond the haunts of civilized men.

This long, familiar intercourse produced the warmest admiration for his noble character, which made him sacrifice friends and relatives to uphold the flag under which he was born, and defend the Constitution of his country"[27]

Periodically, Letterman's frustration surfaced in his *Recollections*. On two occasions he noted General Joseph Hooker had kept much of his medical supplies and ambulances away from the battlefield at Chancellorsville. Without offering a personal perspective, his summation of that battle noted, "I have seen no battle in which the wounded were so well cared for; and had not military necessity deprived us of the use of our ambulance train on the south side of the river, nearly every wounded man could have been comfortably placed in our corps hospitals . . . within twenty-four hours after receipt of his wounds."[28] Later in his *Recollections*, he took direct issue with Hooker on the march toward Gettysburg, when the general reduced medical supplies over Letterman's repeated objections. He called the result "a source of embarrassment and suffering, which might have been avoided."[29]

In three succinct passages, Letterman laid out the core tenets of his military medicine philosophy. Together they formed the foundation that led to the radical overhaul of combat hygiene, diet, battlefield evacuation, and hospital care.

> A corps of Medical officers was not established solely for the purpose of attending the wounded and sick. . . . The leading idea, which should be constantly kept in view, is to strengthen the hands of the Commanding General by keeping his army in the most vigorous health, thus rendering it, in the highest degree, efficient for enduring fatigue and privation, and for fighting.[30]
>
> Without proper means, the Medical Department can no more take care of the wounded than an army can fight a battle without ammunition.[31]

> Even should an army be defeated, it is better to have
> the supplies for proper care and comfort of the wounded
> upon the field, and run the risk of their capture, than that
> the wounded should suffer for want of them. Lost sup-
> plies can be replenished, but lives lost are gone forever.[32]

Dry and almost pedantic, Letterman's publication attracted little notice. Those familiar with Letterman's accomplishments almost sounded disappointed in the brevity of his memoirs. "By reason of native modesty, Dr. Letterman has made his narrative too unassuming; but of one thing he may be assured . . . his claims will never be forgotten by the thousands of sick and wounded who experienced the benefits of the provision inaugurated by him for their care and comfort . . . nor by that large body of civilians who, visiting the army at various times and for different purposes, saw for themselves what he was doing for the welfare of those so unfortunate as to need medical or surgical atten-tion. . . . We regret, however, that the book is no more forcible and striking, as well as more extended, for the material was cer-tainly at hand, and could have been incorporated into the work to make it a standard of authority in all matters pertaining to the care of the sick and wounded," wrote reviewers for the *New York Medical Journal* in September 1866.[33]

Praise for Letterman continued. "From personal observa-tion . . . we unhesitatingly assert to Dr. Letterman . . . more than to any other man, is the army indebted to those radical improvements which brought up the medical department to that thoroughly organized and perfected condition which won so many well deserved encomiums from the military and medi-cal authorities . . . and which enables us to say that never in the whole history of warfare were the sick and wounded so admira-bly and abundantly provided for as in the armies of the United States during the later years of the war of the rebellion."[34]

Letterman probably did not know these reviews would be published in the fall when he met with the principals of Philadelphia & California Petroleum after they had arrived from Philadelphia in spring 1866. They had spent nearly $100,000 in exploratory wells that had not produced commercially viable oil. Highly qualified geologists personally familiar with California natural resources criticized the Silliman samples in scientific journals as possibly fraudulent. It had become clear their investment would not immediately produce a gusher of riches. With limited resources and mounting criticism that diminished stock sales, exploration efforts would have to be reduced.

Letterman's bold dreams had faded to crushing despair. He resigned for the second time in less than two years. A year spent exploring for oil had been a failure. His wife, seven months' pregnant with their second child, and young daughter had endured difficult living conditions and often spent extended periods of time away from him. The Letterman family now lived thousands of miles away from friends and family in Pennsylvania and Maryland. The first documented stock investment in his life had become worthless. His assistant, James DeBarth Shorb, took over the failing operation and wrote that "Letterman . . . trusts we may be successful in obtaining all the damning proofs vs. Sprague."[35]

Meanwhile, Peckham wrote a sobering analysis of his drilling experience on Ojai Rancho. His analysis of the oil seeps marked by desiccated tar-like surface strata revealed "from ten to ninety per cent of grass, leaves, driftwood, and disintegrated soil and rock. . . . I have examined this property with great care, and have been unable to discover petroleum of any description upon it; and all attempts to develop it have thus far failed." Peckham never found the square mile asphaltum that Silliman had described in his evaluation. His largest find was a surface layer a few hundred acres in size at no more than two feet thick.

In July, Peckham quit and booked passage for Providence, Rhode Island, convinced he had become a victim of a scandalous fraud. Letterman abandoned all hope for a career in petroleum and moved his family to San Francisco, the cosmopolitan hub of the West Coast at the time. On July 22, 1866, Ann Madeline was born in San Francisco. Letterman now had a wife who suffered from mysterious ailments and two daughters, an infant and two-year-old, to support. It seemed natural he would return to medicine by establishing his first private medical practice.

As the Lettermans started a new life in San Francisco in the fall, Peckham tested the samples he had collected in California prior to his departure. He was confident the analysis would prove that Silliman's samples had been a fifty-fifty blend of California crude and refined Pennsylvania oil. He spent several months assembling evidence before he felt ready to pit his reputation as a relative newcomer to the oil industry against the national prestige held by Silliman.

Although Peckham had concluded that California oil speculators' "expectations of extraordinary results, that will admit of comparison with those that have been produced in Pennsylvania, must be set aside without the shadow of a hope to rest upon," he did not write off California's oil future. "The expectation of a fair return and a permanently profitable investment may be reasonably entertained; and the application of capital upon this basis to the development of this interest will make it of great importance to the State, and of unequalled importance to that particular section in which the bituminous outcrops occur."[36] That belief was based partially on his laboratory analyses, which had produced a commercially viable kerosene content of 18 percent, compared with Silliman's samples that were 46 percent pure.[37]

In early 1867, Peckham felt ready to publicly contradict Silliman's claim of enormous reserves of California oil waiting to be plumbed. He wrote an article for the *American Journal of Science and Arts*, a preeminent periodical of the American scientific community at the time. Peckham planned an objective analysis of California oil and informed Silliman of his plan, telling him that his article would not amount to an attack against him. Peckham had concluded one or more Californians had tampered with Silliman's samples and that Philadelphia & California Petroleum and California Petroleum stock promoters had either been duped or were parties to the fraud.

His painstaking analysis appeared in the May issue of the *Journal*. It systematically assessed Silliman's samples and conclusions and compared them with the independent analyses of the samples Peckham had collected two years later. It concluded Silliman's samples were not legitimate, but stopped short of naming who he suspected to be the tampering perpetrators. It vindicated California state geologist Whitney's longstanding skepticism and outright criticism of Silliman. The detailed analysis also provided new evidence for a number of disgruntled stockholders, who had already filed lawsuits against Philadelphia & California Petroleum and California Petroleum.

The stockholders had begun filing lawsuits in Philadelphia and New York City three months earlier, seeking damages from what they considered a fraudulent stock offering. Peckham's clinical review not only supported their claim to some degree, it also dealt a new blow to the California oil industry. The oil found to date had been sporadic and of marginal quality. The confirmed reserves fell far short of earlier speculator claims. And that came at a time when increased Pennsylvania production had driven a decline in oil prices of more than 70 percent between 1864 and 1867.[38]

It also spelled the end of Thomas Scott's oil ventures in California. Philadelphia & California Petroleum ceased operations in November 1867, almost a year and a half after California

Petroleum had stopped exploration. Scott's wager on California oil had produced almost no income, national ridicule of his trusted oil consultant, and stockholder lawsuits from coast to coast.

Letterman joined the cast of angry stockholders by filing a lawsuit against Philadelphia & California Petroleum. Of the possible tampering suspects, he believed that Silliman's guide, Thomas Sprague, was the most likely culprit. Sprague was of dubious character and had been desperate to join the California oil bonanza when Silliman visited California. He had finessed his way into a minor partnership position in the Ojai Rancho purchase, probably a welcome relief due to his persistent financial problems. Others, including Scott's California partners and Silliman's laboratory, could have had a hand in the fraud but appear to have had little incentive to do so.[39]

Letterman's role in the venture remained above reproach as the controversy dragged on for years. Whitney and others maintained their public attacks on Silliman's credibility, forcing Silliman to resign one of his Yale professorships, though he remained a medical school professor. They also mounted a campaign to expel Silliman from the National Academy of Sciences, but failed.

Despite his tarnished national reputation, Silliman continued to attract corporate mining speculators. His fees were sometimes based on the amount of minerals he believed a mining claim held, a potential inducement to overestimate reserves, and he continued to overstate various mining propositions. In one case, Senator William Stewart and fellow promoters hired Silliman to write an assessment of the Emma Silver Mine in Alta, Utah. Silliman vastly overstated the ore reserves for a mine that already had played out. His report, along with the endorsement of U.S. ambassador Robert Schenck, induced unsuspecting British investors to buy stock that was nearly worthless.[40]

An 1876 Congressional investigation revealed the swindle. Others received reprimands but were not charged with crimes, but Silliman's reputation did not suffer greatly. Four years later, he became a party to another shady mining venture, this time in New Mexico. He assessed gold ore in Taos and Rio Arriba Counties as equivalent to that discovered in California. Mines in the area never produced substantial quantities of gold and much of it was of marginal quality.

A decade would pass following Letterman's departure from the oil industry before California's oil reserves could be reached and commercialized. By the late 1870s, productive wells near Pico Springs were in operation. Shortly thereafter, major oil production development took place not far from where Letterman and Peckham had searched for oil. One of the earliest oil fields developed by Union Oil was on property once owned by Philadelphia & California Petroleum. By the turn of the century, California had become the nation's largest oil producer.

So it was that Silliman's assessment was ultimately validated long after the Lettermans had moved to San Francisco to begin another new life. After enduring the bloodshed of the Civil War; finding the only love of his life between battles; and embarking on a daring and futile quest in oil exploration, Jonathan Letterman returned to the profession he knew: medicine. The next chapter in his life would be filled with tribute and tragedy.

COMPASSIONATE CORONER

"I have done my duty faithfully."

The face of San Francisco was continuing to change when Letterman returned there with his growing family in 1866. During the war it had developed into the leading port on the West Coast. More than 100 million dollars of gold and silver had been shipped through it. Waves of immigrants, beginning with the Chinese in the 1840s, flooded into an area whose borders were still marked by swamps and tidal inlets. Dirt streets fed paved thoroughfares that carried construction crews bound for waterfront dredging and fill projects to create more usable land and to control tidal flows. San Francisco was transforming itself from an isolated boomtown to a cosmopolitan city.

The city was filled with optimism. Its leaders believed the postwar years would be an era of accelerating prosperity. Agriculture had expanded and prospered during the Civil War, while mining appeared to be a permanent cornerstone of the economy. The year the Letterman family arrived, the city government took control of the wharf from private operators. Soon construction crews leveled a hill on Rincon Point to create 300,000 cubic yards of material to fill in the bay in order to create more developable land and municipally controlled shipping facilities.

The city bought and annexed large tracts of land after ownership disputes were resolved in court. Homes were bought and razed so primary avenues could be widened to accommodate a vibrant commercial district near the waterfront. The bay had become congested with steamer traffic, carrying passengers and freight bound for the East Coast and international destinations such as Panama and China.[1]

Exports had doubled the previous two years. Manufactured goods and agricultural products now exceeded gold production. Major construction projects included a mile-long bridge to expand the metropolitan area and a new seawall at a cost of $1.5 million per mile.[2] The prospect of a transcontinental railroad reaching the West Coast spawned rampant real estate speculation.

In the first year following the Civil War, suffrage for African Americans was a dominant national issue as Congress adopted the second of two constitutional amendments, subject to states' ratification. The Thirteenth Amendment was passed in January 1865, three months before Lee's surrender, and banished involuntary servitude. The Fourteenth, passed in June 1866, granted citizenship to all persons who were born or naturalized in the United States, and prohibited states from abridging citizens' life, liberty, or property ownership without due process.

In San Francisco, however, the paramount post–Civil War issue wasn't the freedom of former slaves. It was how to control thousands of Chinese immigrants, many of whom had come to California to work on the transcontinental railroad in the Sierras. As the railroad neared completion, newly unemployed Chinese swamped the city in the latter 1860s. Enormous anti-Chinese sentiment simmered there while the rest of the nation coped with newly emancipated slaves.

The Anti-Coolie Association, the city's Democratic power structure, and labor unions coalesced out of commonly held fears that the Chinese would take low-paying jobs away from Caucasians and somehow take control of the city. Hysterical claims of the impending degradation of the white race by hordes of Chinese immigrants surfaced in local newspapers. So, optimism contended with divisiveness when the Lettermans arrived. No longer an isolated outpost populated by miners and traders, it struggled with rapid expansion. During this decade, the city's population would skyrocket from 58,800 in 1860 to nearly 150,000, making it the tenth largest city in the nation by 1870.[3]

A stranger to the city, Letterman established a medical practice in the latter half of 1866. Of course, he was far from an anonymous doctor looking to practice medicine in an emerging West Coast city. Two years earlier, he had been highly praised in Washington when Congress institutionalized his philosophy of battlefield evacuation. Reviews of his *Recollections* began to be published in national medical journals and regional newspapers.

He discovered former war colleagues had moved or been transferred to San Francisco, including the former general in chief, Henry Halleck. Halleck had fallen out of favor late in the Civil War and effectively had been exiled to the command of the Division of the Pacific on the West Coast. Although Letterman was a Democrat like McClellan, Halleck's distaste for McClellan did not extend to Letterman.

In the months leading up to his family's move to San Francisco, Letterman's oil exploration efforts had been the subject of regular updates in San Francisco newspapers, reports that usually characterized him as a medical pioneer in the Civil War.

About a year after arriving in San Francisco, Jonathan Letterman decided to reenter public service, this time out of uniform. He sought elective office for the first time in his life when he agreed to run for coroner on the Democratic Party ticket. A man whose intellect ruled his life and who carefully corralled his passions, he might have seemed least likely to be an inspiring candidate. His demeanor was quiet and reserved to the point of aloofness, hardly the stuff of politics. But to fill their San Francisco slate, the Democrats needed a candidate for coroner, whose job was to investigate the causes and manner of death, particularly those of suspicious, unexplained, or violent origin. In Letterman they had a medical professional whose qualifications were beyond question. Their candidate carried a distinguished national reputation as a dedicated and honest medical practitioner and innovative administrator. This was an era in which the electorate typically voted for party slates of candidates, and those at the nonpolitical local level—coroner, harbor master, surveyor, justices of the peace, for example—were not expected to be ideologues.

Letterman made his decision at a time when local politics had grown especially heated and hateful. The Democratic Party was locked in a battle with the Union Party for control of San Francisco and the state of California, where it had wielded power prior to the Civil War and looked to regain it. The Union Party, comprised of Republicans and Union Democrats, sought to retain the political control it had held during the war.

The Democratic Party slate that Letterman joined was headed by Henry H. Haight, a prominent San Francisco attorney, as their candidate for governor. The former state Republican Party chairman in the late 1850s, Haight had become a Union Democrat during the Civil War when he disagreed with some of Lincoln's administrative policies. Previously, he edited a "free soil" newspaper in Missouri and was devoutly religious. He agreed to run as the Democratic Party candidate whose platform emphasized economic development, ethnic purity, and reform.

Letterman had agreed to run for office on behalf of a political party whose platform included a resolution stating: "[W]e believe it impracticable to maintain republican institutions based on the suffrages of the African Americans, Chinese, and Indians, and that the doctrines avowed by the radical leaders of indiscriminate suffrage, regardless of race, color, or qualification, if carried into practice, would end in the degradation of the white race and the speedy destruction of the government."[4] However, Letterman had served in an army dedicated to preserving the Union and ending slavery, and there is no evidence he supported the Democrats' strident and overt racism.

His Union Party opponent was incumbent coroner Stephen Randall Harris, a former mayor of San Francisco in the early 1850s who had returned to politics in 1864. An ambitious reporter new to San Francisco, Samuel Clemens, lobbied for his appointment as coroner to complete the term of his predecessor, who had died in office. In 1865, voters then elected Harris to the post. At the head of the Union slate was George Gorham, as its candidate for governor. Although his party was stalwartly anti-Chinese, Gorham took a pragmatic approach to the issue. He foresaw a future of economic trade with China and noted at the state party convention: "[L]et me suggest that the Chinese now in our midst and those who may come hereafter, must either work, steal, beg or starve. It would be difficult to make an argument to show that the creation of so large a number of street beggars, or of thieves, would be compensated by the fact that none but men of the European race were permitted to earn a livelihood in California. As to starvation, the mere word makes me shudder. So, after all, if we would not have the Chinaman steal, beg, or starve, he must be allowed to work."[5]

On September 4, 1867, voters carried the Democrats and with them Letterman into office on largely white supremacy sentiment. Letterman received 10,509 votes to 7,000 for Harris. Only the county clerk and surveyor's local races produced a wider margin of victory.[6] Mary appeared pleased with the result when she wrote her father, "Dr. Letterman has made his debut in politics and was elected coroner. . . . He found many influential friends in all parties and got many Republican votes. General Halleck was especially kind and is very influential here. The Democrats are encouraged with their victory and a prominent Republican admits 'it was a first.'"[7]

As Letterman prepared to take office six weeks later, on Sunday, October 27, Mary rose early and dressed for a 9:00 a.m. Catholic mass service. Letterman was long accustomed to Mary's devotion to her faith and likely anticipated a routine Sunday morning in the Letterman household. With no warning, convulsive pain erupted from deep within Mary's stomach. She reflexively vomited and crumpled to the floor. Severe cramps and diarrhea followed, leading Letterman to think cholera had struck her. Acute gastroenteritis became more prevalent in San Francisco during the summer and fall, usually due to contaminated food or water, and residents frequently called it "summer's complaint." Typical treatments at the time were laxatives, calomel, and natural diuretics such as smartweed.

They failed to ease Mary's pain as convulsions gripped her body. Concern changed to worry as Letterman sent for two friends, one of whom was a doctor. They, too, grew alarmed and one, prominent undertaker Atkins Massey, spent the night with the Lettermans.[8] It became a night of unbearable agony as Mary suffered. After the vomiting subsided in the early hours of October 28, Jonathan saw clouds of pallid death spread across her face. His wife of four years faded with each passing hour. Mary spoke little at the end, only saying she was prepared to die if it was God's will, and asked Jonathan to raise their small daughters, one-year-old Ann Madeline and three-year-old Mary Catherine, as Catholics. She also asked that if Letterman remarried, it would be to a Catholic.

At 3:00 a.m. on Monday morning Mary died, eleven days after her thirty-fourth birthday. After being responsible for more than 100,000 sick and wounded soldiers, Jonathan Letterman had misdiagnosed his wife's condition. As he treated her for cholera, she slowly bled to death internally. An autopsy the following day revealed a decayed blood vessel near her womb. Letterman buried his wife on October 29 at Lone Mountain Cemetery, a graveyard atop a five-hundred-foot hill in western San Francisco.[9]

In three weeks Letterman would become coroner. The father of two young girls faced a life of practicing medicine during the day and holding coroner's inquests at night. There were no relatives nearby to take care of his daughters. His widowed mother, Anna, was sixty-seven years old. His brother William also was a doctor who had served in the Civil War as a contract surgeon. Now thirty-five years of age, unmarried, and in private medical practice in Baltimore, William was developing a second career as a coal geologist and West Virginia land acquisition agent for firms in Boston, Baltimore, and New York. His other brother, Craig, was an unmarried farmer in Duffau, Texas. Neither were candidates to replace a lost mother.

Letterman turned to his wife's family, the only relatives he knew who had the ability to care for his daughters. Mary's brother, Charles Carroll Lee, was a doctor who had served as an assistant surgeon in the Union regular army in the Civil War. Lee had taken Letterman to the Needwood family home in 1863, where Letterman met his future wife. Charles and his wife, Helen, had moved to New York City in 1867 and had a two-year-old daughter, Sarah. Mary had been close to Charles, and it seemed natural that Jonathan would turn to his brother-in-law, a man he knew well and who had substantial family resources. Cassie and Madeline would be raised by the Lee family in privileged surroundings.

A devastated and lonely Jonathan Letterman took office in November 1867. Just as he had done in the army, he had to separate anguish from duty. The local government provided neither a dedicated office nor a morgue for the city coroner. He practiced medicine during the day and remained on call when a body was discovered in suspicious or unexplained circumstances. Letterman also was responsible for determining the cause and manner of death in cases in which a doctor had not been present. He had the authority to hold inquests in which a jury was impaneled and testimony given, resulting in a verdict that could assign responsibility and influence how a deceased's property was handled. Letterman also was responsible for identifying unknown bodies and making burial arrangements for the unclaimed. With minimal local government resources at his disposal, he asked for favors from Massey and other undertakers when he needed to hold a body pending an autopsy, an inquest, or identification. A veteran of battlefield improvisation, Letterman improvised as coroner.

Night inquests were common, often two in a single evening and frequently attended by newspaper reporters. Most were straightforward and reflected the common lives and tribulations of local residents, and the jury rendered prompt rulings upon evidence presented by Letterman and eyewitness testimony. The following newspaper account, from Letterman's second term as coroner, gives a typical account of the proceedings.

> Coroner Letterman held two inquests last evening. In the case of Elbert Brandt, Otto Johnson, local police officer, testified he heard the report of a pistol, and on the southwest corner of Taylor and Lombard Streets found the deceased lying on the sidewalk, shot through the head and holding a pistol in his right hand. He lived but a few minutes.
>
> Henry Lot testified that he was walking on Taylor Street, between Greenwich and Lombard Streets, about

nine o'clock in the evening, with a girl whom Brandt was courting, when they met him and walking along together. Brandt asked the girl why she did not talk to him, but she made no reply. He then told her that that was perhaps the last time she would see him alive. I told him he must not talk that way; if the girl did not like him he should do no such thing. He said he was crazy to-night, but would not be to-morrow. We then separated and that was the last time I saw him.

VERDICT: The Jury found that Elbert Brand was a native of Germany, aged 27 years, and came to his death from suicide, by shooting himself through the head with a pistol, on or about June 6th, 1871.

In the case of Murray Mitchell, the Jury found that he was a native of Scotland, aged 60 years, and that he came to his death from suicide, by cutting his throat with a razor and jumping into a well, on or about the 29th of May, 1871.[10]

Profound depression and a chronic stomach ailment made his new career more challenging. He had lost his wife and had sent his children to distant relatives with minimal prospects of seeing them in the near future. Persistent dysentery, the signature ailment of Civil War veterans, sapped his energy and potentially could become life threatening. Nearly 300,000 Union army soldiers had suffered from acute and chronic dysentery in the Civil War.[11] Legions of veterans like Letterman faced physical and emotional problems in the years following the war. One postwar study revealed that nearly four in ten Civil War veterans suffered both physical and mental issues. Nearly one in five had heart ailments.[12]

Within a year of being elected, Letterman assumed additional responsibilities. In November 1868, Governor Haight appointed Letterman surgeon general of California's militia, with the rank of colonel. The militia had been reorganized by California's legislature two years earlier to become the state's national guard. Staff organization, training requirements, and equipment and arms provisions were codified. A more formal state military structure required a medical professional to oversee military medical aspects of a new militia. No one in California was better qualified for the position than Letterman.

As Letterman neared the end of his first two-year term, he issued a report to the Board of Supervisors that demonstrated he had developed a remarkably accurate view of his adopted city. He estimated the city population at 150,000 a few hundred more than what the U.S. Census Bureau would give as the city's population less than a year later. His report revealed Letterman's shock at the living conditions of many of those residents, perhaps reminiscent of the squalid army camps he encountered when he took medical charge of the Army of the Potomac.

"Cases have come before me where suicides have been committed (and by men of cultivated intellect), for want of means to procure something to eat. They have been unfortunate . . . too proud to beg, too honest to steal, and prefer to die than do either. These are the persons whose wants should be supplied, and in the vast majority of cases all they ask for is 'work'." He was more distressed by the plight of many Chinese, the community that the Democrats had reviled in their successful quest to win the 1867 election.

"I beg to call your attention to these (Chinese) people . . . it is well worthy of your serious consideration, not only from the filthy condition in which they live, the neglect they undergo from their own people when they are sick and can no longer work, but because they are accumulating in our Almshouses and Lunatic Asylums. While they are able to work they are looked after by the companies which have imported them, but when they become sick, imbecile or dangerously insane, they are left to themselves to lie on a piece of matting and die, or discarded by their own countrymen, taken up by the authorities and sent to the Almshouse or Lunatic Asylum. The companies who bring these people here should be compelled to take care of them when they are unable to take care of themselves."[13]

Letterman's lack of resources had become tiresome for a man who had fought similar battles of professional poverty in the Civil War. "In a city like this, with people from all parts of the world, a great deal of labor devolves upon a Coroner . . . cases involving life depend upon his investigations; and yet he has no office, but must depend upon his own resources and rely on the courtesy of an undertaker to furnish a morgue, or dead-house. A cosmopolitan city like this should have a morgue, where bodies can be preserved (which the ends of justice often require), or until they can be recognized, and where the Coroner can have proper facilities for discharging the important duties devolving upon him."[14]

Anonymous deaths ate at Letterman, perhaps due to his war experience where untold numbers of soldiers—the sons, brothers, and fathers of families afar—were destroyed beyond recognition, never to be individually honored or returned to their shattered families. His report to the supervisors twice sought resources to enable more frequent identification of bodies. A morgue where bodies could be stored would give him more time to identify them. "There is in my mind something exceedingly repugnant in directing a body to be interred and 'unknown' marked upon the grave; and yet under the existing state of things in this city, many persons must be thus buried." Letterman could do nothing in cases of drowning. "No provision is made for the recovery of persons who have been drowned, the Coroner not having the authority to offer a reward for their recovery, or when found to pay the expenses of bringing them ashore. This is all wrong."[15]

Letterman's advocacy was based on the first 443 cases that came to his attention. One-fourth of them resulted in inquests. Overall, about three in four deaths were nonviolent. The most common causes were an embolism, pneumonia, smallpox, apoplexy, and malnutrition. San Francisco was relatively nonviolent at the time. Letterman listed eleven murders in his first two years in office, compared with thirty-nine cases of suicide.

He decided to run for reelection in 1869, when the election at the state level would be less contentious than in 1867, but nonetheless would focus on emancipation and the Fifteenth Amendment. The Thirteenth and Fourteen Amendments had been ratified by the states in 1865 and 1868, respectively. Congress passed the Fifteenth, guaranteeing the right of all U.S. citizens to vote without abridgement based on race or color, on February 26, 1869. Its ratification by the states was considered inevitable but seen by some in California as another challenge to controlling the state's Chinese immigrants. The amendment prohibited states from denying or limiting all citizens' right to vote.

Again, both major political parties in the state adopted strident anti-Chinese planks in their 1869 election platforms. They equated constitutionally mandated African American suffrage with potential Chinese naturalization and access to the right to vote. Many political leaders considered the latter a far greater threat to California society. The Chinese, claimed both parties, were at the root of most of what ailed California. Letterman's party promised to oppose ratification of the Fifteenth Amendment, and took the line that electing Democrats was taking a symbolic stand against Chinese naturalization.

In early 1869, another party took shape, the Taxpayers Union Party, which railed against government mismanagement, extravagance, and dependence upon the two-party system. The slate of candidates it formed for San Francisco offices included

Dr. P. W. Randle, who would run against Letterman for coroner in the fall. Randle was relatively unknown, having served in the 1st California Volunteers as an assistant surgeon in the early days of the Civil War. On September 1, the politics of prejudice prevailed in another Democratic Party victory. Though Letterman's margin of victory was slimmer than it had been in 1867, he received 54 percent of the votes to Randle's 46 percent. At the state level, voters returned Governor Haight to office. The Democrats retained control in San Francisco and Sacramento.

In early 1870, Letterman's health became a more significant issue. In April 1870, newspapers reported he had suffered a broken leg and was confined to his room. The veteran who had escaped the Civil War unscathed had fractured his femur above the knee on February 21, when he was thrown to the pavement while stepping out of a carriage. Complications ensued, including bleeding in his lungs. He didn't return to work until July 21, five months later.[16] But his declining health could not diminish his reputation or weaken his credentials. In November, the University of California regents established a board of medical examiners to screen students applying to medical school. Letterman, who had spent much of his professional life examining and evaluating military doctors, was elected to the board. The year ended on a sad note when Letterman's mother, Anna, fell ill on Christmas Eve and three days later died at seventy years of age.

By 1871, the political and economic climate in San Francisco had shifted. The transcontinental railroad had reached Sacramento, and railroads from Vallejo and Oakland on the east side of the bay to Sacramento had been completed. These new lines drained much of the economic activity away from San Francisco, perched as it was at the end of a peninsula on the west side of the bay. Mining, manufacturing, and agricultural exports now headed east on the railroads instead of being shipped out of San Francisco's port. When the impact of the transcontinental railroad became evident, a real estate bubble created by wild speculation on the prospects of finding mother lodes of mineral wealth burst. Those who borrowed heavily to purchase over-priced real estate lost their property. Some banks failed. Residents who had invested in mining stocks suffered too. The great tide of gold and silver that had carried San Francisco for years evaporated. The city's electorate was in the mood for change.

Letterman again ran for reelection, but the political pendulum had begun to swing against the Democrats. In San Francisco, the Democrat incumbents faced opposition by both the Taxpayers Union and by the Republican Party, two groups that had joined forces in some years and then split in others. In 1871, the Republican candidate for coroner, Dr. W. N. Griswold, withdrew on September 5, throwing his support to Taxpayer candidate J. D. B. Stillman. The Taxpayers Union mounted a vociferous campaign, advocating the abolishment of special-interest commissions.

Along with other Democratic Party candidates, Letterman was turned aside by the voters. His margin of victory in 1869 was reversed in 1871, when he lost to Stillman by a 54 percent to 46 percent margin. Democrats also lost at the state level, when challenger Newton Booth defeated Governor Haight. Letterman resigned his post as California's surgeon general when Booth took office on December 8.

Four days earlier, his term as San Francisco coroner had expired. Letterman turned over the coroner's office on Market Street that he had been authorized to establish by the County Supervisors eight months earlier, in April. His annual workload as coroner had grown to 660 cases in one year, compared with 443 cases the previous two years.[17] After four years, and in the span of one week, Jonathan Letterman's political career ended, and for the most part his career in public service ended. Beginning in 1849, he had spent nineteen of the ensuing twenty-two years as a surgeon, serving either in the army or the city of San Francisco.

Letterman faced an uncertain and empty future in 1872. Service in the army had become a distant memory, as had the time he had spent with his wife. His daughters lived on the East Coast. A few military and medical friends, a small medical practice, and failing health became his universe. He continued to serve in one state-appointed post, as a Commissioner of Lunacy. The commission inspected the state's asylums at a time when twice as many Californians were institutionalized as the national average. Overcrowding was common, according to those who inspected them. "Two of these wards, the second and tenth, intended for thirty patients each, now have about eighty each. These wards are poorly ventilated, low, and uncomfortable in the extreme, and should be erased from the face of the earth and the memory of man. They never were fit receptacles for any human being, and have been tolerated altogether too long." California asylums were utilized to treat the insane as well as for detention of the destitute.[18]

After retiring from public service in late 1871, Jonathan Letterman became critically ill on March 13, 1872. He was visited by Dr. S. A. Ferris and then continued to see patients the following two days. But on March 15 he collapsed and was taken to St. Mary's Hospital. He died later the same day. He was forty-seven years old. Most contemporary newspaper reports indicated Letterman had been in poor health, with what was usually described as a stomach ailment or gastroenteritis. Both were frequent descriptions of chronic dysentery.

Perhaps out of respect for Letterman's wife, his funeral was held in St. Mary's Cathedral near Chinatown, a few blocks inland from the waterfront. A soft breeze floated up from the bay, breaking a days-long hot spell. The towering church had been built twenty-seven years earlier with granite imported from China, New England-minted bricks, local sandstone, and an altar imported from Rome. It was the first cathedral in California. For Letterman's funeral, the church was filled with civic leaders and members of the California military, according to newspaper reports. Jonathan Letterman was buried next to his wife.[19]

Within days of his death, medical and military associations across the country issued proclamations. The California National Guard passed a resolution that summarized Letterman's legacy: "[W]hile in his death the medical profession loses one of its brightest intellects, his life has not been unfruitful of most important results, our late civil war having afforded the opportunity for the exercise of that rare administrative ability which organized and perfected the ambulance system of the Army of the Potomac, a system deemed worthy of adoption in the armies of Europe, and by which it is believed that the unavoidable concomitant horrors of war are greatly ameliorated."[20]

Some of the most passionate tributes came from military officers who had known Letterman early in their careers. In this encomium quoted earlier, W. W. Loring, who had commanded Letterman at Fort Union, New Mexico, wrote: "I never knew an officer who was all the time more ready to render timely aid to the suffering, whether at the summons of an officer or the call of the private soldier. . . . Socially he was modest and retiring, gentle, almost childlike in his character. No one who had the pleasure of knowing him but formed a very high estimate of his ability, and of his varied experience. . . . From my close intimacy with him, I became aware that he was an ardent student, and no man in his corps sought more earnestly to attain the highest knowledge in the scientific advancement of his profession."[21]

Bennett Clements, one of Letterman's medical inspectors who rose to become his assistant medical director, wrote a warm-hearted memoir of him more than a decade after Letterman died. Its detail and tone indicate Clements and Letterman had forged a friendship beyond their association as medical officers. "The writer of this paper, though honored with the friendship of Dr. Letterman, and intimately associated with him in his administration of the Medical Department of the Army of the Potomac, would gladly have left to abler hands the grateful task of endeavoring the rescue from oblivion the record of his able, faithful, and useful services. But there seemed to be no other one to render to his memory this last office of justice and of friendship; and he presents this memoir, however inadequate it may be, to the Army, to the Medical Profession, and especially to the surviving Medical Officers of the Army of the Potomac, as a tribute due to the memory of a most faithful officer, who devoted his great talents and all his energy to the welfare of the men of that Army, and to the honor of his profession and of his corps."[22]

By the time Letterman died, the army's medical department bore little resemblance to the massive organization it had become during the Civil War. As the army demobilized following the war, the medical department withered as well. The 65,000 army patients of June 1865 had dwindled to less than 100 the following year. While the army disbanded the ambulance corps, the government sold surplus hospitals, supply depots, and transports. The medical corps similarly shrank to less than 200 officers responsible for nearly 300 garrisons spread across the country as the Indian War era loomed.[23]

The army recast the medical department to its earlier military-outpost-medicine structure, which Letterman had encountered twenty-three years earlier when he had entered military service. Renewed shortages of medical officers forced the department to rely on contract civilian surgeons to augment the regular army medical corps. Yet some key aspects of military medicine had been fundamentally changed by the wartime experience.

Letterman's mentor, Surgeon General William Hammond, had laid the groundwork for what would become the nation's foremost medical library. He bought medical books and journals for the surgeon general's library and made sure each regimental surgeon received five of what Hammond considered the most relevant medical texts. In 1864, one of Letterman's surgeons, John Shaw Billings, had been assigned to the surgeon general's office, in part to manage a library collection that had grown to more than 2,000 books and periodicals by the close of the war.

The collection, together with volumes of wartime surgeon and medical officer reports— including those written by Letterman—was critical to another landmark initiative. Hammond's successor, Joseph K. Barnes, assigned medical officers to compile a comprehensive *Medical and Surgical History of the War of the Rebellion*. When the first two of six volumes had been published in 1870, they were based on the medical records of more than 200,000 wounded army patients, and relied on much of the library's 10,000 volumes of reference material.[24]

Jonathan Letterman's daughters, Cassie and Madeline, never returned to San Francisco. Charles Carroll Lee raised his two nieces along with three daughters and two sons in New York City. He rose to prominence as a gynecologist, ultimately serving as the president of the Medical Society of the County of New York. It was a privileged life, in which Letterman's daughters became young women who mingled with New York City's most prominent citizens.

In 1906, Cassie moved her parents' bodies to Section C in Arlington National Cemetery. The text at the base of her father's tombstone, a tall white cross, is as concise as Letterman was direct. "Jonathan Letterman. Who brought order and efficiency to the medical service and was the originator of modern methods of medical organization in the armies." Mary Letterman lies interred next to Jonathan. Her tombstone reads, "Blessed are the dead who died in the Lord." They lie along a ridge overlooking Washington, DC, the city he helped protect more than forty years earlier.

Cassie Letterman achieved a fleeting degree of notoriety in the early 1900s, when she became the social secretary for Helen "Nattie" Taft, the wife of President William Taft, in 1910. Nattie had suffered a stroke in 1909 and temporarily lost her ability to speak. Cassie Letterman, Nattie's daughter, and three sisters managed the First Lady's affairs until she regained some degree of speech by 1911. In a White House era of formality, musicals, formal dinners, and garden parties, Cassie became known as "Washington's 'Chatty Knollys,'" a reference to England's Queen Alexandra's personal assistant, Charlotte Knollys, widely known as "Chatty."[25]

When the Taft presidential term ended in 1913, Cassie became director of the American Women's Club in Berlin. Neither daughter developed a public profile following that posting, and they appeared to remain close throughout their lives. Madeline spent much of her life in Europe. Public records indicate the sisters were residents of New Mexico shortly after World War II and spent the remainder of their lives in the Albuquerque area. In 1957, both were hospitalized at Presbyterian Hospital. Neither left the hospital. Cassie died on October 14, and her sister followed on December 15.[26]

Letterman, however, had not been forgotten by the American military. During the Civil War, his bold reorganization prior to Antietam had quickly earned praise ranging from the surgeons at aid stations to Washington politicians. "You can't imagine how deeply we all are indebted to Letterman for telling us what to do, and showing us how to do it," volunteer surgeon Sam Holman told Letterman's assistant medical director and memoirist, Bennett Clements. Within months of taking medical command of the Army of the Potomac, the nation's military medical corps recognized the ramifications of his administrative genius. "How thoroughly Dr. Letterman performs his duties, may be in part judged from the important orders emanating from him. . . . His reorganization of the field hospital and ambulance corps is a signal proof of his ability and fitness to credibly fill his position. . . . In a quiet, unobtrusive way, with that modesty that is indicative of true greatness, Dr. Letterman has done, and is doing much to place the medical department of the Army of the Potomac on a footing that will challenge the admiration of the country. In this important work he has the countenance and hearty co-operation of the energetic surgeon-general. We trust that through their influence Congress will remove the clogs that prevent the medical department of our army from accomplishing all the good that it is capable of," wrote a reporter for the *Medical and Surgical Reporter*.[27]

That respect extended well into the next century. In 1911, the War Department renamed a 300-bed San Francisco military hospital Letterman General Hospital. The pavilion-style hospital, remarkably similar to the design Letterman helped establish with Surgeon General William Hammond in the Civil War, had been built from 1899 to 1902 to treat Spanish-American War troops. Seven years later, the Board of Regents of the Smithsonian Institution wrote in its annual report, "The name of Jonathan Letterman should always be remembered by military surgeons as the greatest sanitary organizer of modern times."

In World War II, fluid battle lines, amphibious assaults, and troop movements across continents placed a premium on mobile

and well-organized combat medical care. Despite the mechani-
zation of the army that had first taken place in World War I, the
fundamental principles forged by Letterman remained as valid
as when they had been pioneered decades earlier. The nation
took notice. In June 1943, nearly on the eightieth anniversary
of Gettysburg, American troops prepared to invade Sicily. In the
eighteen months America had been at war, Letterman's accomplishments once again had become evident. "Jonathan Letterman, medical director of the Army of the Potomac ... could not
tell surgeons to beware of bacteria, because Pasteur and Koch
had still to do their great work and Lister had not yet shown the
importance of asepsis. But Letterman could reorganize the medical services of the army and reorganize them he did. Four days
before Antietam he collected supplies and thirty ambulances, so
that he was able to move 10,000 to shelters within twenty-four
hours. He made military history. Every army in the world profited by his example," wrote a *New York Times* reporter.[28]

As chief surgeon for the European Theater of Operations
and later medical chief of the Veterans Administration, Major
General Paul R. Hawley, grew passionate about Letterman's
contributions. "Compared with what Letterman did for the
wounded soldier, the contributions of Florence Nightingale
seemed small," he said following World War II. "There is not a
day during World War II that I did not thank God for Jonathan
Letterman. He was truly a surgeon for the soldiers."[29]

12

AN ENDURING LEGACY

"War is a terrible thing at best."

Over the course of eight generations, more than 40 million Americans have served in times of crises and conflict. Nearly 1.5 million have survived wounds received on the battlefield. "War is a terrible thing at best; and all the horrible things you read of it are inseparable from it," wrote surgeon J. Franklin Dyer of the 19th Massachusetts Regiment on July 17, 1863, two weeks after Gettysburg.[1] Yet it is also true that through the horrors of the battlefield, military medicine has validated and sometimes pioneered advances in medicine.

War strategist Karl von Clausewitz wrote that organization is fundamental to the order of battle. Military organization takes time to develop, but in most of the wars America has entered, the military medical department has been undermanned, outdated, poorly equipped, and unprepared. In each new generation of war, it has fallen to a relatively small number of innovative thinkers to manage human carnage of an unimagined scale, and in the Civil War the task fell to William Hammond and Jonathan Letterman.

Horrific suffering by the wounded and dying may have been inevitable, but the chaotic, poorly organized battlefield evacuation and inadequately coordinated post-battle care that exacerbated and cruelly prolonged it could not be allowed to continue. Letterman responded to what he saw as a doctor devoted to the compassionate care of the sick and wounded. He also was motivated to arm his commanding officer with a healthy and sound fighting force that could contribute to a more prompt end to the war. In eighteen months, the introspective and unassuming doctor from Pennsylvania forged a legacy through his exceptional organizational ability, which enabled him to recast the military's medical corps into a professional, recognized, and accountable entity essential to battlefield victory.

On July 4, 1862, it fell to Letterman to create order out of chaos in the face of a diseased and dispirited Army of the Potomac. Following the failed Peninsula Campaign, more than one in three soldiers in the staggered army were ill. The chaotic river of wounded, sick, and cowardly to hospitals far from the battlefield threatened the fighting force from the rear. Letterman discovered one-fifth of the soldiers who had retreated to hospitals at Fortress Monroe were fit for duty.[2] He realized he had to focus first on the health of his army in camp, long before it met the enemy on the battlefield. Within three weeks of his arrival Letterman rewrote the standards of military camp hygiene; living conditions; diet; and the process of authorizing transfer to hospitals in the rear; and he delineated who would be held accountable for enforcement. The benefits of Letterman's approach to preventive medicine appeared quickly. Within a month, the sickness rate in the Army of the Potomac decreased to 20 percent.

He described the results as follows: "It is impossible to convey in writing to any one not mingling with the troops a true idea of the improvement which took place in the health of the troops while we were encamped at that place . . . there are many ways in which improved health manifests itself that cannot be adequately described. There was so much in the appearance, in the life and vivacity exhibited by the men in the slightest actions, even in the tone of the voice, which conveyed to one's mind the impression of health and spirits, of recovered tenacity of mind and body, of the presence of vigorous and manly courage, an impression which to be understood must be felt—it cannot be told."[3]

Letterman stood in a unique position to improve the health, morale, and fighting strength of the army. Every soldier wants to be fed well and know that he will be taken care of if he falls wounded on the battlefield. Letterman turned his attention to the latter. Within a month of taking medical command, he rewrote battlefield evacuation. He codified a system establishing a dedicated ambulance corps that included a leadership structure, command responsibilities, organization on the march, and supply. The ambulance corps he created became a strategic element of the army, not a tactical afterthought.

But the wounded could only be cared for by well-supplied medical officers. Both the availability of medical supplies and wagons to carry them must be organized, and officers had to be accountable for both. Letterman knew that stacks of supplies without adequate transportation "were lost, and in various ways wasted; and not unfrequently all the supplies of a regiment were thrown away by commanding officers, almost in sight of the enemy, that the wagons might be used for other purposes."[4] After his first battle at Antietam, Letterman rewrote medical supply requirements, mandating that medical officers have fewer supplies on hand but were authorized to order resupply more efficiently. This just-in-time inventory management reduced waste and made his army's medical facilities more mobile.

A few weeks later, in October 1862, Letterman completed his overhaul of battlefield medicine by recasting the military hospital system. He established field hospitals at the division level close to the battlefield. Now his stretcher bearers could evacuate the wounded to aid stations on the battlefield, knowing an organized ambulance corps could transport them from there to field hospitals not far away. This missing link, between aid stations and general hospitals far to the rear, proved critical to battlefield survivability. Ambulances could make regular runs between aid stations where the wounded had been collected and division hospitals, rather than scavenge the battlefield for survivors. The field hospitals' effectiveness improved significantly when Letterman's system also established organizational structure by assigning doctors to specific duties such as triage, surgery, administration, and supply.

In less than four months, Jonathan Letterman had eliminated much of the anarchy of getting the wounded off the battlefield. He had organized a system of tiered hospital care, from the aid station to the general hospital in a large city many miles away. He had made sure medical supplies could be reliably procured at each stage of the process and had established a measure of independence and control of transport between each level of care. He had organized and professionalized a medical corps that some commanding officers deemed a necessary evil by creating a corps that directly improved those officers' ability to defeat the enemy.

As one measure of his system, 37 percent of the Army of the Potomac was unable to report for duty in July 1862, due to sickness, but a year later only 9 percent were sick. Similarly, the mortality rate of wounds dropped from 26 percent the first year to 15 percent and then 10 percent the next two years.[5]

The role of General McClellan and Surgeon General Hammond in Letterman's overhaul cannot be overstated. McClellan and Letterman became more than senior officers and colleagues. Letterman earned McClellan's strong backing within weeks of joining the Army of the Potomac and developed a friendship that extended beyond their time together in Virginia, Maryland,

and Pennsylvania. He also had a staunch ally in Hammond. They shared an analytic approach to medicine as well as a propensity to question and challenge established procedures and protocols. The support from McClellan and Hammond enabled Letterman to reorganize care on perhaps the most scrutinized battlefield of the Civil War, the region mostly spanning Maryland and Virginia between Washington and the Confederate capital, Richmond, less than one hundred miles away. In the aftermath of battle, newspaper reporters, humanitarian commission representatives, politicians, and President Lincoln himself visited where the two armies, often with a combined fighting strength of 175,000 men, had collided.

Letterman's work also came in the midst of ongoing political intrigue and Machiavellian plots at the highest levels of the Union army. In eighteen months, the Army of the Potomac was handed to four commanding officers who could not have been more different in their ability to command and in their leadership style. The diminutive George McClellan was armed with an outsize ego and disdain for his commander in chief. His hesitancy to aggressively attack General Lee led to Ambrose Burnside taking command, a general who didn't want the responsibility. A friend of McClellan, he clumsily reorganized the army, feared he was unworthy of the job, and lost the confidence of some senior officers to the extent they attempted a coup in Washington. His feud with General in Chief Henry Halleck led to his dismissal and the appointment of the raucous Joseph Hooker. Hooker unwound Burnside's "grand division" scheme, was popular among the troops for improving their living conditions, but also feuded with Halleck, so that Lincoln again concluded he had to make a change in command. Once again Letterman's commanding officer was a near polar opposite of his predecessor. Only days before Gettysburg, George Meade, a pensive, thoughtful, short-tempered man some officers called

"Old Brains" took command. Few medical officers had to deal with a more fluid and unpredictable cast of commanding officers was than did Jonathan Letterman. Similarly, William Hammond had battled against the secretary of war while humanitarian commissions sought to exert their influence on how soldiers should be treated and cared for.

Armies around the world paid careful attention to America's Civil War. Several sent observers to learn from the American experience and from the high-profile Army of the Potomac in particular. British inspector general Edward Muir visited Letterman shortly after Antietam and reportedly was impressed with what became widely known as "The Letterman System." British surgeon general Thomas Longmore wrote a book in 1869 on the care of sick and wounded soldiers, and his argument was significantly influenced by Letterman and the book Letterman had published three years earlier. Two Prussian physicians, Rudolf Virchow and Theodore Billroth, similarly were impressed. They later were influential in the Prussian army's adoption of Letterman's philosophy of battlefield care.

Observers also drew on the bulk of the Civil War medical legacy, and in some areas, where advances had not been achieved outright, anecdotal progress was gained. Medical officers knew diet and hygiene were critical in the war against disease but did not understand the micro-organism agents of illness, an enemy that killed far more soldiers than rifle and artillery fire. Reliance on mercury- and opium-based medicines remained prevalent. Without understanding the scientific basis for it, doctors serving in the war saw that improved hygiene standards, healthier food preparation techniques and a more nutritious diet reduced the incidence of disease, lessons they took home after the war. Sickness rates for diarrhea and dysentery generally declined throughout the war, although mortality rates in the ranks of the weakened armies increased.

Many of those who survived, like Letterman, faced a lifetime of disability. Civil War veterans were more than fifty times more likely to suffer from diarrhea and dysentery than civilians and suffered significantly higher rates of heart ailments and rheumatism, among other maladies.[6]

Civil War surgeons did not understand the agents of infection any more than they did the agents of disease. But anecdotal experience demonstrated that regularly cleaned wounds and a well-ventilated environment facilitated recovery from wounds. Wounded soldiers generally fared better in barns and tents than in farmhouses. Noting that well-ventilated hospitals also held fewer cases of infection, Hammond and others developed a pavilion-style design that influenced civilian hospital design over the next seven decades. That innovation became a major step in military medicine's battle against hospital gangrene, a ghastly complication that was frequently fatal and nearly always disfiguring.

Surgeons performed tens of thousands of amputations, giving rise to a national debate over their frequency. Given the almost certain infections that resulted from being wounded, Letterman and others believed amputation was often the advisable medical approach in order to reduce the chances of fatal infection from a dirty wound,. He noted: "From my observations I am convinced that if any fault was committed it was that the knife was not used often enough."[7] Surgeons learned that prompt surgery, within forty-eight hours of battle, improved the odds of surviving the subsequent infection. That became an early step in the progressive realization by twentieth-century surgeons that "the golden hour" after suffering a wound was critical. Today, twenty-first century military surgeons recognize that "the platinum ten minutes" for trauma care is even more critical to survivability.

The nature and location of the wound in the Civil War largely dictated a soldier's odds of survival. Fatal infections from amputation ranged from 20 percent for arms to more than 80 percent for amputations at the hip. The abundance of amputations and infections was ample opportunity for surgeons to learn the value of ligature, tying off arteries as part of the amputation process. A wound to the torso was devastating, with 62 percent of chest wounds becoming fatal and nearly 90 percent of abdominal wounds producing death.[8] The first widespread use of anesthesia for surgeries, principally chloroform, produced a death rate of five per thousand cases.[9] Although the wounded now could be safely anesthetized, surgeons were still limited in what kinds of severe wounds they could effectively treat.

Thousands of Civil War soldier case histories document the horrors that both the wounded and their surgeons endured. For example, John Peters of the 11th Pennsylvania Volunteers reached a Washington hospital on June 15, 1863, after being wounded thirty-three days earlier at Chancellorsville. He had been shot through the thigh, broken his femur, and suffered a skull fracture. "His general condition is not promising," wrote the attending physician.

> His tongue is red and dry, his pulse frequent and feeble, his spirits somewhat depressed, and he has but little appetite.
>
> June 27: The wound in the head is again suppurating (oozing pus) and he has no fever. Removed from the thigh a detached fracture splinter about one inch in length.
>
> July 1: The discharge of pus from the wounds in the thigh is profuse. He looks pale and anemic.
>
> July 18: He has diarrhoea.
>
> July 25: He has loose stools occasionally, which are controlled by the use of opium.
>
> July 28: Removed another detached splinter from the thigh.

August 10: His general condition has much improved. The fracture of the femur has united, but necrosed (dead) bone is discernable on exploration of the thigh wound.

September 11: There is swelling, redness, and pain in his thigh. Ordered lead and opium wash to be applied to it.

December 20: He complains of debility and want of appetite; is pale and anemic, and the thigh continues to discharge freely. Prescribed extract. Nucis vomicae gr 1/6 (strychnine).

February 14: The diarrhoea continues. Ordered (opium) and comphorae to be taken after each stool.

April 14: The patient was transferred to Philadelphia, Pa., being in good flesh and spirits, and abundantly able to stand the journey. The injured limb is recovering from atrophy occasioned by the long disuses, that is, it is increasing in size, and the patient is rapidly regaining use of it. The limb was shortened about three inches.[10]

Peters spent nearly one year in the hospitals recovering from his wounds.

Other medical advances included limb immobilization (notably the Hodgen splint) and the birth of medical specialties. Surgeon General Hammond dedicated one hospital exclusively to the treatment and study of neurological injuries. Another was devoted to venereal disease. Plastic surgery became an emerging specialty as some soldiers survived horrifically disfiguring injuries and their ensuing infections. Hammond also created the Army Medical Museum, sending doctors into the field to collect thousands of specimens. The multivolume *Medical and Surgical History of the War of the Rebellion* that took more than a decade to compile and publish remains an unprecedented chronicle of disease, trauma, and their treatment in mid-nineteenth century war.

Yet, as the army and its medical department returned to out-post assignments and isolated Indian battles, much of the mass-casualty medical knowledge acquired in the Civil War became more academic than practical. "While all other nations made haste to apply the lessons of our war and to remodel their medical organizations in accordance with them, our own Medical Department reverted to antebellum conditions and went backward. The hospital stewards were the only permanent enlisted personnel and all nursing and other work about the hospitals was done by an uninstructed and constantly changing personnel of men detailed from the companies," wrote a reporter for the *Journal of the American Medical Association* in 1904.

In fact, the army's medical department in the decades following the Civil War became saddled with many of the same issues that Letterman had confronted. The lack of trained medical personnel persisted until 1887, when a hospital corps was established. Medical officers with military rank implemented training programs, but, like Letterman's medical staff, faced resentment by some line officers for having an officer's rank that the line officers deemed unworthy. At the start of the Spanish-American War, the army medical department again was unprepared for a military force that stood to increase tenfold to approximately three hundred thousand men. Volunteer regiments with civilian doctors unfamiliar with the demands of military medicine produced many of the same challenges Letterman had faced.

Disease remained the deadliest enemy. Five times more soldiers died from disease than from enemy fire during the Spanish-American War. Malaria, yellow fever, and typhoid fever decimated some units. Secretary of War Russell Alger noted, "More than ninety per cent of the volunteer regiments developed (typhoid fever) within eight weeks after their enrolment; and the deaths from this camp scourge alone amounted to more than eight per cent of the total deaths from disease."[11] Appalled at the deaths caused by disease, President William McKinley appointed a post-war commission to investigate. The Dodge Commission issued a set of recommendations that called for additional commissioned officers, trained support staff, and greater surgeon authority to secure medical supplies. All were challenges faced by Letterman, and Congress addressed none of the Commission's recommendations when it reorganized the army in 1901.

Alger concluded that "camp pollution" was the culprit of rampaging disease and was due to either the inexperience or negligence of officers and enlisted men. On April 25, 1898, Surgeon General George Sternberg issued Circular No. 1, which was practically a rewrite of the report Letterman submitted to General McClellan two weeks after Letterman had taken medical command of the Army of the Potomac in 1862. Army camp conditions had required Letterman's immediate attention to improve soldiers' diet, sleeping conditions, work schedule, food preparation, personal hygiene, and officer accountability. Like Letterman, Sternberg urged that camps be established on well-drained high ground and required that human waste sinks be carefully located, covered regularly, and discontinued before fecal waste reached the surface. Both Letterman and Sternberg recommended rest during the hottest portion of the summer day. Like Letterman, Sternberg also believed in hot coffee and recommended it prior to going on duty at night or early in the morning.[12]

The first full-scale test of "The Letterman System" came in World War I, along front lines that extended from the English Channel to the Swiss Alps. Stagnant war with weapons of vastly increased lethality presented new challenges to the Letterman philosophy of rapid battlefield evacuation and treatment as close to the fighting as possible. During the world's first industrialized war, the army medical department refined the Civil War–era division hospital by establishing more specific levels

of care, including collection stations, field hospitals, and evacuation hospitals that often were permanently built near rail lines.
Yet despite that development in World War I, the U.S. Army
found it necessary in 1923 to issue Regulation 1427, which
again prohibited the non-medical use of vehicles intended to be
ambulances— another reissue of a standard that Letterman had
fought to establish.[13]

With each ensuing war, many of the medical lessons of the
previous war were forgotten. Now, as world affairs have evolved
from massive wars around the world to more isolated and marathon regional wars, military medical philosophies, protocols, and
advances have similarly evolved. Today, the National Museum of
Civil War Medicine is preserving and teaching the fundamental
lessons of past wars to modern-day military medical professionals.
Under the leadership of executive director George Wunderlich
and museum founder Gordon Dammann, the museum's Letterman Institute has taught more than 4,500 medical professionals from the Army, Navy, Air Force, and Veterans Administration,
and other public safety personnel the value of linking battlefield
medicine with military field command. To these new medical
professionals, the institute imparts the golden lesson that integrated decision-making processes save lives and contribute to
accomplishing command missions. Jonathan Letterman's legacy
is the basis of the successful training program.

Nearly 150 years ago, Jonathan Letterman's fellow medical officers proved clairvoyant when they petitioned Congressional recognition for Letterman. They instinctively knew
that in less than two years of war he had created a legacy that
would benefit countless future generations of wounded. "We
may search history in vain for campaigns of equal severity, for
battles of equal magnitude, with those of this Army for the past
eighteen months, and we challenge history to produce a battle
wherein the hundreds of wounded have been so well and so

rapidly provided for, as the thousands in the great battles of this Army (of the Potomac)."[14]

It is a legacy that has continued to instruct and inspire subsequent generations of military medical officers. As warfare evolves, the wounded soldier lies on the battlefield still, desperately hopeful that someone will race toward enemy fire, slide to a stop, and say, "It's okay, I've got you." Every word of encouragement and care is an echo of Jonathan Letterman's legacy.

So, too, is the ongoing appreciation by the community of military medicine for what Letterman accomplished within the enveloping chaos and cacophony of war. "When (Letterman) assumed charge, he did not proceed by precedent, but had the vision to see what was wrong, and the energy and courage to carry out those reforms that he deemed necessary. Undoubtedly he was prepared when the opportunity came to do those things which are demanded of all military men when the supreme moment comes—to efficiently and thoroughly do the job. May his life actions be an example to us all."[15]

13

EPILOGUE

"Today I am used up."

An estimated 3.5 million Americans fought in the Civil War. There are no reliable statistics reflecting the number who served as career, volunteer, or contract surgeons. A minority of those who did were career military officers, summoned from remote outposts. Many more volunteered or sold their medical services to the U.S. Army. Some of the career medical officers, like Letterman, resigned during the war, while others endured to war's end and either left the service or received orders for another outpost. Some of the others served only with the aim to survive and return home. Others willingly risked their lives in a spirit of unity and emancipation.

It would be hard to believe that the horrors of the Civil War did not leave scars on every man. Those whose lives crossed Letterman's path met fates as varied as the roles they played throughout his life and on the battlefield.

LETTERMAN FAMILY

Although Jonathan Letterman had little use for them, the Union army's contract surgeons included Letterman's younger brother, William Henry. Like Jonathan, William excelled at Jefferson

Medical College, graduating in 1856 as president of his class.
Four years earlier, in 1852, when he lived with his mother a few
blocks from Jefferson College during his undergraduate education, he cofounded Phi Kappa Psi.

After practicing medicine in Pennsylvania, he moved to Baltimore where he suffered from a heart condition. After eight years
in failing health, and despondent over his mother's death, William
moved to Cotton Hill, West Virginia, in 1871. Diary entries reflect
a man at a loss with life. "The lovely waters of the Ohio are
peaceful, but I am plunging amidst the tumultuous stream of life
which flows within. How little we know those around us. The
smile or the laugh may come from a heart that is bowed down.
May God grant true wisdom unto me and good health, and may
I be prospered far beyond my hopes and anticipation. May those
dear ones at home be preserved and may we meet again."[1]

William developed an interest in geology. He became an
expert in coal deposits and purchased coal land for mining
interests. In 1875, at forty-three years of age, he met and married Laura Slaughter. But his health continued to plague him. A
move to Missouri near her family led to another move to Texas
in 1878 with Laura and two young daughters. His family joined
the third Letterman brother, Ritchie, who also had graduated
from college and become a Texas farmer.

William started a medical practice and helped establish a
local medical society and a Masonic Lodge. In 1881, another
move became necessary, this time to the Gulf, in search of
better health. Prior to leaving, an exhausted William wrote
his father-in-law. "Today I am used up right sharp—does not
express my case too strong. . . . Your next, if answered, will
direct you to Austin. Good-by. Love to all, W. H. Letterman."[2]
William Henry Letterman died nine days later on May 23,
1881, at the age of forty-eight. He was buried near Ritchie's
farm, in Duffau, Texas.

MEDICAL SCHOOL

Jonathan Letterman received one of the best medical educations possible before enlisting in the army. Several members of the medical faculty at Jefferson Medical College achieved national recognition in their respective fields following the war. Dr. Thomas Mutter taught surgery to Letterman and then retired seven years later, in 1856, due to poor health. He donated a collection of more than 1,300 medical specimens and a $30,000 endowment to the College of Physicians in Philadelphia, which remains one of the foremost medical-specimen museums in the country. Like William, he died at forty-eight years of age, two years later.

Dr. Charles Meigs became a widely recognized expert in pediatrics. He also spent much of his professional life translating medical journals and texts from French. Cultured, and full of humor, Meigs favored poetic phrases and mixed philosophy with his instruction. A colleague, Dr. John Mitchell, likewise was a man of literature. A published specialist in several diseases, he also published such diverse works as poetry, treatises on nature, and "The Means of Elevating the Character of the Working Classes." Both writers were topped by Dr. Robley Dunglison, another professor of Letterman. His works ultimately sold more than 150,000 copies. Although he became known as "the father of American physiology," Dunglison delved into many aspects of society in America and abroad. The one-time dean of the medical school published works on English fashion, word construction, superstitions, and languages, as well as a dictionary for the blind.

EARLY MEDICAL CAREER

Fellow officers who developed close friendships while spending long months at isolated outposts sometimes later found themselves

on opposite sides of the battlefield during the Civil War. Early in
his career, Letterman refused to get involved in a dispute between
a young officer, Thomas Jackson, and the commanding officer of
Fort Meade in Florida where Letterman served as medical officer.
Jackson resigned from the army shortly thereafter and became
a professor at Virginia Military Institute. Early in the Civil War,
Jackson demonstrated his verve, audacity, and leadership for the
Confederates, becoming known as Stonewall Jackson after his
inspirational bravery at the first Battle of Bull Run. He died from
friendly Confederate fire when Letterman and the Army of the
Potomac fought at Chancellorsville, a loss General Robert E. Lee
considered irreplaceable.

Letterman treated his first wounds inflicted by enemy fire—
several arrow wounds after an Indian engagement as Loring
sought marauding Apaches—in 1857, on an expedition led by
Colonel William Loring. Loring had served in the Mexican-
American War and later fought for the Confederacy throughout
the Civil War. After the war, Loring was hired by the Egyptian
army, where he rose to prominence before being dismissed in
1878. The North Carolina native moved to Florida and practiced law. He died in 1886, after unsuccessfully running for the
U.S. Senate.

Prior to the Civil War, Letterman participated in one other
expedition against an Indian tribe, the Paiutes. Under the command of James Carleton at Fort Tejon (north of Los Angeles),
Letterman served as the medical officer on an extended march in
search of Paiute leaders. Again he treated arrow wounds, suffered
in a battle near Camp Cady in the Mojave Desert. Carleton spent
most of the Civil War commanding the California Volunteers,
guarding the Southwest against Confederate incursion. Following the war, Carleton commanded the Department of New
Mexico. He ordered the forced relocation of 8,000 Navajos to
a reservation. The march became a failure when many Navajos

returned to their homeland. In 1867, he was transferred to San Antonio, where he died from pneumonia in 1873.

THE FRINGE OF WAR

When Letterman was transferred to the Department of West Virginia as medical director in January 1862, another medical officer arrived the same month. Introductions were not necessary, as William Hammond had attended Jefferson Medical College at the same time as Letterman. Their career paths had taken different routes in the ensuing thirteen years. Letterman worked in relative anonymity at various military outposts, while Hammond had developed a national reputation as a military medical officer, scientist, and researcher. They worked together for four months before Hammond became surgeon general.

They remained close friends after Hammond was removed from office in 1864, following his conviction of conduct unbecoming an officer and not following medical-supply purchase procedures. Many thought Hammond's conviction was based more on politics than evidence, because he had made a number of powerful enemies in Washington. He moved to New York in the Civil War's final year, borrowed money to start a medical practice, and again rose to national prominence in the emerging field of neurology. During the next ten years he held a series of medical-school professorships before launching a successful campaign in 1878 to overturn his military conviction.

An act of Congress restored his rank as brigadier general and placed him on the army's retired list as surgeon general. Hammond spent the next decade studying mental diseases, established a sanatorium in Washington, and resumed his prolific writing. A cardiac problem led to his death in 1900 at seventy-one years of age.

In West Virginia, Hammond and Letterman were under the command of General William Rosecrans. An intellectual of varying interests, Rosecrans had served in the army for twelve years until 1854, before resigning to become an architect, engineer, and inventor. He volunteered at the start of the Civil War and served with modest distinction until the close of the war. His largest contributions came in West Virginia, where he and Letterman worked on an improved ambulance design and where Hammond and Letterman built one of the first pavilion-design hospitals, a design that influenced hospital construction for the remainder of the nineteenth century. At one time a possible running mate of Abraham Lincoln, Rosecrans moved to Los Angeles following the war and became minister to Mexico. He developed mining operations, was elected to Congress, and bought speculative real estate in downtown San Diego. He also served as register of the Treasury before dying in Los Angeles in 1893.

Almost as soon as William Hammond became surgeon general, his clash with Secretary of War Edwin Stanton affected Letterman. Stanton refused Hammond's recommended appointment of Letterman as a hospital inspector in Washington, a precursor of Stanton's insistent role in surgeon general and Army of the Potomac affairs. Stanton remained secretary of war until the end of the Civil War.

Lincoln tolerated the sometimes disrespectful Stanton, admiring his tenacity, organization, and work ethic. Generals, colleagues, and employees found him opinionated, supremely self-confident, insensitive, and short-tempered. As Letterman made preparations to leave the army in late 1864, Stanton lobbied for an appointment to the Supreme Court. Lincoln demurred, believing his irascible confidant was more valuable as secretary of war.

Following Lincoln's assassination, Stanton's relationship with President Johnson deteriorated quickly. When Stanton refused to leave his office after President Johnson fired him, the Senate attempted to impeach Johnson in the belief that Stanton's dismissal required Congressional approval. When impeachment fell one vote short, Stanton promptly resigned. He planned to resume a lucrative law practice, but when another Supreme Court vacancy occurred, Stanton was named to the bench by Johnson's successor, President Ulysses S. Grant. However, Stanton died before he took his seat on the bench, five days short of his fifty-fifth birthday.

BATTLE SCARS

Jonathan Letterman fought the war on several fronts. He had to build a medical department on the march, comprised of volunteer regiments, civilian doctors, intrusive humanitarian organizations, and a relative handful of military surgeons, most of whom were strangers. Four different commanding officers held authority to either facilitate or foil his ability to treat thousands of wounded men. He had to earn their respect and trust quickly after each change of command. The surgeon general likewise wielded significant power in dictating Letterman's ultimate effectiveness. The cast of characters on and near the battlefield sometimes played key roles for only a few months, but some held sway for extended periods of time. Their final fates were as varied as the roles they played in Letterman's battlefield career.

Charles Tripler, Letterman's predecessor as the Army of the Potomac's medical director, never completely recovered from the disastrous Peninsula Campaign, in 1862, that cost him his job. After losing the confidence of both his commanding officer and the surgeon general, Tripler was granted his requested transfer to Detroit in the Department of the Lakes. Five years later, he developed a brain tumor and died in 1866. His *Manual of the Medical Officer of the Army of the United States* became his professional legacy and the universal guide for recruit examiners for the next half century.

After running a half-hearted campaign and losing to Abraham Lincoln in the 1864 presidential election, General George McClellan and his family spent several years traveling throughout Europe. He returned in 1868 and began a prosperous career as an engineer before becoming president of the Atlantic and Great Western Railway. He returned to politics in 1873 and was elected governor of New Jersey. He wrote and traveled extensively in the final years of his life. He died in 1885 from heart failure, believing much of the criticism of his leadership in the Civil War was unfounded.

McClellan's replacement, General Ambrose Burnside, served in the army for the remainder of the Civil War without significant distinction. He also rebounded from losing command of the Army of the Potomac to achieve political success. In 1866, Burnside was elected governor of Rhode Island. Eight years later, the Republican was elected to the U.S. Senate, where he served as chairman of the Committee on Education and Labor. He died while holding that office in 1881.

Burnside's replacement, General Joseph Hooker, fared poorly in the years following his removal from the Army of the Potomac as it approached Gettysburg. He was a corps commander in the Atlanta campaign before suffering a stroke in November 1865. He recovered enough to return to duty but suffered another stroke before resigning from the military in 1868. He traveled despite reliance on a cane and physical assistance during his trips. Some believed the term "hooker" came from Hooker's lifestyle, although there is evidence of its use prior to his army command. Hooker died in 1878 from what his physician called paralysis of the heart.

General George Meade also suffered from poor health following his command at Gettysburg. When Ulysses S. Grant was appointed general in chief of the Union army in 1864 and established his headquarters with the Army of the Potomac, Grant essentially took over Meade's command. Meade retained nominal authority of his army until the conclusion of the war, but suffered from bouts of pneumonia and jaundice in 1864 and 1865. Despite chronically poor health, he held several post–Civil War commands before collapsing and dying in November 1872. An autopsy revealed an enlarged liver that showed scar tissue on a path similar to a bullet wound Meade had suffered in the war.

The Army of the Potomac's debacle in the 1862 Peninsula Campaign led to more than Letterman taking medical command. President Lincoln named Henry Halleck his general in chief to coordinate the Union's armies. Halleck became an outspoken critic of what he considered an overly cautious McClellan. As Letterman worked to develop his battlefield care system between battles, Halleck often urged McClellan to take the fight to the enemy more aggressively. Later, Halleck was accused of the same timidity by President Lincoln and Secretary of War Stanton. Toward the end of the war, Halleck's authority had been eviscerated to the point that he believed he was little more than an advisor to the president and secretary of war. After falling out of favor in Washington, Halleck transferred to the Department of the Pacific in San Francisco following the war. He helped Letterman win his race for coroner before transferring to the Department in the South. He died at his post in Louisville in 1872, leaving an estate of more than $400,000.

POSTWAR LIFE

Thousands of physicians benefited from the experience they gained in the Civil War. Contract and volunteer surgeons returned to their private lives, while the careers of military officers took many paths after the army demobilized. Some of the physicians Letterman worked with and relied upon became leaders in their specialties, while others completed their medical careers in relative anonymity.

John Shaw Billings was one of hundreds of surgeons at Gettysburg. Battle so exhausted Billings that he took a month's sick leave before returning to the Army of the Potomac. In late 1864, he transferred to the surgeon general's office. He became a widely renowned medical administrator in the years following the Civil War and built a medical library that became one of the largest in the world. He helped design and establish the Johns Hopkins Medical School and in 1883 became curator of the Army Medical Museum. Following his retirement from the military, Shaw led the creation of the New York Public Library. He died in 1913, the day before his seventy-fifth birthday.

Dr. William W. Keen had recently graduated from medical school when he reported to Letterman in late 1862. Keen treated hundreds of casualties following Gettysburg and within a year had become a battle-toughened surgeon. He pursued his medical education in Europe following the war and became one of the first surgeons in the United States to adopt antiseptic techniques. Many acknowledged him as the first brain surgeon following a successful brain tumor surgery in 1887. A prolific writer, he published more than 650 articles, editorials, and books. He wrote and updated medical textbooks and became the Civil War's most internationally recognized surgeon.

Letterman's counterpart in General Robert E. Lee's army, medical director LaFayette Guild, followed a path similar to Letterman. Guild graduated from Jefferson Medical College one year ahead of Letterman, enlisted in the army, and served at several outposts. He was stationed in California at the outset of the Civil War and was dismissed from the army when the Alabama native refused to take the oath of allegiance. Guild and Letterman met personally to resolve the stalemate over returning more than 1,000 wounded Union soldiers in the aftermath of Chancellorsville. Guild supervised the evacuation of moderately ambulatory Confederate wounded after Gettysburg, while Letterman organized Union hospitals in the area to treat thousands of wounded men from both sides. Following the war, Guild moved to San Francisco and worked for the Board of Health as a city and county hospital visiting surgeon near the end of Letterman's second term as coroner. Guild died on July 4, 1870, the eighth anniversary of Letterman taking medical command of the Army of the Potomac, at forty-four years of age.

Dr. Bernard John Dowling Irwin held a number of medical posts following his opportunistic use of abandoned tents as the first field hospital near the battlefield at Shiloh. Letterman expanded on that concept and systemized it, creating a field hospital structure that provided a critical link between aid station and general hospital. Following the war, Irwin remained in the army, serving at West Point and in the Departments of Dakota and Arizona. He retired in 1894, wrote a number of articles, and rarely mentioned the Medal of Honor he had received prior to the war for bravery in an Indian battle against the Apaches near Fort Buchanan. He was buried at West Point after dying at his vacation home in Canada in 1917.

CALIFORNIA CALLING

Jonathan Letterman shocked his friends and colleagues when he resigned from the army in 1864 to accept a job offer in a field in which he was completely inexperienced: oil exploration. But railroad baron Thomas Scott wasn't looking for an experienced wildcatter. He could hire oil rig crews from Pennsylvania. He needed a proven organizer and administrator to build a company and oil-drilling operation in Southern California. In addition, Letterman knew the region from his posting at Fort Tejon. The venture failed in little more than a year amid accusations of fraudulent oil samples. Scott spent many years following the Civil War in court, defending his group of promoters against unhappy stockholders.

Benjamin Silliman, the nationally recognized expert whose reports had painted bright California oil prospects, suffered a tarnished reputation when it became clear that his samples had been tainted by an unknown party. Other mine prospecting cases followed, in which Silliman was accused of overstating reserves in various mining ventures. Like Scott, he spent years defending himself, largely against Josiah Whitney and other critics in the scientific community.

California state geologist Josiah Whitney, who was skeptical of oil reserves in California, later established a school of mines at Harvard and was a professor there the rest of his life. He was a founding member of the National Academy of Sciences. His skepticism proved unfounded, when California became a major oil producer by the time he died in 1896. Stephen Peckham, the chemist who became skeptical of the samples allegedly collected in the region he and Letterman were drilling, became an academic following his brief oil exploration career. He taught chemistry, physics, and geology at universities in Pennsylvania, Ohio, and Minnesota. One of the nation's leading experts on bitumens, he wrote an exhaustive analysis on the production, manufacture, and potential of oil and related products. Letterman's assistant superintendent, James De Barth Shorb, abandoned the oil industry shortly after Letterman, married into a wealthy local family, and went into the vineyard business.

Jonathan Letterman's fate, of course, was born of the battlefield. It defined his life and its final chapters. He, too, became a casualty of war and likely would have agreed with the reflections of General George McClellan, his first commanding officer and his friend, when McClellan wrote his wife in 1862:

"I am tired of the sickening sight of the battlefield

with its mangled corpses & poor suffering wounded.

Victory has no charms for me when purchased at such cost."[3]

NOTES

Introduction

1. Jonathan Letterman, *Medical Recollections of the Army of the Potomac* (New York: Appleton & Company, 1866), 100.

2. George Stevens, *Three Years in the Sixth Corps* (Albany, NY: S. R. Gray, 1866), 154.

3. Ibid., 340–341.

4. Anne Leland, *American War and Military Operations Casualties: Lists and Statistics* (Washington, DC: Congressional Research Service, Sept. 15, 2009).

Chapter 1

1. Benjamin Cook, *History of the Twelfth Massachusetts Volunteers (Webster) Regiment* (Boston: Twelfth (Webster) Regiment Association, 1882), 73.

2. Blaine Ewing, *Canonsburg Centennial, 1802–1902* (Pittsburgh: Pittsburgh Printing Company, 1903), 72.

3. Ibid., 73.

4. Boyd Crumrine, *History of Washington County, Pennsylvania with Biographical Sketches of Many of Its Pioneers and Prominent Men,* (Philadelphia: L. H. Leverts & Co., 1882), 601–611.

5. Alfred Creigh, *History of Washington County* (Harrisburg, PA: B. Singerly Printer, 1871), 221.

6. Extended correspondence with Canonsburg historian James Herron of the Jefferson College Historical Society. Subsequent references: Herron, Correspondence.

7. Creigh, *History of Washington County*, 221.

8. Washington City was reorganized as the District of Columbia in 1871.

9. Crumrine, *History of Washington County*, 601–611.

10. Ledermann is the original family name and is of German origin, from an era when family names often reflected the nature of the tradesman in the family. Later it became Leatherman, the surname of Jonathan's father. Early records of Jonathan Letterman reflect both Leatherman and Letherman. As late as 1856, he submitted a military report to the Smithsonian Institution under the name of Letherman. Shortly thereafter, he was listed as Letterman in Army documents and that spelling remained for the rest of his life. For clarity throughout, Jonathan Letterman is referred to as Letterman while Leatherman refers to his father.

11. Herron, Correspondence.

12. Ibid.

13. Public announcement, *The Reporter*, March 20, 1823.

14. Although property deeds are unclear, local tax records indicate Leatherman had moved from the house next to his father-in-law to this location in 1822.

15. *1820 United States Census*, U.S. Census Bureau.

16. Herron, Correspondence.

17. Ibid.

18. *Catalogue of the Officers and Students* (Jefferson College, 1845), 13.

19. Herron, Correspondence.

20. *Catalogue of the Officers and Students*, 15.

21. James Herron, "Beta Theta Pi," *Jefferson College Times*, November 1976.

22. Ibid.

23. H. M. Brackenridge, "The Annual Address Delivered Before The Philo and Franklin Literary Societies, 1838," 10.

24. *Catalogue of the Officers and Students*, 13–15.

25. Ibid.

26. Some historical records indicate Jonathan and Anna also had a daughter, Elizabeth, but do not list her dates of birth or death. It may be that she died as an infant, a common occurrence in the early 1800s.

27. *Catalogue of the Officers and Students*, 10–15.

28. Letterman Papers Collection of Gordon Dammann, founder of the National Civil War Medicine Museum. Subsequent references: Letterman Collection of Gordon Dammann

29. George Milbry Gould, *The Jefferson Medical College of Philadelphia, benefactors, alumni, hospital, etc. Its founders, officers, instructors, 1986–1904: A History* (Philadelphia: Thomas Jefferson University, 2009), 113–115.

30. Frederick B. Wagner, MD, *Thomas Jefferson University: Tradition and Heritage* (Philadelphia: Thomas Jefferson University, 1989), 23–24.

31. *Annual Announcement of Jefferson Medical College of Philadelphia 1847–1848*, 15.

32. Wagner, *Thomas Jefferson University*, 41, 43–44.

33. Gould, *The Jefferson Medical College of Philadelphia*, 108.

34. Wagner, *Thomas Jefferson University*, 53.

35. Ibid.

36. Ibid., 47–48.

37. John Simon, *Personal Memoirs of John H. Brinton, Civil War Surgeon, 1861–1865* (Carbondale: Southern Illinois University Press, 1996), xvii.

38. Wagner, *Thomas Jefferson University*, 54.

39. Mary C. Gillett, *The Army Medical Department 1818–1865* (Washington DC: Center for Military History, U.S. Army, 1987), 4.

40. George Worthington Adams, *Doctors in Blue* (Baton Rouge, LA: Louisiana State University Press, 1980), 50.

41. Herron, Correspondence.

42. Gabriel and Metz, *A History of Military Medicine*, 134.

43. Ibid., 132.

44. Ibid., 133.

45. Richard A. Gabriel and Karen S. Metz, *A History of Military Medicine* (Westport, CT: Greenwood Press, 1992), 180.

46. Charles Ayars, "Some Notes on the Medical Service of the Army, 1812–1839," *The Military Surgeon*, May 1922, 506.

47. Public announcement, *The Reporter*, March 20, 1823.

48. Ayars, "Some Notes on the Medical Service," 524.

49. Gillett, *The Army Medical Department 1818–1865*, 95.

50. Gabriel and Metz, *A History of Military Medicine*, 180.

51. Ibid.

52. Gillett, *The Army Medical Department 1818–1865*, 117.

53. Ibid., 124.

54. *Catalogue of Jefferson Medical College of Philadelphia 1849–1850*, 14.

55. Letterman Collection of Gordon Dammann.

56. Joseph T. Smith, "A Review of the Life and Work of Jonathan Letterman, M.D." *Johns Hopkins Hospital Bulletin*, August 1916, 243.

Chapter 2

1. Michael Schene, "Not a Shot Fired: Fort Chokonikla and the 'Indian War' of 1849–*1850*," *Tequesta* (1977, no. 37): 24.

2. Guy Henry, *Military Record of Civilian Appointments of the United States Army* (New York: Carleton Publishers, 1869), 2–4.

3. Canter Brown Jr., *Fort Meade 1849-1900* (Tuscaloosa: University of Alabama Press, 1955), 7.

4. Schene, "Not a Shot Fired," 31.

5. "Surgeon General Lawson Annual Report, 1839," *The Eclectic Journal of Medicine* vol. IV, no. 6 (1840): 193–200.

6. Surgeon General William Hammond later cited Fort Meade's original hospital as typical of the poorly located and inadequately constructed outpost hospitals that often contributed to the chronic poor health of soldiers.

7. Henry, *Record of Civilian Appointments*, 8, 10.

8. Ibid., 13.

9. Ibid., 10.

10. Gillett, *The Army Medical Department 1818–1865*, 75, 128.

11. Ibid., 128–129.

12. Richard H. Coolidge, MD, *Statistical Report of the Sickness and Mortality of the Army of the United States* (Washington: A.O.P. Nicholson, 1856), 310.

13. Gillett, *The Army Medical Department 1818–1865*, 10.

14. Ibid.

15. James Roberts, *Stonewall Jackson* (New York: MacMillan, 1997), 106.

16. Brown, *Fort Meade*, 9–11.

17. Jonathan Hood, *Jonathan Letterman and the Development of a Battlefield Evacuation System* (PhD Dissertation, 2004: Texas Tech University, http://library.ttu.edu/about/collections/theses_dissertations.php, accessed January 2, 2010), 28–29.

18. George C. Tanner, *History of Fort Ripley, 1849–1859* (Minnesota Historical Society, 1905), 179–202.

19. Ibid.

20. Peter Boulay, *History of Weather Observations, Fort Ripley, Minnesota 1849–1990* (Minnesota State Climatology Office, 2006), 6.

21. Compilation of Minnesota weather records dating to 1820, http://www.climatestations.com, accessed May 16, 2010.

22. Boulay, *History of Weather Observations*, 8.

23. Coolidge, *Statistical Report of Sickness*, 318, 320.

24. Hood, *Jonathan Letterman*, 24–31.

25. Maurice Frink, *Fort Defiance & the Navajos* (Boulder, CO: Pruett Press, 1968), 3.

26. Ibid., 20, 22.

27. Gillett, *The Army Medical Department 1815–1865*, 15, 17.

28. Frank R. Freemon, *Gangrene and Glory* (Chicago: University of Illinois Press, 2001), 21.

29. Ibid.

30. Jonathan Letterman, *Sketch of the Navajo Tribe of Indians, Territory of New Mexico (1856)* (Washington: Smithsonian Institution, 1856), 287.

31. Ibid., 294.

32. Bennett A. Clements, "Memoir of Jonathan Letterman, M.D.," *Journal of the Military Service Institution,* September 1883, 26.

33. Letterman, *Sketch of the Navajo*, 221.

34. Ibid.

35. Ibid., 222.

36. John V. Quarsten, *Fort Monroe, The Key to the South* (Charleston, SC: Arcadia Publishing, 2000), 9.

37. William and John Gorenfeld, "Carleton at Bitter Spring," *Wild West,* June 2001, http://www.musketoon.com/2005/01/15/bvt-major-james-carleton-at-bitter-spring-1860, accessed September 14, 2010.

38. Hood, *Jonathan Letterman*, 35.

39. George Worthington Adams, *Doctors in Blue* (Baton Rouge: Louisiana State University Press, 1980), 5.

40. "The Call for Volunteers," *Harper's Weekly*, April 27, 1861.

41. Louis C. Duncan, *The Medical Department of the United States Army in the Civil War* (Washington, DC: U.S. Army, 1910), 5.

42. Ibid., 4.

43. Ibid., 5.

44. Emma Edmonds, *Nurse and Spy in the Union Army: The Adventures and Experiences of a Woman in Hospitals, Camps, and Battle-Fields* (Hartford, Connecticut: W. S. Williams and Co., 1865), 43.

45. Letter by surgeon Frank H. Hamilton, *American Medical Times*, July 27, 1861.

46. Ibid.

47. William Howard Russell, *My Diary North and South* (Ann Arbor: University of Michigan, 2005), 467.

48. Duncan, *The Medical Department*, 33.

49. *Medical & Surgical History of the War of the Rebellion* (Washington: Government Printing Office, 1870), vol. 2, 334–345.

50. Adams, *Doctors in Blue*, 26.

Chapter 3

1. Charles J. Stille, *History of the United States Sanitary Commission* (Philadelphia: J. B. Lippincott), 49.

2. Adams, *Doctors in Blue*, 27.

3. Gillett, *The Army Medical Department 1818–1865*, 163.

4. Adams, *Doctors in Blue*, 12.

5. Ibid., 11.

6. John Y. Simon, *Personal Memoirs of John H. Brinton, Civil War Surgeon, 1861–1865* (Carbondale: Southern Illinois University Press, 1996) 357.

7. Stille, *Sanitary Commission*, 33.

8. *Medical & Surgical History*, vol.12, 928.

9. Stephen W. Sears, *George B. McClellan, The Young Napoleon* (New York: Da Capo, 1988), 116.

10. Duncan, *The Medical Department*, 38.

11. Jeffry D. Wert, *The Sword of Lincoln, The Army of the Potomac* (New York: Simon & Schuster, 2005), 43.

12. Hood, *Jonathan Letterman*, 53.

13. *Medical & Surgical History,* vol. 12, 177–178.

14. "Report of the Sanitary Commission," *Harper's Weekly*, August 24, 1861, 542.

15. Stille, *Sanitary Commission, 103.*

16. Ibid., 169–170.

17. Between October and December 1861, more than 3,900 men were discharged from the Army of the Potomac for lack of their physical fitness; about 2,900 of them were disabled at the time they enlisted. Tripler considered them frauds who cost the government nearly $200,000 a month before they were sent home.

18. Duncan, *The Medical Department*, 84.

19. William A. Hammond, *A Treatise on Hygiene With Special Reference to the Military Service* (Philadelphia: J. B. Lippincott., 1863), 349–350.

20. Stille, *Sanitary Commission*, 113.

21. The Sanitary Commission did not get everything it sought in the new legislation. The provision of medical supplies and wagons remained the province of the quartermaster corps, for example.

22. William Quentin Maxwell, *Lincoln's Fifth Wheel* (New York: Longmans, Green & Co., 1956), 126.

23. Stille, *Sanitary Commission*, 131.

24. Adams, *Doctors in Blue*, 32.

25. Gillett, *The Army Medical Department 1818–1865,* 184.

26. Alfred Jay Bollet, MD, *Civil War Medicine Challenges and Triumphs* (Tucson, AZ: Galen Press, 2002), 350.

27. Charles S. Tripler, *Report of Surgeon Charles S. Tripler, Army of the Potomac, August 12, 1861 to March 17, 1862* (Washington, DC: Government Printing Office, 1880–1901), 10.

28. Letterman Collection of Gordon Dammann

29. Freemon, *Gangrene & Glory*, 68–69.

30. Bollet, *Civil War Medicine*, 120.

31. Adams, *Doctors in Blue*, 60–61, 69.

32. John T. Greenwood, "Hammond and Letterman: A Tale of Two Men Who Changed Army Medicine," *The Landpower* Essay, June 2003, 3.

Chapter 4

1. Bollet, *Civil War* Medicine, 8 9.

2. Clements, "Memoir of Jonathan Letterman, M.D.," 2.

3. Letterman, *Medical Recollections*, 8.

4. Ibid., 7.

5. Clements, *Memoir of Jonathan Letterman*, 4.

6. Maxwell, *Lincoln's Fifth Wheel*, 161.

7. Sears, *George B. McClellan*, 230–231, 236.

8. Adams, *Doctors in Blue*, 194–195.

9. *Medical & Surgical History*, vol. 11, 214.

10. John Davis Billings, *Hardtack and Coffee*, (Memphis, TN: General Books, 1887), 112.

11. Ibid., 115–135.

12. *Medical & Surgical History*, vol. 14, 351.

13. Adams, *Doctors in Blue*, 210.

14. Maxwell, *Lincoln's Fifth Wheel*, 42.

15. Billings, *Hardtack and Coffee*, 81.

16. Hood, *Jonathan Letterman*, 80.

17. "Character of Wounds," *Harper's Weekly*, June 11, 1864, 379.

18. *Medical & Surgical History*, vol. 11, 218.

19. Letterman, *Medical Recollections*, 24–25.

20. Ibid., 24–30

21. *Medical & Surgical History*, vol. 2, 934.

22. Letterman, *Medical Recollections*, 32.

23. Adams, *Doctors in Blue*, 75.

24. Ibid., 76.

25. Louis Duncan, "Pope's Virginia Campaign," *The Military Surgeon*, January 1913, 11.

26. Duncan, *The Medical Department*, 41.

27. Freemon, *Gangrene and Glory*, 76.

28. Letterman, *Medical Recollections*, 33.
29. Ibid., 34.

Chapter 5

1. Alonzo Hill, *In Memoriam. A Discourse for Lieut. Thomas Jefferson Spurr, Fifteenth Massachusetts Volunteers* (Boston: John Wilson and Son, 1862), 19.
2. Letterman, *Medical Recollections*, 34.
3. Hood, *Jonathan Letterman*, 97
4. Letterman, *Medical Recollections*, 35.
5. Ibid.
6. Maxwell, *Lincoln's Fifth Wheel*, 171.
7. Letterman, *Medical Recollections*, 35.
8. Ibid., 36.
9. Ibid., 39.
10. Duncan, *The Medical Department*, 23–24.
11. Ibid., 24.
12. Wert, *The Sword of Lincoln*, 159.
13. Ted Ballard, *Antietam* (Washington, DC: Center of Military History, U.S. Army, 2006), 39.
14. John Tooker, MD, "Antietam: Aspects of Medicine, Nursing and the Civil War," *Transactions of the American Clinical and Climatological Association* 118 (2007): 218.
15. Stevens, *Three Years*, 153.
16. *1860 United States Census*, U.S. Census Bureau.
17. Duncan, *The Medical Department*, 27.
18. James Greiner, *A Surgeon's Civil War* (Kent, OH: Kent State University Press, 1994), 23.
19. Lewis H. Steiner, MD, *Diary Kept During the Rebel Occupation of Frederick MD and an Account of the Operations of the U.S. Sanitary Commission* (New York: Anson D. F. Randolph, 1862), 31–32, 41.
20. *Antietam National Battlefield: Letters and Diaries of Soldiers and Civilians* (National Park Service), http://www.nps.gov/anti/forteachers/upload/Letters%20and%20Diaries%20of%20Soldiers%20and%20Civilians.pdf, accessed June 4, 2010.

21. A little more than a year earlier at Bull Run, it took the Army of the Potomac's medical department a week to evacuate about one-fourth as many casualties from the battlefield.

22. Letterman, *Medical Recollections*, 41.

23. Ibid., 44–45.

24. Pry House Museum Exhibit, National Civil War Medicine Museum, Antietam, MD.

25. Pry House Museum Exhibit, National Civil War Medicine Museum, citing the *Indianapolis Weekly Sentinel*, January 26, 1863.

26. Letterman, *Medical Recollections*, 47–48.

27. Greiner, *A Surgeon's Civil War*, 38.

28. Stille, *Sanitary Commission*, 262–263.

29. Maxwell, *Lincoln's Fifth Wheel*, 173.

30. Steiner, *Diary Kept*, 36.

31. Gillett, *The Army Medical Department 1818–1865*, 193.

32. Letterman, *Medical Recollections*, 50.

33. Greiner, *A Surgeon's Civil War*, 27.

Chapter 6

1. *1860 United States Census*, U.S. Census Bureau.

2. Donald C. Pfanz, *War So Terrible* (Richmond, VA: Page One History Publications, 2003), 14.

3. Wert, *The Sword of Lincoln*, 175.

4. Letterman, *Medical Recollections*, 51.

5. *Medical & Surgical History*, vol. 3, 711–712.

6. Letterman, *Medical Recollections*, 57–58.

7. Ibid.

8. Ibid., 60.

9. Gabriel and Metz, *A History*, 190.

10. Letterman, *Medical Recollections*, 63.

11. Adams, *Doctors in Blue*, 153.

12. Mary A. Livermore, *My Story of the War* (Williamstown: Corner House, 1978, original edition 1887), 325.

13. "The Army of the Potomac from Warrenton," *The New York Times*, December 13, 1862.

14. Ibid.

15. Pfanz, *War So Terrible*, 16.

16. "The Army of the Potomac," *The New York Times*.

17. Ibid.

18. Stille, *Sanitary Commission*, 368.

19. Pfanz, *War So Terrible*, 22.

20. Duncan, *The Medical Department*, 176.

21. Gordon W. Jones, "The Medical History of the Fredericksburg Campaign: Course and Significance," *Journal of the History of Medicine and Allied Sciences,* vol. 18, no. 3, 248.

22. Greiner, *A Surgeon's Civil War*, 54.

23. Duncan, *The Medical Department*, 180.

24. Pfanz, *War So Terrible*, 82.

25. Ibid.

26. Based on personal research conducted throughout the town of Fredericksburg and on the battlefield.

27. Pfanz, *War So Terrible*, 95.

28. Duncan, *The Medical Department*, 180.

29. Franklin B. Hough, "New York Infantry Surgeon's Fredericksburg Oral History," Fredericksburg & Spotsylvania National Military Park Archives.

30. David Chamberlain, "Letter by 4th Michigan Regiment's Surgeon," Fredericksburg & Spotsylvania National Military Park Archives.

31. Pfanz, *War So Terrible*, 102.

32. Letterman, *Medical Recollections*, 89.

33. John Brinton, "History of the Army of the Potomac from Oct: 1 to Dec. 20, 1862," National Archives Record Group 94, Entry 628.

34. Stille, *Sanitary Commission*, 371.

35. Alfred Jay Bollet, MD, "The Truth About Civil War Surgery, *Civil War Times*, October 2004, 370.

36. Stevens, *Three Years*, 180.

37. Clements, *A Memoir of Jonathan Letterman*, 11.

38. Hood, *Jonathan Letterman*, 100.

39. Greenwood, *Hammond and Letterman*, 3.

Chapter 7

1. Gary Gallagher, *Chancellorsville* (Chapel Hill: University of North Carolina Press, 1996), 181.

2. Letterman, *Medical Recollections*, 91.

3. Coincidentally, when Letterman was transferred from Fort Defiance, Arizona, to Fort Union, New Mexico, nearly ten years earlier, he replaced Irwin, who had taken Letterman's place earlier at Fort Defiance.

4. Adams, *Doctors in Blue*, 82.

5. Simon, *Personal Memoirs*, 173–174.

6. Letterman, *Medical Recollections,* 94. The following month, Washington hospital was transferred to a new medical department so Letterman could not follow through on his medical data collection initiative.

7. Ibid., 109.

8. Maxwell, *Lincoln's Fifth Wheel*, 202.

9. Letterman, *Medical Recollections*, 102–103.

10. Ibid., 97.

11. Ibid., 99–100.

12. *The Medical & Surgical Reporter*, May 16, 1863.

13. Letterman, *Medical Recollections*, 110.

14. Ibid., 115.

15. Gillett, *The Army Medical Department 1818–1865*, 210.

16. Letterman, *Medical Recollections*, 125.

17. Gallagher, *Chancellorsville*, 187.

18. Wert, *The Sword of Lincoln*, 254.

19. Letterman, *Medical Recollections*, 138.

20. Gallagher, *Chancellorsville*, 190.

21. Russel H. Beatie, *Army of the Potomac, McClellan Takes Command September 1861–February 1862* (New York: Da Capo, 2004), 433.

22. Ibid., 435.

23. Simon, *Personal Memoirs*, 234.

24. Ibid., 235.

25. Letterman, *Medical Recollections*, 129.

26. *Medical & Surgical History*, vol. 27, 195.

27. Stephen R. Taaffe, *Commanding the Army of the Potomac* (Lawrence: University of Kansas, 2006), 180.

28. Billy Arthur, *Gettysburg Staff Ride Briefing Book* (Fort McNair, DC: U.S. Army Center of Military History), 90.

29. Ibid., 90.

30. Taaffe, *Commanding the Army*, 110.

31. Letterman, *Medical Recollections*, 165.

Chapter 8

1. Arthur, *Gettysburg Staff Ride*, 5.

2. Gregory A. Coco, *A Vast Sea of Misery* (Gettysburg, PA: Thomas Publications, 1988), 188.

3. Russell Stewart, *The United States Army and the Forging of a Nation, 1775–1917* (Washington, DC: United States Army, 2005), 2.

4. Extended author interviews and battlefield tour with certified Gettysburg guide Phil Lechak.

5. Stewart, *The United States Army*, 3.

6. Gregory A. Coco, *Strange and Blighted Land, Gettysburg: The Aftermath of a Battle* (Gettysburg, PA: Thomas Publications, 1995), 153.

7. Philip Andrade, *A Survey of Union and Confederate Casualties at Gettysburg* (Gettysburg, PA: The Battle of Gettysburg Resource Center), 7.

8. Stille, *Sanitary Commission*, 377.

9. Duncan, *The Medical Department*, 212.

10. Arthur, *Gettysburg Staff Ride*, 12.

11. Andrade, *A Survey*, 5.

12. Jonathan Letterman, *Gettysburg Report* (Culpeper Courthouse, VA, October 3, 1863).

13. Gettysburg received 1.39 inches of rain by 4:00 p.m. on July 4, 1863, with the rain far more intense that night.

14. Duncan, *The Medical Department*, 217–218.

15. Coco, *Strange and Blighted Land*, 210.

16. Ibid., 173.

17. Sarah Broadhead, *The Diary of a Lady at Gettysburg* (privately published, 1864), 20.

18. Cornelia Hancock, *South After Gettysburg* (Philadelphia: University of Pennsylvania Press, 1937), 6–8.

19. Andrew Boyd Cross, *Battle of Gettysburg and the Christian Commission* (publisher not listed, 1865), 25.

20. Stephen Sears, *The Civil War Papers of George B. McClellan* (New York: Ticknor & Fields, 1989), 340.

21. Gerard A. Patterson, *Debris of Battle* (Mechanicsburg, PA: Stackpole Books, 1997), 49.

22. Hood, *Jonathan Letterman*, 133.

23. Fatout, *Letters of a Civil War Surgeon*, 70.

24. Coco, *Strange and Blighted Land*, 253.

25. Ibid., 243–244

26. Ibid.

27. Stevens, *Three Years*, 214.

28. Patterson, *Debris of Battle*, 96.

29. Robert N. Scott, *The War of the Rebellion: A Compilation of Official Records* (Washington, DC: U.S. Government Printing Office, 1889), vol. 27, 197.

30. The typical costs for sending the dead home for burial were $15 for embalming, $5 for the wood box, and about $24 for transportation.

31. Office of the Surgeon General Letters and Endorsements, vol. 4, record group 112, National Archives.

32. Patterson, *Debris of Battle*, 160.

33. Ibid., 190–191.

34. Michael B. Chesson, *The Journal of a Civil War Surgeon* (Lincoln: University of Nebraska Press, 2003), 108.

35. Letterman, *Medical Recollections*, 169–170.

36. Samuel D. Gross, *Autobiography of Samuel D. Gross* (Philadelphia: George Barrie Printers, 1887), 285.

37. Ibid., 55.

38. Ibid. 281.

39. This was the equivalent of the entire population of the nation's capital at the start of the Civil War.

Chapter 9

1. Letterman family letters. Thomas Sim Lee Collection, Catholic University, Washington, DC.

2. Ibid.

3. Letterman Collection of Gordon Dammann.

4. In early October, President Lincoln had established the Thanksgiving holiday by proclamation, in part asking the "Almighty Hand to heal the nation and restore it as soon as may be consistent with the Divine purposes to the full enjoyment of peace, harmony, tranquility and Union."

5. Letterman, *Medical Recollections*, 182.

6. Ibid., 183.

7. Joseph Smith, "A Review of the Life and Work of Jonathan Letterman, M.D.," *John Hopkins Hospital Bulletin* 27 no. 299: 245.

8. Letterman, *Medical Recollections*, 185–186.

9. Ibid., 183.

10. Glenn E. Billet, *The Department of the Susquehanna* (Lancaster, PA: L. B. Herr & Son, 1962), 9, 13.

11. Scott, *War of the Rebellion*, vol. 33, 382.

12. Ibid., 380.

13. Ibid. 379–383.

14. Horace Hillery, *Putnam County in the Civil War* (Patterson, NY: typewritten essay, 1961), unnumbered.

15. A memorial was a statement included in the official Congressional Record that was a public recognition of an individual or organization.

16. Clements, *A Memoir of Jonathan Letterman*, 21.

17. Ibid., 14.

18. "Dispatches," *The New York Times*, December 6, 1863.

19. Duncan, *The Medical Department*, 259.

20. Ibid., 260.

21. "Government Care of the Soldier Hospitals and Supplies," *The New York Times*, August 8, 1864.

22. "Letters," *The New York Times*, December 20, 1863.

23. Duncan, *The Medical Department*, 270.

24. Ibid., 272.

25. *Official Register of the Officers and Cadets* (West Point, NY: U.S. Military Academy, June 1864).

26. Letterman family letters. Thomas Sim Lee Collection, Catholic University, Washington, DC.

27. Letterman Collection of Gordon Damman.

28. "Hammond Trial," *The New York Times*, August 23, 1864.

29. Simon, *Personal Memoirs*, 310.

30. Sears, *George B. McClellan*, 386.

31. Sears, *The Civil War Papers*, 623.

32. Gillett, *The Army Medical Department 1818–1865*, 229.

33. Bollet, *Civil War Medicine*, 188.

Chapter 10

1. Arthur Wright, "Biographical Memoir of Benjamin Silliman," National Academy of Sciences Paper Presentation, April 1911.

2. Benjamin Silliman, Jr., *A Description of the Recently Discovered Petroleum Region in California with a Report on the Same* (New York: Francis & Loutrei Printers, 1865), 2.

3. Ibid., 22.

4. Ibid., 18–19.

5. Gerald T. White, *Formative Years in the Far West, A History of Standard Oil Company in California and Predecessors* (New York: Appleton-Century-Crofts, 1962), 2–9.

6. *The Philadelphia and California Petroleum Company Prospectus* (Philadelphia: Crissy & Markley Printers, 1865), 4–6.

7. Martin D. Saltzman, "Who Salted the Sample," *Chemistry & Industry*, January 1, 1996, 9.

8. J. Williamson, *Professor Silliman's Report Upon the Oil Property of the Philadelphia and California Petroleum Company* (Philadelphia: E. C. Markley & Son Printers, 1865), 5.

9. Ibid., 9.

10. Alfred Jay Bollet, MD, "An Analysis of the Medical Problems of the Civil War," *Transactions of the American Clinical & Climatological Association*, 103: 131.

11. Stewart Brooks, *Civil War Medicine* (Springfield, IL: Charles C. Thomas Publishing, 1966), 116.

12. California Petroleum Company shares were offered at $40 each. Extensive research did not locate an initial stock offering for Philadelphia & California Company, but given the near-identical nature of the two companies, their timing, and property to be explored, it's likely the $40 offer was the same for both companies.

13. John Schertzer Hittell, *A History of the City of San Francisco* (San Francisco: A. L. Bancroft & Company, 1878), 322–324.

14. Ibid., 336–338.

15. "Notes on a Tour Through the Southern Coast Counties of California," *Daily Alta California*, June 7, 1865, 1.

16. "City Items," *Daily Alta California*, July 3, 1865, 1.

17. Joseph D. Weeks, *The Production of Petroleum in 1894* (Washington, DC: Government Printing Office, 1895), 373.

18. "Notes," *Springfield Republican*, March 25, 1865.

19. Gerald T. White, "The Case of the Salted Sample: A California Oil Industry Skeleton," *Pacific Historical Review,* May 1966, 158.

20. Letterman family letters. Thomas Sim Lee Collection, Catholic University, Washington, DC.

21. Ibid.

22. Ibid.

23. White, "The Case of the Salted Sample," 164.

24. Stephen Peckham, "Examination of the Bituminous Substances Occurring in Southern California," *Geology of the Coast Ranges,* 1882, 66.

25. Letterman, *Medical Recollections*, Preface.

26. Ibid., 185.

27. Although a Southerner, Davis was a devout Unionist. Two of his brothers fought in the Army of Northern Virginia and were killed in battle.

28. Letterman, *Medical Recollections*, 129.

29. Ibid., 153.

30. Ibid., 100.

31. Ibid., 156.

32. Ibid., 157.

33. "Reviews and Bibliographical Notices," *New York Medical Journal,* September 1866, 453–455.

34. Ibid.

35. White, "The Case of the Salted Sample," 179. It wasn't until the 1870s that oil exploration experience, coupled with advances in equipment, enabled wildcatters to tap extensive oil deposits in the Los Angeles, Ventura, Kern, and Santa Barbara Counties.

36. Peckham, "Examination of the Bituminous," 73.

37. Saltzman, "Who Salted the Sample," 9.

38. White, "The Case of the Salted Sample," 175.

39. Ibid., 177–180.

40. In Congressional testimony, Silliman acknowledged he was paid a $5,000 advance for his report, plus $10,000 to $20,000 when completed.

Chapter 11

1. Hittell, "A History of the City of San Francisco," 357–360.

2. Ibid., 366–368.

3. *1870 United States Census,* U.S. Census Bureau.

4. Ralph Shaffer and Sheila Skjeie, *California and the Coming of the Fifteenth Amendment.* Vol. I: *California Racism and the Fifteenth Amendment.* http://www.csupomona.edu/~reshaffer/Books/black/amend_xv.htm, accessed October 23, 2011.

5. Winfield J. Davis, *History of Political Conventions in California* (Sacramento: Sacramento Society of California Pioneers, 1893), 242.

6. "Vote of San Francisco," *Daily Alta California Newspaper,* Sept. 11, 1867.

7. Letterman Collection of Gordon Dammann. Following its convention, the Union Party was hurt by defectors, who broke away to form the Republican Party, effectively dividing the Union Party vote. Following the 1867 election the Union Party dissolved. In future elections, Letterman faced Republican Party opponents.

8. A native of Pennsylvania, Massey was an accomplished cabinetmaker before he joined the California gold rush in 1849 and then settled in San Francisco to become one of its foremost undertakers.

9. Letterman's brother, William Henry, visited Letterman in the days following his wife's death. He later wrote the only known account of Mary's death in correspondence with his family.

10. "Inquests," *Daily Alta California,* June 28, 1871.

11. Charles Kieffer, "Tropical Diseases," *The Philadelphia Medical Journal,* February 7, 1908, 252.

12. JoAnn Prause, Roxanne Cohen Silver, Judith Pizarro, "Physical and Mental Health Costs of Traumatic War Experiences Among Civil War Veterans," *Archives of General Psychiatry* 63 (2006), 196.

13. Jonathan Letterman, *The Coroner's Report 1868–1869 to the Board of Supervisors (City and County of San Francisco).*

14. Ibid.

15. Ibid.

16. "Notices," *Sacramento Daily Union,* July 20, 1870.

17. "Annual Report of Coroner Letterman," *Daily Alta California,* August 5, 1871.

18. E. T. Wilkens, MD, *Insanity and Insane Asylums for the State of California* (Sacramento: T. A. Sprixger, State Printer, 1871), 136–137.

19. *Stockton Daily Independent,* March 16, 1872, *Sacramento Daily Union,* March 18, 1872.

20. "Obituary Notice of Dr. Letterman," The Western Lancet, April 1872, 232–233.

21. Clements, *A Memoir,* 25–26.

22. Ibid., 27.

23. Mary Gillett, *The Army Medical Department 1865–1917* (Washington, DC: Center for Military History, U.S. Army, 1987), 11–13.

24. Wyndham D. Miles, *A History of the City of San Francisco* (San Francisco: A. L. Bancroft & Company, 1878), 25–34.

25. "Notices," *Washington Post,* October 22, 1911.

26. "Miss Letterman Rites Planned in Baltimore," *Albuquerque Tribune,* December 17, 1957, 13.

27. "Important Orders by the Medical Director of the Army of the Potomac," *The Medical and Surgical Reporter,* November 15, 1862, 186.

28. "Our Medical Army Does a Vast Job," *The New York Times,* June 13, 1943. American troops suffered approximately 15,600 wounded in thirty-eight days' fighting on Sicily. By contrast, Letterman had been

responsible for approximately 12,000 wounded in only three days' fighting at Gettysburg.

29. "Medicine: All-American Surgeon," *Time*, November 24, 1947.

Chapter 12

1. Chesson, *The Journal of a Civil War* Surgeon, 105.
2. Letterman, *Medical Recollections*, 21.
3. *Report of Surgeon Jonathan Letterman to Brigadier General S. Williams, March 1, 1863.*
4. Letterman, *Medical Recollections*, 51.
5. Freemon, *Gangrene and Glory*, 215–222.
6. Gillett, *The Army Medical Department 1865–1917*, 276–278.
7. *Letterman Report to Brigadier General S. Williams.*
8. Gillett, *The Army Medical Department 1865–1917*, 280–286.
9. Ibid., 286.
10. Harold Straubing, *In Hospital and Camp* (Harrisburg, PA: Stackpole Books, 1993), 90–93.
11. Russell Alger, *The Spanish-American War* (New York: Harper & Brothers, 1901), 411.
12. Ibid., 412–414.
13. Hood, *Jonathan Letterman*, 194–197.
14. Clements, *A Memoir*, 21.
15. Rudolph Bloom, "Surgeon Jonathan Letterman, U.S.A.," *The Army Medical Bulletin*, October 1937, 85.

Chapter 13

1. *The Centennial History of the Phi Kappa Psi Fraternity*, vol. 1, appendix 2, 497–500.
2. Ibid.
3. Sears, *George B. McClellan*, 196.

BIBLIOGRAPHY

Books

Adams, George Worthington. *Doctors in Blue*. Baton Rouge: Louisiana State University Press, 1980.

Baxley, Haughton. *The Evolution of Preventive Medicine in the United States Army, 1607–1939*. Washington, DC: Government Printing Office, 1968.

Beatie, Russel H. *Army of the Potomac, Birth of Command November 1860–September 1861, Volume 1*. New York: Da Capo, 2002.

———. *Army of the Potomac, McClellan's First Campaign March–May 1862*, vol. III. New York City: Savas Beatie, 2007.

———. *Army of the Potomac, McClellan Takes Command September 1861–February 1862*. New York: Da Capo, 2004.

Billet, Glenn E. *The Department of the Susquehanna*. Lancaster, PA: L. B. Herr & Son, 1962.

Billings, John Davis. *Hardtack and Coffee*. Memphis, TN: General Books, 1887.

Blustein, Bonnie Ellen. *Preserve Your Love of Science*. New York: Cambridge University Press, 1991.

Bollet MD, Alfred Jay. *Civil War Medicine Challenges and Triumphs*. Tucson, AZ: Galen Press, 2002.

Brooks, Stewart. *Civil War Medicine*. Springfield, IL: Charles C. Thomas Publishing, 1966.

Brown Jr, Canter. *Fort Meade 1849–1900*. Tuscaloosa: University of Alabama Press, 1995.

Bucklin, Sophronia, *In Hospital & Camp*. Philadelphia, PA: John E. Potter & Co., 1869.

Byrne, Frank L., and Andrew T. Weaver. *Haskell of Gettysburg; His Life and Civil War Papers*. Kent, OH: Kent State University, 1989.

Camp Letterman, The Lost Legacy of Gettysburg's "Hospital Woods." Gettysburg, PA: Gettysburg Battlefield Preservation Association, 1997.

Caton, Bruce. *The Army of the Potomac: Mr. Lincoln's Army.* Garden City, NY: Doubleday & Company, 1951

Chesson, Michael B. *The Journal of a Civil War Surgeon.* Lincoln: University of Nebraska Press, 2003.

Coco, Gregory A. *A Vast Sea of Misery.* Gettysburg, PA: Thomas Publications, 1988

———. *Strange and Blighted Land, Gettysburg: The Aftermath of a Battle.* Gettysburg, PA: Thomas Publications, 1995.

Coddington, Edwin B. *The Gettysburg Campaign.* New York City: Simon & Schuster, 1968.

Coolidge MD, Richard H. *Statistical Report of the Sickness and Mortality in the Army of the United States, 1839–1855.* Washington: A.O.P. Nicholson, 1856.

———. *Statistical Report of the Sickness and Mortality of the Army of the United States, 1855–1860.* Washington: George W. Bowman, 1860.

Creigh, Alfred. *History of Washington County.* Harrisburg, PA: B. Singerly Printer, 1871.

Cross, Andrew Boyd. *Battle of Gettysburg and the Christian Commission.* Publisher not listed, 1865.

Crumrine, Boyd. *History of Washington County, Pennsylvania with Biographical Sketches of Many of Its Pioneers and Prominent Men.* Philadelphia: L. H. Leverts & Co., 1882.

Davis, Winfield J. *History of Political Conventions in California.* Sacramento: Sacramento Society of California Pioneers, 1893.

Deaderick, Lt. Col. Robert D. *Field Medical Support of the Army of the Potomac at Gettysburg.* Carlisle Barracks, PA: U.S. Army War College, 1989.

Denney, Robert E. *Civil War Medicine.* New York: Sterling Publishing, Co., 1994.

Duncan, Louis C. *The Medical Department of the United States Army in the Civil War.* Washington, DC: U.S. Army, 1910.

Ellis, Thomas. *Leaves from the Diary of an Army Surgeon.* New York: J. Bradburn, 1863.

Ewing, Blaine. *Canonsburg Centennial, 1802–1902.* Self-published, 1903.

Fatout, Paul. *Letters of a Civil War Surgeon.* West Lafayette, IN: Purdue University Studies, Humanities Series, 1961.

Forrest, Earle R. *A History of Washington County, Pennsylvania.* Chicago: S. J. Clark Publishing, 1926.

Frazer, Robert W. *Mansfield on the Condition of Western Forts 1853–54.* Norman: University of Oklahoma Press, 1963.

Freemon, Frank R. *Gangrene and Glory.* Chicago: University of Illinois Press, 2001.

————. *Microbes and Minie Balls.* Cranbury, NJ: Associated University Presses, 1993.

Frink, Maurice. *Fort Defiance & The Navajos.* Boulder, CO: Pruett Press, 1968.

Gallagher, Gary. *Chancellorsville.* Chapel Hill: University of North Carolina Press, 1996.

Gabriel, Richard A., and Karen S. Metz. *A History of Military Medicine.* Westport, CT: Greenwood Press, 1992.

Gardner, Mark. *Fort Union National Monument.* Tucson, AZ: Western National Parks Association, 2005.

Gillett, Mary C. *The Army Medical Department 1818–1865.* Washington, DC: Center of Military History, U.S. Army, 1987.

————. *The Army Medical Department 1865–1917.* Washington, DC: Center of Military History, U.S. Army, 1995.

Gould, George Milbry. *The Jefferson Medical College of Philadelphia, Benefactors, alumni, hospital etc. Its founders, officers, instructors, 1826–1904.* Volume 1. *A History.* Philadelphia: Thomas Jefferson University, 2009.

Greenleaf, Charles R. *A Manual for the Medical Officer of the United States Army.* Philadelphia: J. B. Lippincott, 1864.

Grefenstette, Jerry. *Images of America, Canonsburg.* Charleston, SC: Arcadia Publishing, 2009.

Greiner, James M. *A Surgeon's Civil War.* Kent, OH: Kent State University Press, 1994.

Gross, Samuel D. *Autobiography of Samuel D. Gross.* Philadelphia: George Barrie Printers, 1887.

Guthrie, Dwight Raymond. *John McMillan, The Apostle of Presbyterianism in the West, 1752–1833.* Pittsburgh: University of Pittsburgh Press, 1952.

Hammond, John Martin. *Quaint and Historic Forts of North America.* Philadelphia: J. B. Lippencott Company, 1915.

Hammond, William A. *A Treatise on Hygiene With Special Reference to the Military Service.* Philadelphia: J. B. Lippincott & Co., 1863.

Hancock, Cornelia. *South After Gettysburg.* Philadelphia: University of Pennsylvania Press, 1937.

Hart, Paul J. *Old Forts of the Far West.* Seattle, WA: Superior Publishing Company, 1965.

Haskell, Franklin. *Battle of Gettysburg.* Madison, WI: Democrat Printing Company, 1908.

Hemmeter MD, John C. *Diseases of the Intestines.* Philadelphia: P. Blakiston's Son, 1901.

Henry, Guy. *Military Record of Civilian Appointments of the United States Army.* New York: Carleton Publisher, 1869.

Hittell, John Schertzer. *A History of the City of San Francisco.* San Francisco: A. L. Bancroft, 1878.

Hunt, Aaurora. *The Army of the Potomac, 1860–1866.* Mechanicsburg, PA: Stackpole Books, 2004.

La Garde, Louis A. *Gunshot Injuries: How They Are Inflicted, Their Complications and Treatment.* New York: William Wood, 1914.

Lechak, Phil. *A Blue & Gray Sea of Misery.* Gettysburg, PA: Self-published, 2010.

Letterman, Jonathan A. *Medical Recollections of the Army of the Potomac.* New York: D. Appleton & Co., 1866.

Manny, Solon W. *History of Fort Ripley, 1849–1859.* Minnesota Historical Society, 1905.

Mansfield, Joseph. *Mansfield on the Condition of Western Forts, 1853–1854.* Norman: University of Oklahoma Press, 1963.

Maxwell, William Quentin. *Lincoln's Fifth Wheel.* New York City: Longmans, Green & Co., 1956.

McGaugh, Scott. *Battlefield Angels, Saving Lives Under Enemy Fire From Valley Forge to Afghanistan.* Oxford: Osprey Publishing, 2011.

Miles, Wyndham D. *A History of the National Library of Medicine.* Bethesda, MD: U.S. Department of Health & Human Resources, 1982.

The Military Surgeon. Washington, DC: Association of Military Surgeons of the United States, 1922.

Morris, William. A. *A Manual of Ambulance Transport.* London: Harrison & Sons, 1893.

Nietz, John Alfred. *Old textbooks: spelling, grammar, reading, arithmetic, geography, American history, civil government, physiology, penmanship, art, music, as taught in the common schools from colonial days to 1900.* Pittsburgh: University of Pittsburgh Press, 1961.

Operations of the Sanitary Commission During and After the Battle of Gettysburg. Philadelphia: William C. Bryant & Co., 1863.

Patterson, Gerard A. *Debris of Battle.* Mechanicsburg, PA: Stackpole Books, 1997.

Pfanz, Donald C. *War So Terrible.* Richmond, VA: Page One History Publications, 2003.

Quarsten, John V. *Fort Monroe The Key to The South.* Charleston, SC: Arcadia Publishing, 2000.

Rex, Millicent Barton. *Life at Jefferson College in 1850.* Canonsburg, PA: Phi Kappa Psi, 1966.

Richardson, R. G. *Larrey—What Manner of Man?* Proceedings of the Royal Society of Medicine, vol. 70, July 1977.

Robertson, James. *Stonewall Jackson*. New York: MacMillan, 1997.

Rutkow, Ira M. *Bleeding Blue and Gray*. New York: Random House, 2005.

Sears, Stephen W. *Chancellorsville*. Boston: Houghton Mifflin, 1996.

———. *The Civil War Papers of George B. McClellan*. New York: Ticknor & Fields, 1989.

———. *Controversies & Commanders*. Boston: Houghton Mifflin, 1999.

———. *George B. McClellan, The Young Napoleon*. New York: Da Capo, 1988.

———. *Gettysburg*. Boston: Houghton Mifflin, 2004.

Simon, John Y. *Personal Memoirs of John H. Brinton, Civil War Surgeon, 1861–1865*. Carbondale, IL: Southern Illinois University Press, 1996.

Steiner, Lewis H. *Account of the Field Relief Corps of the U.S. Sanitary Commission in the Army of the Potomac*. A compendium of public addresses, 1857–1875, with no designated publisher or publication date.

Stevens, George T. *Three Years in the Sixth Corps*. Albany, NY: S. R. Gray, Publisher, 1866.

Stille, Charles J. *History of the United States Sanitary Commission*. Philadelphia: J. B. Lippincott, 1866.

Storkel, Yda Addis. *A Memorial and Biographical History of the Counties of Santa Barbara, San Luis Obispo and Ventura, California*. Chicago: The Lewis Publishing Company, 1891.

Stewart, Russell. *The United States Army and the Forging of a Nation, 1775–1917*. Washington, DC: United States Army, 2005.

Straubing, Harold. *In Hospital and Camp*. Harrisburg, PA: Stackpole Books, 1993.

Swasey, W. F. *The Early Days and Men of California*. Oakland, PA: Pacific Press Publishing, 1891.

Swinton, William. *Campaigns of the Army of the Potomac*. New York: Charles Richardson, 1866.

Taaffe, Stephen R. *Commanding the Army of the Potomac*. Lawrence: University Press of Kansas, 2006.

Taylor, Frank. *Philadelphia in the Civil War, 1861–1865*. Philadelphia: Dunlap Printing, 1913.

Trudeau, Noah Andre. *Gettysburg, A Testing of Courage*. New York: HarperCollins, 2002.

Wagner MD, Frederick B. *Thomas Jefferson University: Tradition and Heritage*. Philadelphia: Thomas Jefferson University, 1989.

Wafer, Cheryl A. *A Surgeon in the Army of the Potomac*. London: McGill-Queen's University Press, 2008.

Welsh, MD, Jack D. *Medical Histories of Union Generals*. Kent, OH: The Kent State University Press, 1996.

Wert, Jeffry D. *The Sword of Lincoln, The Army of the Potomac*. New York: Simon & Schuster, 2005.

White, Gerald T. *Formative Years in the Far West, A History of Standard Oil Company in California and Predecessors*. New York: Appleton-Century-Crofts, 1962.

Wilbur, C. Keith. *Civil War Medicine*. Guilford, CT: Pequot Press, 1998.

Wilkins, MD, E. T. *Insanity and Insane Asylums for the State of California*. Sacramento: T. A. Sprixger, State Printer, 1871.

Woodwar MD, Joseph. *Chief Camp Diseases*. Philadelphia: J. B. Lippincott, 1863.

Wooster MD, David. *The Pacific Medical and Surgical Journal,* vol. IV. San Francisco, 1861.

Wormeley, Katharine Prescott. *The Other Side of the War with the Army of the Potomac*. Boston: Ticknor and Company, 1889.

Articles, Essays, and Historical Documents

Andrade, Philip. *A Survey of Union and Confederate Casualties at Gettysburg*. The Battle of Gettysburg Resource Center, 2004.

"The Army Medical Department: A Sketch of Its History, Its Organization and Its Work." *The Journal of the American Medical Association,* May 7, 14, 21, 28 and June 4, 1904. Reprinted as a booklet in 1904.

"The Army of the Potomac From Warrenton." *The New York Times,* December 13, 1862.

Arthur, Billy. *Fredericksburg Staff Ride Briefing Book,* U.S. Army Center of Military History, undated.

Arthur, Billy. *Gettysburg Staff Ride Briefing Book,* U.S. Army Center of Military History, undated.

Ayars, Charles W. "Some Notes on the Medical Service of the Army, 1812–1839." *The Military Surgeon,* May 1922; 505–524.

Ballard, Ted. "Antietam." Center of Military History, U.S. Army, 2006.

Billings, John S. "Medical Reminiscences of the Civil War." *Transactions of the College of Physicians of Philadelphia*. Third Series, vol. 27, 1895: 115–121.

Blaisdell, F. William. "Medical Advances during the Civil War." *Annals of Surgery,* 1988: 1045–50.

Bollet MD, Alfred Jay. "An Analysis of the Medical Problems of the Civil War." *Transactions of the American Clinical & Climatological Association,* 103: 128–141.

Bollet MD, Alfred Jay. "The Truth about Civil War Surgery." *Civil War Times,* October 2004.

Boulay, Peter. "History of Weather Observations, Fort Ripley, Minnesota 1849–1990." Minnesota State Climatology Office, 2006.

Brinton, John. *History of the Army of the Potomac from Oct. 1 to Dec. 20 1862.* NARA Record Group 94, Entry 628.

"Canonsburg Salutes Who's Who of 1802." *Pittsburgh Press,* February 26, 1976: 2.

"Catalogue of the Officers and Students, Jefferson College." Jefferson College, 1845.

Chamberlain, David. Letter by 4th Michigan Regiments' Surgeon. Fredericksburg & Spotsylvania National Military Park Archives, December 23, 1862.

Churchill, James O. "Wounded at Fort Donelson: A First Person Account." *Civil War Times,* July 1869: 18–26.

Clem, Richard E. "Misery Lasts Long After Antietam Battle." *Washington Times,* September 22, 2007.

Clements, Bennett A. "Memoir of Jonathan Letterman, M.D." *Journal of the Military Service Institution,* September 1883.

Delaney, Robin. "Combat Medicine in the War of 1812." *Fort Madison Daily Democrat,* September 5, 2007.

Desjardin, Thomas A, "Self-Imposed Work of Mercy: Civil War Women of the Maine Camp and Hospital Association, 1861–1865." Unpublished manuscript, Main State Archives, Records of Maine Soldiers Relief Agency.

Fahey, John H. "Bernard John Dowling Irwin and the Development of the Field Hospital at Shiloh." *Military Medicine,* May 2006.

Figg, Laurann and Farrell, Jane. "Amputation in the Civil War: Physical and Social Dimensions." *Journal of the History of Medicine and Allied Sciences,* 48: 454–475.

Fitts, Deborah. "Antietam's Pry House to Open as Seasonal Medical Museum Site." *Civil War News,* April 2005.

"Gettysburg Battlefield." *Atlantic Monthly,* November 1865.

Greenwood, John T. "Hammond and Letterman: A Tale of Two Men Who Changed Army Medicine." *The Landpower Essay,* June 2003.

Hawk, Allan. "An Ambulating Hospital: Or, How the Hospital Train Transformed Army Medicine." *Civil War History,* vol. 48, no. 3: 197.

Herron, James. "Beta Theta Pi." *Jefferson College Times,* November 1976: 7–15.

Herron James. (no title) *Jefferson College Historical Society Newsletter*, March 1973: 2–5.

Hill, Alonzo. "In Memoriam. A Discourse for Lieut. Thomas Jefferson Spurr, Fifteenth Massachusetts Volunteers." Boston: John Wilson and Son, 1862.

Hood, Jonathan D. "Jonathan Letterman and the Development of a Battlefield Evacuation System." PhD Diss. Texas Tech University, 2004. http://etd.lib.ttu.edu/theses/available/etd-07012008-31295019800837/unrestricted/31295019800837.pdf (accessed January 2, 2010).

Hough, Franklin B. 97th New York Infantry' surgeon's Fredericksburg oral history. Fredericksburg & Spotsylvania National Military Park Archives, December 1862.

Jones, Gordon W. "The Medical History of the Fredericksburg Campaign: Course and Significance." *Journal of the History of Medicine and Allied Sciences,* vol. XVIII, no. 3.

Keen MD, W. W. "Surgical Reminiscences of the Civil War." *Transactions of the College of Physicians of Philadelphia.* Third Series, vol. 27, 1905: 115–121.

Kieffer, Charles. "Tropical Diseases." *Philadelphia Medical Journal.* February 7, 1908: 252–256.

Lechak, Phil. Personal tour daylong interview on Gettysburg battlefield, Sept. 15, 2010.

Letherman, Jonathan. "Sketch of the Navajo Tribe of Indians, Territory of New Mexico (1856)." Smithsonian Institution, 1856.

Letterman, Jonathan. "The Coroner's Report 1868–1869 to the Board of [San Francisco] Supervisors."

Letterman, Jonathan. "The Coroner's Report 1871 to the Board of [San Francisco] Supervisors."

Letterman, Jonathan. "Report of the Operations of the Medical Department, July 4 to November 7, 1862." *Official Records of the War of the Rebellion.* Washington: GPO, 1880–1901. Series 27, vol. 19,106–117.

McClellan, George B., *George Brinton McClellan Papers.* Manuscript Division, Library of Congress, Washington, DC.

McCormick, Robert W. "A Union Army Medical Inspector: Norton Townshend." *Yale Journal of Biology and Medicine,* vol. 74: 169–177.

"Medicine: All-American Surgeon." *Time,* November 24, 1947.

"Miss Letterman Rites Planned in Baltimore." *Albuquerque Tribune,* December 17, 1957.

"Notice." *The Reporter,* March 20, 1823.

O'Connell, P. A. 9th Army Corp Medical Director's Fredericksburg Campaign Report. Fredericksburg & Spotsylvania National Military Park Archives, December 1862.

Ortiz, Jose M. "The Revolutionary Flying Ambulance of Napoleon's Surgeon." *U.S. Army Medical Department Journal,* October–December 1998: 17–25.

Peckham, Stephen. "Examination of the Bituminous Substances Occurring in Southern California." *Geology of the Coast Ranges, vol. II.* John Wilson & Son University Press, 1882.

Phalen (U.S. Army, ret.), Colonel James M. "Dr. Charles Stuart Tripler." *The Army Medical Bulletin,* April 1942: 176–181.

The Philadelphia and California Petroleum Company Prospectus. Crissy & Markely Printers, Philadelphia, 1865.

Pizarro, Judith; Cohen Silver, Roxanne; Prause, JoAnn. "Physical and Mental Health Costs of Traumatic War Experiences Among Civil War Veterans." *Archives of General Psychiatry,* vol. 63, 2006.

Rubenstein, David. "A Study of the Medical Support to the Union and Confederate Armies During the Battle of Chickamauga: Lessons and Implications for Today's U.S. Army Medical Department Leaders." U.S. Army, 1990.

Saltzman, Martin D. "Who Salted the Sample?" *Chemistry & Industry,* January 1, 1996.

Sartin MD, Jeffrey, and Douglas Lanska MD. "Surgeon General William A. Hammond (1828–1900): Successes and Failures of Medical Leadership." *Gundersen Lutheran Medical Journal,* vol. 5, number 1, July 2008.

Schene, Michael. "Not a Shot Fired: Fort Chokonikla and the 'Indian War' of 1849–1850." *Tequesta,* 1977 no. 37: 19–37.

Shryock, Richard H. "A Medical Perspective of the Civil War." *American Quarterly,* 1962: 161–173.

Silliman, Jr., Benjamin. "A Description of the Recently Discovered Petroleum Region in California With a Report on the Same." Francis & Loutrei Printers, February 1865.

Skjeie, Sheila and Shaffer, Ralph. *California and the Coming of the Fifteenth Amendment.* Vol. I: *California, Racism and the Fifteen Amendment, 1849–1870.* 2005 http://www.csupomona.edu/~reshaffer/Books/black/amend_xv.htm

Smith, Joseph T. "A Review of the Life and Work of Jonathan Letterman, M.D." *Johns Hopkins Hospital Bulletin* 27, no. 299: 243–247.

Steiner MD, Lewis H. "Diary Kept During the Rebel Occupation of Frederick, MD and an Account of the Operations of the U.S. Sanitary Commission." New York: Anson D. F. Randolph, 1862.

Tooker MD, John. "Antietam: Aspects of Medicine, Nursing and the Civil War." *Transactions of the American Clinical and Climatological Association,* vol. 118, 2007: 215–223.

Tripler, Charles S. "Report of Surgeon Charles S. Tripler, Army of the Potomac, August 12, 1861 to March 17, 1862." *Official Records of the War of Rebellion.* Washington: GPO, 1880–1901. Series I, vol. 5.

Wagner Jr., M.D., Frederick B. "Thomas Jefferson University: Tradition and Heritage." Thomas Jefferson University, 1989, 1022–23.

The War of the Rebellion. A Compilation of the Official Records of the Union and Confederate Armies. 128 volumes. Washington, D.C, 1882–1900.

Ward, James A. "J. Edgar Thomas and Thomas A. Scott: A Symbiotic Relationship." *Pennsylvania Magazine of History & Biography,* vol. 100, number 1, January 1976: 37–65.

Welch, Abraham. 4th New York Infantry Surgeon's Letter. Fredericksburg & Spotsylvania National Military Park Archives, December 27, 1862.

White, Gerald T. "The Case of the Salted Sample: A California Oil Industry Skeleton." *The Pacific Historical Review,* vol. 35, no. 2 (May 1966): 153–184.

Williamson, J. "Professor Siliman's Report Upon the Oil Property of the Philadelphia and California Petroleum Company." E. C. Markley & Son Printers, 1865.

Online/Other Sources

Air Force. "Military Medicine Through the Eighteenth Century (MD0405)." http://www.au.af.mil/au/awc/awcgate/milmedhist/chapter2.html (accessed December 30, 2009).

"Antietam: Eyewitness to Battle, Part 2." National Park Service, http://www.nps.gov/anti/historyculture/eyewitness-to-battle-part-2.htm (accessed July 28, 2010).

"Antietam National Battlefield: Letters and Diaries of Soldiers and Civilians." http://www.nps.gov/anti/forteachers/upload/Letters%20and%20Diaries%20of%20Soldiers%20and%20Civilians.pdf (accessed August 4, 2010).

Bollet MD, Alfred Jay. "Some Considerations of the Quality of American Medicine at the Time of the Civil War." http://www.civilwarsurgeons.org (accessed February 12, 2010).

"Caring for Men, The History of Civil War Medicine." http://www.civilwarhome.com/medicinehistory.htm (accessed December 6, 2009).

Goellnitz, Jenny. "Civil War Medicine: An Overview of Medicine." http://www.library.vcu.edu/tml/bibs/civilwar_medicine.html (accessed December 2, 2009).

Leland, Anne. "American War and Military Operations Casualties: Lists and Statistics." Congressional Research Service, September 15, 2009.

Lincoln Institute, The. "Simon Cameron (1799-1889)." http://www. mrlincolnandfriends.org/inside_search.asp?pageID=84&subjectID=7 &searchWord=Simon%20%Cameron (accessed December 23, 2009).

Melowney, Georgeann. "The Leatherman Family of Washington County, Pa."   http//www.chartiers.com/raybell/1991-Leatherman.html (accessed March 1, 2010.)

Ohio State Unviersity. "Civil War Statistics." http://ehistory.osu.edu/ uscw/features/medicine/cwsurgeon/statistics.html (accessed January 2, 2010).

Price, Angela. "Whitman's Drum Taps and Washington's Civil War Hospitals."   http://xroads.virginia.edu/~CAP/hospital/whitman.html (accessed November 30, 2009).

Research trip to Fredericksburg (both the town and battlefield) in September, 2010.

INDEX